Fenton Glass
The Third Twenty-Five Years
1956-1980

by william heacock

Edited by
James Measell and Frank M. Fenton

Fenton History written by
Dr. Eugene C. Murdock

Photography & Printing by
Richardson Printing Corporation
Marietta, Ohio 45750

Produced with cooperation of the members of the
Fenton Art Glass Collectors of America, Inc., and its Education Committee.

Copyright 1989 by O-Val Advertising Corp.

ALL RIGHTS RESERVED

ISBN 0-915410-36-2

Published and Distributed by:
O-VAL ADVERTISING CORP.
P.O. Box 663
Marietta, Ohio 45750

2

IN MEMORIAM

William R. Heacock
1947-1988

William R. Heacock, 41, died at 12:10 a.m., Sunday, August 14, 1988, in a Pittsburgh hospital after a year-long illness.

He had a warm, caring personality, easily hurt but also very sensitive to others' feelings. He had a great need to be loved and wore his heart on his sleeve. He wasn't always responsible, but he was honest and wanted to do the right thing by everyone. He just couldn't say no and consequently was forever getting himself into promises he couldn't keep and deadlines he couldn't meet. And he'd feel remorseful and depressed for days on end afterward because he'd let somebody down.

He was sincere and dedicated to his craft and in his prime was absolutely the best at glass attribution. He was a full time researcher, author, and lecturer; he gave his adult life to glass history and teaching us about glass.

There was never anyone else like him before, there isn't now and probably never will be again. He encouraged me to start publishing a magazine just for his kind of people (glass collectors) and lent me his help at every turn. He was special and he was my friend and this book which he began but was never able to complete is dedicated to his memory.

David E. Richardson
President

TABLE OF CONTENTS

FOREWORD

At the time of his death (August 14, 1988), William Heacock was working on several book-length projects devoted to American glass. Among those endeavors was this book, called "Fenton 3" in his files. Having told the stories of Fenton's first (1905-06 in Martins Ferry and 1907-1932 in Williamstown) and second (1930-55) twenty-five year periods in separate books, Bill was looking forward to recounting the 1956-1980 segment, perhaps because he had seen some of the glass of the 1970s actually being made and, of course, because he had become extraordinarily fond of Fenton glass, particularly Jade Green.

With his customary enthusiasm, Bill had super-vised the color photography and was writing the captions and attending to countless other details he felt were essential to this book when he became unable to continue his many projects. Bill's working notes and files for "Fenton 3" were used in preparing this book. The Table of Contents he planned has been followed.

Although I am responsible for some of the finishing touches to the research and a few of the words printed here, this book is really Bill's.

I hope he will be pleased.

James Measell
March 1989

ACKNOWLEDGMENTS

There are so many people to thank for their help and encouragement on this book that I hardly know where to begin. It involved much time and thought for two years of my life, and at times I felt it would never be completed. Certainly, it would not have been published without the commitment of Frank M. Fenton, whose unwavering support during the difficult periods of production gave me the faith to forge on with my efforts.

This book is a cooperative effort between myself and the Fenton Art Glass Collectors of America, Inc. This organization of collectors agreed to "sponsor" the book, providing me with a number of volunteers to help with the arduous photography, editing and the price guide. I must single out David Nielsen and Willa Norman for their priceless contributions of time, knowledge and energy in the completion of this book. The FAGCA, Inc., has offices within the complex of the Fenton factory at Williamstown, W. Va., but the group is composed of thousands of spirited glass lovers from every region in this country, with smaller "regional" chapters from coast to coast. When illness forced a postponement of publication of this book in 1987, and cancellation of my appearance at their annual National convention, this group rallied a sense of love and support in my direction which far surpassed their disappointment over the delay on the book. My recuperation was unquestionably accelerated by the many words of encouragement received from members of this selfless group of collectors.

For loans of glass, or time or advice, I would like to thank the following fine fellow Fenton friends:
Mr. & Mrs. Otis Rice
Mr. & Mrs. Neil Unger
Mr. & Mrs. Bill Ehrsam
Mr. & Mrs. James Stage
Mr. & Mrs. Joseph Humphrey
Mr. & Mrs. Dale Robinson
Mr. & Mrs. Richard Staats
Mr. & Mrs. Bud Johnson
Mr. & Mrs. Marvin Rose
Mr. & Mrs. David Nielsen
William Voss
Dorothy Ludeke
Betty Broughton
Dorothy Frazee
Carolyn Kriner
Tom Burns
Betty Hardman
Kay Wahl
Cheryl Robinson
Mildred Coty

Some of the glass shown in this book was borrowed from special displays at the annual convention. My appreciation to those who loaned glass from the 1986 FAGCA convention: Mr. & Mrs. Chris Fernimen, Mr. & Mrs. Alvin Wolfgram, Mr. & Mrs. Jess Fravel, Irene Smith, Tom Collins, Mr. & Mrs. Bill McMichael, Mr. & Mrs. Bill Gray, Ruth Ann Ujcich, Glenn Huguet, Kari McMichael, Mary Clapper, John Binegar, Diane Wolfgram.

Although individual members of the chapters are not listed below, some glass was borrowed from Club Displays at the 1986 FAGCA Convention. These include the Mid Ohio Valley, Toledo, Ohio Area, Buckeye State, Southwestern Ohio, Buckeye Town & Country, Maryland, Michigan, Wisconsin.

For her help transcribing much of the data needed in this book and for her continued encouragement, I also want to thank Faith Siegel. And a final thanks to my publisher, David Richardson, for his faith in me when the odds seem insurmountable getting this project finished.

William R. Heacock
August 1987

PUBLISHER'S INTRODUCTION

In all of the previous books that we have published I never felt it was necessary to include an explanatory introduction. Because of the unusual circumstances surrounding the production of this book, I believe that its readers are entitled to an insider's look at what has happened to get this publication into your hands. First I'll give you a little ancient history, then some recent history and finally, some concluding remarks.

In 1977 Frank Fenton approached William Heacock about writing and publishing a book on the Fenton company. Mr. Heacock was very reluctant to say yes to this undertaking because his financial resources were insufficient and because he felt he knew nothing about the subject. It wasn't Victorian Glass and he felt unqualified to write about it. Mr. Fenton then asked me if the Richardson Printing Corporation or one of its divisions would be interested in acting as the publisher if we could persuade Mr. Heacock to research and write the book. I answered in the affirmative and I spent the next several days convincing Bill he could do the job. He finally agreed and we began working on *Fenton: The First Twenty-Five Years.*

As Bill got deeper into the subject he became more fascinated. He found that his love of glass allowed him to appreciate the products of The Fenton Art Glass Company even though much of their production was not from his beloved Victorian era. Mr. Heacock was not particularly keen on working on any part of the book that was not directly glass related, so the historical section of the book was given to Dr. Eugene Murdock, a history professor from Marietta College. That first book was published in 1978, less than twenty months from concept to finished book. It sold very well and it considerably broadened Mr. Heacock's horizons.

An interesting side note related to the publication of this first book was that it coincided with the founding of a Fenton Art Glass Collector's Society of America. As *Fenton: The First Twenty-Five Years* was nearing completion Mrs. Ferill Jeane Rice and Mr. Frank Fenton came up with the idea that my company print an application for membership in the FAGCA and tuck one of these brochures in every book that was shipped. We were more than happy to do this and it proved to be a great boon to the rapid growth of FAGCA. (Included in this book on *Fenton: The Third Twenty-Five Years* is a current brochure and application for anyone interested in joining the Fenton Art Glass Collectors of America. If its gone, call or write to the address given on the copyright page).

The first book in the series sold so well that it was followed in 1980 by *Fenton: The Second Twenty-Five Years.* It, too, sold well, but after that one was published, Bill told me that he would never do a book on the third twenty-five years. "Nothing that has been produced in the last thirty-five years is old enough to qualify as an antique and I only write books about antiques." Nonetheless, in the spring of 1985 Frank and I persuaded him to begin work on the last book in the trilogy.

Photography was started that year, with much of it being done at the 1985 August FAGCA convention. The project got off to a flying start at the convention with all the exhibitors enthusiastically lending us prize glass samples and their advice. With this type of support and Mr. Fenton's considerable knowledge and energy at his disposal, Mr. Heacock believed the book would be done in less than a year. Unbeknownst to any of us, including Mr. Heacock, the debilitating disease which would ultimately take his life, was already at work destroying his body and impairing his mind.

A year came and went and to the outside observer not much was accomplished during that time period. At the 1986 convention it was reported that the volume of glass produced during the third twenty-five years was making the task a bit more difficult than anyone first believed it would be. In the spring and summer of 1987, Mr. Heacock's illness was wreaking havoc with his ability to concentrate and to mentally organize data. Each time he would sit down at his computer to work on the book his thoughts would be so jumbled that he could never get much accomplished. By the 1987 convention although sixty-four pages of color were photographed, separated and in proofing form, only thirty-six pages of text was written and none of the color page captions had been composed.

At that convention in 1987, when the collectors gathered for dinner and to hear the banquet speaker, they were surprised to find that it wasn't William Heacock as they had expected. Instead they got a short presentation by his publisher. In that short speech I made Bill's apologies for him and indicated to the public for the first time that Bill was seriously ill. I tried to give some indication of when I thought the book could be completed, but in my heart I really didn't have any idea. As it turned out, during Bill's last twelve months he was unable to do anything on this book, but was very reluctant to admit this to either me or himself. I fully understood his condition and I knew he was unable to continue, but rather than hurt his feelings and destroy his will to live, I let the project languish. I really felt there wasn't much else that could be done.

Shortly before he passed away, Bill finally admitted that he was going to be unable to finish this book. He asked me what was going to happen to his last five uncompleted manuscripts. I told him that I would do whatever was necessary to see that they were completed and published and that they would be done so under his name as author. (Besides this book on Fenton, he was also working on the eighth book in his Encyclopedia of Victorian Pattern Glass Series, *More Stained Glass from A to Z* and a trilogy on Northwood, *Northwood — The Early years, Northwood — The Later Years* and *Dugan-Diamond.*) With Bill's knowledge and consent, I began looking for people to help in the completion of these works. And in the case of this book on Fenton, I didn't have to look very far.

One of the reasons which I wanted to include a Publisher's Introduction in this work is so that you, the reader and collector, could understand the different points of view which you will get by reading through this book. For you see this book is not the work of one man but rather, four men (five, if you count me). And the disparity of their perspectives, as well as their writing styles and word choices become apparent if you read the book from cover to cover.

The first person who I called upon was Frank Fenton. Mr. Fenton was very close to Bill and knew that we would have to find an editor to help pull all of Bill's notes together into final book form. Frank's first suggestion was that Dr. Eugene Murdock, the college professor who wrote the history chapters in the first two books, be called upon to perform the role of historian once again. This was agreed upon immediately and accomplished with a phone call. Dr. Murdock has done a wonderful job in completing this part of the book as you will soon see when you begin to read it.

In regards to the role of editor, I suggested to Frank that we talk to Dr. James Measell, a professor at Wayne State University in Michigan. Dr. Measell had previously done some writing and editing for me and I was very impressed by his knowledge, his organizational abilities and his competence. To this suggestion Frank readily agreed. The team I needed to complete the book was taking shape, but one more key player was missing. I knew that the book could not possibly be done without Frank's help and he knew it too, so of course, he graciously offered to do whatever was necessary to bring Mr. Heacock's vision into reality.

Next I had to try to determine what all Mr. Heacock had accomplished. To that end I enlisted the help of Bill's business associate, Nick Daemus. We poured through the filing cabinets, shelves of books and boxes of notes which comprised Bill's office/research library. The computer with its millions of bytes of information was also tapped. Everything was loaded into a van and brought to Marietta where each book's notes could be gone through and prepared for publication. The outline for "Fenton3"—Bill's code word for this book,

was retrieved and sent (with the computer) to Jim Measell in Michigan. The catalogue reprint pages and the color plates were taken to Frank for review and Dr. Murdock was given Bill's Table of Contents which showed how many pages had been allotted for the history. As each of us began working on "Fenton3" we were all acutely aware of Bill—his handwriting and his thoughts were everywhere we looked; his outline for the book, his comments on its progress and his frustrations at his own inabilities to make any progress—his emotions were as real as if he had been there working with each of us.

I think its fair to say that we have all strived to do this book as Bill wanted it done. And I think we've accomplished that. He chose the items to be photographed; he chose the catalog reprints to be reproduced; he outlined the book and gave it its character. All we have done is carry out his plan. I believe that this was a task that we all accepted and completed out of respect for Bill.

To Dr. Gene Murdock and Dr. Jim Measell I would like to offer my thanks. It was a pleasure to work with you, gentlemen and I feel your writing and editing was first rate. To Mr. Frank Fenton, who devoted so many hours of time and effort to putting the finishing touches on this book, I say "thank you." All of us who love the products of The Fenton Art Glass Company, owe you an immense amount of gratitude for your unselfish work in seeing this vision of Mr. Heacock's come to pass. It was Frank's years of experience and intimate knowledge of Fenton Glass which gave this book its authenticity and its meat—the information for which collectors hunger.

And to the readers and collectors of The Fenton Art Glass Company, to all of you who have waited so patiently or impatiently for this book to become a reality I say "enjoy".

David E. Richardson
President
March 1989

INTRODUCTION

During the past twenty years, the glassware made by the Fenton Art Glass Company, called simply "Fenton glass," has become increasingly popular. Those who favor antique glass, especially carnival glass, have been interested in "early" Fenton (1907 through the 1920s) for many years. The many depression glass clubs and publications have focused much attention upon the Fenton products of the 1930s and 40s.

The Fenton Art Glass Collectors of America, through its meetings and *Butterfly Net* newsletter, has both enlarged the circle of Fenton aficionados and heightened interest in Fenton glass made in the 1950s-70s, as well as current production. In their own way, glass collectors' clubs devoted to the other great American factories (Cambridge, Duncan Miller, Fostoria, Heisey, and Imperial) have also stimulated interest in Fenton, as sharp-eyed collectors and researchers have pondered the similarities and differences among the products of those tableware factories whose working lives span much of the twentieth century.

This book is devoted to the "third" twenty-five years of the Fenton Art Glass Company (1956-1980). Other books by William Heacock have covered the two previous twenty-five year segments: *Fenton Glass: The First Twenty-Five Years* (1978) and *Fenton Glass: The Second Twenty-Five Years* (1980). Like the previous publications, this book separates the glassware from the history for ease of discussion. Once more, the Fenton history is told by Dr. Eugene C. Murdock, Emeritus Professor of History at Marietta College.

Each of the color plates is supported by extensive captions which provide detailed information regarding pattern names, item numbers, colors, years of production, etc. In the early 1950s, the Fenton Art Glass Company began to use both two-letter color codes and four-digit ware numbers to facilitate order-taking. A designation such as "No. 3886 MI" refers to the Fenton ware number 3886 (a candy box) in milk glass (MI).

Several sources were used to make the information in this book as complete as possible. Well-illustrated Fenton catalogues were issued about every two years between 1956-80, and "catalog supplements" appeared at regular intervals, too. Both the catalogs and the catalog supplements contain listings of Fenton color codes. These two-letter codes were used for particular glass colors (for instance, CP stood for Colonial Pink in 1962-68) as well as surface treatments such as satin (RS stood for Rose Satin in 1974-78) and decorations (CW signifies the handpainted Cardinals in Winter). Some letter combinations were used more than once over the years: BC stood for both Blue Crest (1963) and Black Crest (1970), and it was also used for the handpainted decoration Bluebirds on Custard (1977-79). A listing of the color codes used between 1956-1980 begins on p. 144.

In addition to color codes, the Fenton firm also used four-digit ware numbers between 1956-80. Since several different articles were often made from the same mould (see the Cactus items on p. 66), each separate article, *not* each mould, was assigned an individual ware number. A Cactus mould for a round bowl (No. 3424) was also used as the basis for five additional items: No. 3401 epergne; No. 3411 plate; No. 3422 footed bowl; No. 3425 banana bowl; and No. 3430 basket.

For the most part, the first two digits of a ware number are the same within a given pattern line. The Valencia pattern, for instance, always has "83" as the first two digits in the four-digit ware number. The Hobnail line contains so many different articles that its ware numbers encompass most of the available designations from 3600 through the 3900's.

There is also some noticeable consistency across pattern line ware numbers in the second two digits: vases usually have ware numbers ending in 50's, and baskets are frequently in the 30's, but there are many exceptions and no internal coherence built into the system. Collectors should realize that ware numbers (and color codes) are arbitrary, shorthand designations used by the Fenton Art Glass Company to facilitate customers' orders, and also to keep production and inventory records within the company.

Although they contain no illustrations, original Fenton price lists were invaluable sources in documenting the extent of pattern lines and the production of certain colors. Only in the Fenton price lists can one discover all of the articles and colors produced. Unlike the Fenton catalogues and catalogue supplements, which picture only selected articles from the lines, the Fenton price lists record each and every article offered for sale through Fenton's extensive dealer network. Since an article might continue in the line for a year or more, all the price lists from 1956-1980 were consulted to determine production dates. When an item is captioned "1956-58," this means that the item was listed in the color shown throughout the time period, in Fenton price lists and/or catalogs.

Some of the items shown in the color pages do not appear in either Fenton catalogs or Fenton price lists, but they were undoubtably made by the Fenton Art Glass Company. There are several situations in which this occurs, one of which is so-called "private" production. Private work has been frequent in the pressed and blown glassware industry for many years. In brief, glass factories often make articles for some other party, usually a wholesaler who then resells the ware. The wholesaler chooses whether or not to reveal that Fenton made the ware. When the Levay Distributing Company commissioned Fenton to produce several lines in the late 1970s, the Fenton name was mentioned prominently in promotional materials and advertising. In contrast, the many items made by Fenton for L. G. "Si" Wright were not attributed to their manufacturer. Fenton's production for Wright was considerable, beginning about 1937 and continuing into the 1980s, although most dates from the 1940s-60s.

Incidentally, private work should not be construed as an attempt to deceive the glass collector. From the company's perspective, private work keeps the plant active and its workers employed when demand for the company's own lines might prove insufficient. Furthermore, the private production is "sold" directly to one customer, so inventory storage and marketing/advertising costs are not incurred. In turn, the wholesaler is assured of quality products.

Documenting Fenton's private work proved to be challenging and interesting. Fortunately, two highly reliable sources were available—Frank M. Fenton's remarkable memory and a production card file maintained at the factory. When Mr. Fenton was examining the color photography and assisting with the captions, he pointed to articles which were not "in the line" (these would not appear in either catalogs or price lists). Often, he recalled the name of the firm or individual which had ordered the article.

The production card file is maintained by using ware numbers in sequence. A single ware card records the following: dates of production; skilled and unskilled manpower required; quantities of acceptable ware produced and amounts of rejects; and mathematical calculations related to productivity and costs of production. When private production took place, it was duly noted on the ware cards.

Another sort of selective production needs to be mentioned. Like any successful glass company, the Fenton Art Glass Company is continually developing innovations in colors as well as design concepts. Along the way, some experimentation and sampling is necessary. In order to test the working properties and characteristics of a glass color under development, the Fenton firm must "try out" the color under ordinary factory conditions with a working mould. The result is often a very limited number of finished articles, and these may go unrecorded in the production card file, particularly if several different moulds are used for short periods during production trials. These may be stored for a time and eventually make their way into the "One-of-a-Kind" sales at the Fenton Gift Shop.

Two final circumstances of selective production must be mentioned. On occasion, several shops of workers, particularly in pressed ware, will be working simultaneously, producing various articles in different colors. One shop may encounter unworkable, "bad" glass and be shifted over to another nearby pot which contains production-ready glass of a different color. Within a short time, salable articles have been produced, albeit of a kind not scheduled for production. These may find their way into the Fenton Gift Shop, too.

Finally, when a small quantity of glass remains in a pot, it could be "ladled out," freeing the pot for its next melt. Rather than allow this glass to go to waste, the production foremen may put a shop to work "using up" the glass which would be discarded if ladled out. Like the situation described above, this circumstance will result in a few small articles which do not appear in catalogs or price lists and may go unrecorded on the production file cards.

Despite the situations recounted above, virtually all of the Fenton Art Glass Company's production items between 1956 and 1980 can be dated and documented with some specificity. Bear in mind that this book does not discuss everything made by Fenton from 1956-80. This book does picture many of the patterns and items most likely to be encountered by today's Fenton glass collectors as well as some of the more unusual articles which have turned up. Both should serve as a stimulus to the collecting of Fenton glass.

James Measell
March 1989

Fenton History
1956-1980

Chapter Ten
IN FIRM CONTROL

Readers of *THE SECOND TWENTY-FIVE YEARS* of Fenton history may recall that Frank M. and Bill Fenton assumed control of the Fenton Art Glass Company in 1948, a rather trying moment. They were young and inexperienced and the hand glass industry was entering a down period. They inherited from their father and uncle, Frank L. and Robert, a company based on a conservative business philosophy, a physical plant which was becoming outdated, and a management structure which was rather rudimentary. They had little experience with design, were unfamiliar with the sales organization, and were to lose their veteran glassmaker, Paul Rosenthal, in 1949. A serious strike closed the factory down for 17 days in September 1950.

Readers may also remember Richard Slavin's "formula for failure" of small hand glass plants, discussed at the end of the last volume. He wrote of a time—the 1950s—when 16 glass companies had lately expired and a dozen more were on the brink of expiration. A study of these defunct enterprises revealed several reasons for their collapse. Tariff policies, death of the owners, union pressures, and natural disasters all played a part. More important than any of these, however, particularly in family-owned companies, was the transition in management from the older to the younger generations and the failure to adopt modern bookkeeping and accounting methods. If any company was ticketed for oblivion, according to the Slavin prescription, it was the Fenton Art Glass Company.

But that did not happen. The young Fentons fought their way forward, not always sure of what they were doing or where they were going, but with what proved to be an unerring instinct for survival. They recognized that it would be fatal to stand pat, so they began to experiment with this and that. They dropped jobbers and turned to sales representatives. They went from annual financial reports to quarterly and then monthly statements. They modernized their raw materials handling system. Frank began to frequent antique shows to study what other companies had been doing and gradually developed a "feel" for design and what the market might be interested in. He brought in Stan Fistick who developed "contemporary" designs, although these were things the market was not interested in. FAGCO purchased moulds from closed plants to broaden its line. It revived old patterns and introduced new ones.

By the end of its second 25 years Fenton had survived the Depression, World War II, an industry decline, and a change of leadership. The early 1950s saw the new leaders struggle to master the hand glass business. But at the time of the 50th anniversary, noted in the last volume, "as the company faced the second half century of its history, it was prepared to write an even more successful chapter than those which have been written before." Frank M. and Bill Fenton were now in firm control.

* * *

The third 25 years of Fenton history was the most profitable quarter century it had yet enjoyed. With very few exceptions, sales and earnings moved up annually. According to studies made by the Glass Crafts Association, Fenton's share of the hand glass business averaged between 15 and 20 per cent throughout those years. At times it was the leader in the field in this regard, and when it was not, it was right behind the leader.

To start the new age, 1956 was reported as a good year with sales reaching $1,900,000. Prospects for the future were so promising that hot metal facilities had to be enlarged to meet the anticipated increase in orders. It was necessary that year to build a new pot arch and add a lathe for the mould shop. By June 1957, predictions were made that 1957 would be a record year in both sales and earnings. And indeed it was. Sales reached $2,300,000 and while profit data was not listed, the figures were said to be very good. The prospect for 1958 was excellent and FAGCO's position was described as very strong. Expenditures for plant improvements to further strengthen its position were outlined at the January directors' meeting.

This strong beginning of the third 25 years continued unabated. 1958 proved to be another record year with sales up 18 per cent—to $2,700,000—and profits advancing accordingly. 1960 was also a record year in both sales and profits. Although overall growth was steady, a kind of two-step forward and one-half step backward pattern prevailed in the late 1950s and early 1960s. As 1959 fell below the record year of 1958, so 1961 fell below the record year of 1960. This growth in company operations led to necessary additions in management personnel and physical facilities. In 1960 Fenton spent over $120,000 for new buildings and equipment.

In 1963 Fenton enjoyed its greatest year in history, exceeding everything that had gone before. It was more like three steps forward this time. In reporting to the directors in June, Frank Fenton said that the first six months of the year had been very good and the prospects for the last six months appeared bright. He confirmed his preliminary statement when he told the directors in November that it seemed almost certain that records for both sales and earnings would be broken. His report to the stockholders in January 1964 made it official: 1963 had been FAGCO's most successful year, setting new highs for sales and profits. The sale of more items to the trading stamp companies, such as Sperry and Hutchinson and J. C. Penney's, and a general improvement in the line were the principal factors contributing to the record figures. Overtime work had been necessary in the first six months to meet the large demand and maintain inventories. The company president predicted that sales would continue to increase in 1964.

1964 and 1965 continued the upward trend. There were no steps backward. In April 1964 Frank Fenton reported to the directors that the first quarter of the year was a good one despite the loss of production capacity in January due to furnace repairs. Sales remained high through the summer and fall and in November it was reported that they would exceed those of the previous year while earnings would be about the same as in 1963. A substantial sales hike in the first quarter of 1965 over that of 1964 augured well for that year. Indeed, 1965 broke all previous records both in sales and earnings, sales reaching $4,691,648, a 23.4 per cent jump over 1964. "It is believed," Frank Fenton reported to an appreciative group of stockholders in January 1966, "that we are now the second largest handmade glass manufacturer in the United States."

* * *

It has been hinted that with this tremendous growth in sales, [a discussion of Fenton's sales organization has been reserved for chapter 12, "Selling the Product"] FAGCO was in urgent need of upgrading and expanding its facilities. There had been times during this "sales explosion" that production capacity could not keep up with shipping orders. Management was well aware of the developing dilemma and moved, as quickly as conditions permitted, to deal with the problem. The two most important improvements—expansion of the Hot Metal Department and the expansion and relocation of company offices—came in the middle 1960s. Sales having more than trebled in the previous decade, obviously, expansion of the production facilities was the top priority.

Prior to that time, however, numerous other improvements had been made, one new building had been put up, and one major innovation had been instituted. The new building was the first of four warehouse facilities, attached to the west side of the original factory building along Elizabeth Street. It was constructed in 1958. The main reason for the new building was the need to have a place to house the flow-rack conveyor. Perhaps the largest of its kind in the glass industry at that time, the conveyor system was developed over a two-year period by plant superintendent Joe Ehnot, industrial engineer William R. "Bud" Johnson, and plant engineer Floyd Showalter. The system was the key element in a larger materials handling and packaging process, which hastened the preparation of orders for shipment and cut down on labor costs.

When this $250,000 project was approved by FAGCO management, the call for bids went out and Jeffords and Moore of Charleston, a division of Rapids-Standard of Grand Rapids, Michigan, was awarded the job. They sent a man named Frank Uteck to Williamstown to work with the Fenton people in building the new system. "He was of tremendous help in getting the equipment we needed to do the job," said Johnson. "I would show him a drawing of what we wanted to do and he would come up with the equipment to do it."

In addition to the conveyor, a "modular packing system," which saved time and conserved packing space, was installed. Glassware was housed in bins behind the walkways on either side of the flowracks. As the cartons came down the racks, packing clerks reached behind, took the numbered pieces from the bins, and put them in the cartons—each item in an individual carton, the smaller cartons then placed in the master cartons. A new IBM computer proved invaluable in organizing the orders in sequence, so the clerks had no problems in filling the orders correctly.

Frank M. and Wilmer C. (Bill) Fenton—1958.

The carton moved along the flow-rack until it was filled, at which point the sealing clerk sealed it shut and pushed it on to the weigh station where it was weighed and stamped with the buyer's address. The system was operational by June 1959.

In 1960 the Fenton company set another record by spending $120,000 on plant improvements. Over half of this was to pay off the new warehouse where the conveyor system was located. Also, the pre-packaging area was enlarged, more office equipment was purchased, the parking lot was expanded, and a new ruby oven was installed. Plans for 1961 included relocation of the railroad siding farther west to expedite the unloading of raw materials, expansion of the mixing room and glass research facilities, and replacement of the floors in the hot metal department.

When the first warehouse was completed, Frank and Bill Fenton strolled through the cavernous structure almost gawking at its immensity. "Bill," said Frank, "I can't think that you or I will ever need any more space than this." It was only a couple of years before he realized that additional warehouse space was badly needed. The problem was where to build? The company owned no land beyond the one warehouse which was already in place. It would either have to cross over Elizabeth Street and build on property it owned there or purchase land to the west of its current boundary. Two acres facing Elizabeth and Poplar streets were owned by one Bronny Bronson Bee. FAGCO preferred to build on Bee's property, but the company and Bee had not agreed on a sale price. No offer had been made by either party. At length a decision had to be made—to either go south [across the street], or west [on Bee's land]. Both parties met in the Fenton offices one morning in 1960. Frank made the company's first and only offer for the property. He felt it was a fair offer. He added that they must have the answer by noon that day. The engineers were prepared to move, one way or another, at that time.

"I want to go home and talk to my wife," Bee replied.

"I think," chuckled Bill Fenton, "he must just have gotten back into his house when he picked up the phone. 'I'll take it,' he said."

The remaining three warehouses were constructed over the next 14 years on Bee's former property. The final building, which abutted on Poplar Street, was twice as big in floor space as the others and was designed so that if more space was needed, an additional story could be built on top of it.

With the company's rapid growth in the early 1960s it became necessary to plan carefully ahead. Early in 1962, for the first time, we read about long-range planning. In November of that year, Frank Fenton presented to the directors a tentative five-year plan for annual expenditures for plant improvements. Of course, the plan was subject to change depending on unforeseen developments, but at least it provided a rough idea of what monies were going to be needed and for what purpose in the near future. The figures were:

1963 —	$243,000
1964 —	190,700
1965 —	183,800
1966 —	112,000
1967 —	74,000
	$803,500

Tentative as the plan was, Frank Fenton explained management's thinking:

Each year we tried to look five years ahead. We thought that if we continued to grow, we must know what kinds of things we would need as we grew. Perhaps more lehr capacity, or expand this or that, whatever it might be. And with each thing that we thought we ought to do, we would have to anticipate the cost and the right time to do it. So some things which were in the first year were pretty firm, while those in the fifth year were only loosely set.

When the preliminary statistics came in for 1963, it was found that $20,000 had been saved by rebuilding an old lehr rather than buying a new one. But a lack of time and personnel prevented completion of work planned on new batch-handling and crushing equipment. Everything else was on schedule. This included a new lehr—in addition to the rebuilt one, a new mixer, new scales, a print-weigh hopper to check weights, and the relocation of the railroad siding. This had been planned a year or two before, but was not completed until this time. Also the area formerly used by the old railroad siding was enclosed. It was estimated that expenditures would exceed $200,000 for the year, although no final sum was included in the minutes. Unfinished improvements were rescheduled for the following year.

The June 12, 1964 directors meeting was devoted almost exclusively to the expansion and improvements of the physical plant. Frank Fenton pointed out that, "As the company grows and diversifies, it will be necessary for us to expand our physical facilities even more. Most of this expansion is already set up in the long range capital improvement program. The toughest part of this sort of scheduling is to be ready with the facilities when we need them and yet not build anything that we won't need." It was at this time that the company president emphasized the pressing importance of the expansion of the Hot Metal Department. "We are now selling more than we can produce," he said, "and are withholding from the market items which could add even more to sales. It seems desirable to proceed at once with the Hot Metal expansion just as soon as detailed drawings can be prepared."

Fenton went on to discuss the other high priority item, relocation and expansion of company offices. Business growth had made obsolete the small office facilities which had hardly been enlarged since the

The Fenton Art Glass Factory building as it looked in 1967. Notice the brick stack and water tank.

factory was built 60 years before. "The second step," he continued, "involves the construction of a second floor over the present offices, gift shop, finishing department and mould shop. The gift shop would then be expanded and the major part of the offices would be moved to the second floor. We now need additional office space," he emphasized.

Reconstruction of the Hot Metal Department got under way early in November 1964 at a time when sales were peaking. Frank Fenton commented that "if the new facilities had been available this fall, with the skilled personnel to use them, much more business could have been accepted and shipped." Work continued on through the winter and spring. They were ready for use by June 1965.

Meanwhile, bids for construction of new offices were considered high. At the suggestion of plant engineer Floyd Showalter, the company decided to become its own general contractor and to sub-contract the steel work, roofing, and other parts of the project. This worked out very well. The steel work, for example, was all put up in one day, a Saturday. The footers had already been poured and the steel brought in on Friday. The workers started in early on Saturday and finished the job by dusk, so there was no interruption in office work. Frank Fenton credits the ease with which the job was done to Showalter, who had planned the details. "He did an excellent job," he said of the native Williamstowner. Showalter had worked some years before in the factory and then went into construction before he returned to the company as plant engineer. The new offices were completed by the end of the year. 1965 was a record year for sales, which was due in no small part to the new production facilities. Total expenditures for plant improvements in 1965 came to $350,000.

The author well remembers the construction of the new offices at the Fenton factory. It was at this time that he was doing his research for the first two volumes of the company history. He began working downstairs in the old offices and finished working upstairs in the new offices. It was dangerous work downstairs. With holes in the floor and steel I-beams projecting from the walls in unexpected places, one had to be forever vigilant to avoid a serious mishap. But when the work was done, what an improvement!

A near mishap occurred to Frank Fenton during those days of reconstruction. He was sitting in his office one day, innocently attending to business, when it happened. Let him tell the story:

All that we had done so far [in the reconstruction] was to cut holes in the floors and pour footers where the steel columns were going to go up. We went outside and dug around the building to pour footers there for the new outer walls. They were digging around my office which was in the corner of the building. Then we had a very hard rainstorm and the water went in and washed out the footers of the building. I was sitting in my office talking to somebody when I heard a cracking sound—a cracking in the wall. I looked over at the window frame and I could see nails appearing as the wall pulled away from the window frame. The wall was collapsing because there was no support underneath it—it had been washed out in the rainstorm. I said to whoever it was, "Let's get out of here. I don't want to be here when the roof falls in."

He went into the next office and phoned the maintenance department. Shortly, several men arrived, and using two-by-fours, propped the wall back up. Plywood walls were installed for temporary service.

1965 was the most expensive year yet with respect to plant improvements. The final figure was $410,000. But FAGCO was not finished with its program of physical expansion and the addition of new facilities. At the January 1966 stockholders meeting Frank Fenton outlined plans for the coming year. They included the purchase of a new lehr and the installation of a complete cullet crushing operation. Moreover, the blacktopping of the parking lot on the north

GHOST TOWN SHOP FIRST TO ORDER FULL CARLOAD FROM FENTON ART GLASS

VIRGINIA'S Gift Shop of Buena Park, Calif., recently became the first gift shop in the country to purchase a full freight carload of Fenton Art Glass — some 10,000 pounds of merchandise packed in over 700 individual cartons.

Such volume buying is all the more amazing when you consider that Virginia's operates in a ghost town. Fortunately for the shop, however, this ghost town attracts people, not poltergeists. As part of the famous Knott's Berry Farm, a re-created California Gold Mining Community circa 1850, Virginia's gets a sales shot at more than two million tourist-customers a year.

It takes three people to unload freight carload of glass — Ray Cole (center) and John Fopma do the lifting while buyer Glenna Schleiderer checks shipment.

side of 4½ Street, east of Caroline, was in the works. The latest long-range planning figures were

1966 — $240,500
1967 — 297,000
1968 — 137,000
1969 — 160,000
1970 — 205,000

* * *

Joe Ehnot was a natural addition to the developing management team at Fenton. Next to Frank and Bill Fenton, and perhaps a few workers in the Hot Metal Department, his links with the company go back farther than anyone else. He went to work there on July 17, 1949, between his junior and senior years at Marietta College. He worked part-time at FAGCO through his senior year, occupied with "design drawings and various other assignments, one being the lehr adjustment project." His one dollar an hour wage aided him to pay his college expenses and support his young family. He had a two-year old daughter. After graduation in June 1950 he took a full-time job at the company at $65 a week. He stayed on until December 1952 working in "developing sales analysis techniques and marketing information, and doing advertising work and some selling." He was classed as an "advertising manager" at the time of his departure.

Ehnot did not leave Fenton because of any disenchantment with the company. Rather, "I thought I needed to broaden my experience and got that opportunity with Joseph M. Cook and staff." Joseph M. Cook was the consulting firm Fenton had brought in to advise it on building a management organization and Ehnot had done a good bit of work with them. He stayed with Cook for two years and nine months. The understanding was that he would return to Fenton when he felt he had acquired sufficient experience away from the company. He came back "into the fold," you might say, on August 1, 1955. He was given the title at the time of plant engineer and moved steadily up the managerial ladder until his departure on January 1, 1972, to become president of Armstrong Custom Fabricators. Ehnot remained plant engineer through 1957 and in 1958 became superintendent of the Cold Metal Department, a post he held until 1961. He then became works manager, or manager of manufacturing. In February 1968 he was elected vice-president of the company. By this time he was dividing his work load between FAGCO and Armstrong, which had been acquired in the fall of 1966. (See footnote on page 20).

Ehnot played a central role in the expansion of the physical plant at the company during the late 1950s and 1960s. The construction of the warehouses, the installation of the flow-rack and packaging system, and other additions and innovations went through his hands. "When I rejoined Fenton in 1955," he recalled, "I was involved in the bricks and mortar stage of rebuilding old buildings, remodeling and expanding the physical plant with new structures, and installing improved furnaces and new equipment." This construction and reconstruction placed something of a burden on the day-to-day operations of the factory, but it was all carried out with little disruption in the regular operations. At the time of Ehnot's elevation to the vice-presidency, a company bulletin stated that,

Joseph Ehnot, newly elected Vice President, and Don E. Alexander, newly elected Secretary/Treasurer — 1968.

"Much credit for the growth of the company must go to Joe for the way he has applied his organizational and planning talents. He has consistently urged us to plan ahead and to build for the future." "It would have been difficult to do without Joe during those years," reflected Bill Fenton.

Another important addition to the management team, in the front office, was Don E. Alexander, who also joined FAGCO in 1955. A native of Marietta, Alexander graduated from Marietta High School in 1940 and spent three and one-half years in the armed services in World War II. Following the war he took a position with Vanguard Paints in Marietta where he rose to the position of chief accountant. He came to Fenton as an accountant and, according to a company bulletin, "gradually assumed the responsibilities for handling all accounting, auditing, insurance, tax returns, forecasting, and other office procedures." Alexander became the company's first controller in 1959. At the time Ehnot became vice-president, in January 1968, Alexander was elected secretary-treasurer, while retaining the position of controller. Ehnot and Alexander were the first non-Fenton family company officers in 35 years. Alexander retired from FAGCO in 1977.

The hiring of psychologist Dr. Robert Fischer on a part-time basis in 1957, marked what for those days was a rather innovative step in corporate management. Fischer had come to Marietta College in 1947 as associate professor of psychology and with the further purpose of establishing a counseling clinic at the college. It was thought that he could be helpful in assisting the older servicemen, who were then returning to school, to adjust to civilian life. As the years passed, and as the veterans finished school, he found that he was spending more time counseling than with his academic responsibilities. Consequently, in 1952, he left the college and devoted full time to counseling.

Fischer opened an office located in the Parish Hall of the Episcopal Church in Marietta and "hung out his shingle" as a "consulting psychologist." He had come to know Frank Fenton and they had talked about some of the conditions or needs at the company, which Fischer might be able to handle. They discussed such things as the selection of employees, testing, problems of training, evaluations of people who were having

Robert P. Fischer, Director of Personnel Research.

difficulties but did not have the resources to go to a professional person, and other similar matters. The president was having a particular difficulty at the time with one of his management personnel, whom he felt was rather severe with the people underneath him. He thought this individual might have a problem and wanted Fischer to test him. So that this would not appear too conspicuous, everyone in management was tested. It was then, in 1957, that Fischer came to work at Fenton on a part-time basis.

In 1962 the Parish Hall was taken down and he had to decide whether to find a new office or to return to the academic field. But then another option developed at Fenton, when Frank invited him to come to work full-time for the company. "You can have an office in our building and we need to test new employees and job applicants." Fischer joined the staff in 1962, remaining until his retirement in 1979. "We looked around for a name for my position," he recalled, "something that would not threaten people emotionally, so I took the title of Director of Personnel Research."

Fischer worked out well for FAGCO. "Any employee who was having a problem of any sort," Frank Fenton remarked, "could come and talk to Bob about it at no cost to the employee. Management people who at times got frustrated could go to him and sound off. And he would listen." Fischer did a number of other things besides testing and listening to complaints. He wrote letters to employees about company policy and various things, he wrote advertising copy, he wrote some materials for the catalog, and he wrote identifying captions for rare pieces of glass. It was an unstructured position, "a kind of free-wheeling situation with no time cards to punch. But I wanted to appear busy. If I happened to be thinking about a problem in my office, where it might appear to someone passing by the door that I was doing nothing, I always had a pencil and a pad of paper in front of me. And if I went over to town, I always carried a briefcase with me even though I might only have my lunch in it."

Other duties went with the job, although these were not written into the contract; they were merely understood. These dealt with community service. The Fenton company has always been a firm supporter of the diverse sides of social and economic life in Williamstown. Through the people it employs, the tourist trade it attracts, the Fenton Foundation grants, and in untold other ways, it has contributed substantially to make the town such a pleasant place to reside and raise families. The ancillary use of Fischer's professional expertise was an example of this spirit. Part of his time was to be spent tending to the emotional needs of institutional units in town. "If a minister had someone who needed psychological counseling," commented Frank, "he knew he could send the person to Bob. The schools did the same thing. He also helped the police department. He used his office here at the factory, or people might go to his home. The idea was that part of his time would be devoted to things of that type."

A number of additional people went to work for FAGCO in management or supervisory positions as business continued to grow. Floyd R. Showalter was hired in November 1956 as plant engineer. Arthur R. Edwards, who later became manager of quality engineering and control, went to work for the company in May 1959. James E. Martin arrived in October 1960 as office manager, succeeding Robert L. Simms who had departed about a year before. Chemist Charles Goe, who had worked at Fenton in his Marietta College years, much like Ehnot, was hired in September 1960. Carnick Hamperian, who would succeed retiring mould shop foreman Francis Lehew in 1965, was employed only a couple of weeks after Goe in September 1960.

In 1966 another group of management people came to the company. Howard E. Seufer, an engineer who had worked for various companies, most recently O. Ames in Parkersburg, was named methods engineer. In January 1969 he was appointed manager of data processing. Richard E. Zimmermann, a Marietta College Phi Beta Kappa graduate with a degree in economics, was named assistant controller. In May 1970 he succeeded Don Alexander as controller. Another in the class of 1966 and another Marietta College graduate was Richard J. Blauvelt, who was appointed to head the shipping department.

An important management newcomer from the class of 1966 was Joseph Voso, Jr., who was hired on March 1 of that year. Like Fischer, Voso's duties were loosely-drawn and he became involved in many things. He was called director of industrial relations. "The attractive thing to me about coming here," he recalled,

Floyd Showalter, Plant Engineer and James E. Martin, Credit and Office Manager.

William R. (Bud) Johnson, Cold Metal Superintendent and Arthur E. Edwards, Quality Control Manager and Special Products Manager.

Howard E. Seufer with Subodh Gupta.

Richard Blauvelt, Shipping Foreman.

"was that, in industry, when you have been at a job for awhile, it tends to get boring. In big companies you don't have a variety of things to do; you do one thing—you're a specialist. I liked the Fenton job because it would give me a variety of things to do. No two days would be alike. The job had to do with labor relations and negotiations, with safety, with security, with hiring."

"Did you train for these kinds of tasks in college?" inquired the author.

"I trained to be an ordained Baptist minister."

In 1955, after serving nine years in the ministry in New Martinsville, West Virginia, Voso was invited by Pittsburgh Plate Glass, which had a chemical plant in the small town of Natrium north of New Martinsville, to join its industrial relations staff. He accepted the offer and became training director for the plant. "By early 1963," Voso said, "I was getting pretty bored. I put the training program on 50 times and by the 45th time I was becoming tired. I needed a change." At the time PPG needed to hire some engineers and it was difficult to attract them to a small town such as Natrium, so Voso was appointed college recruiter. He spent the next three years traveling about the country visiting colleges as far west as Nebraska, as far south as Clemson, South Carolina, and throughout New England. This work, too, began to pall.

To improve on his skills in industrial relations, in the early 1960s Voso and several friends from PPG formed a car pool and came down to Marietta College where they enrolled in a couple of courses. He remembers a good course he had from Paul Theisen in labor relations and another good one from Bob Fischer in industrial psychology. In the fall of 1965 Fischer, who had come to know Voso well, invited him to talk to the Rotary Club of Marietta. Frank Fenton was the actual program chairman and he had enlisted Fischer to help line someone up for this meeting. The talk went over very well. When the program was concluded, a Dravo official said to Fenton, "Frank, I don't know where you're getting speakers like this from, but you're making it hard on me. I'm the next program chairman, you know."

This talk initiated Fenton's interest in Voso, who came to work for the company the following spring. As has been mentioned, his job was ill-defined, which troubled him. "I couldn't find the job definition I was looking for. Nothing was spelled out for me and I pretty much had to make my own job." Security and safety were two areas which, while listed on the organization chart, did not seem to be in anyone's particular charge. So Voso began involving himself in those matters, training guards to secure the factory. He played a part in the formation of a discipline committee [composed of the president, plant manager, hot or cold metal department superintendent, foreman of the particular department, and Voso] which set up standard procedures to avoid having people wrongfully fired or punished. Often, in disciplinary hearings, Voso would represent the accused employee in an effort to strike a balance between the two disputants, the foreman and the worker.

Voso played an important role in handling labor grievances. In every such instance, he would draft the initial statement of the grievance and then, with Frank Fenton, prepare the answer to the grievance. The union would reply to the answer and the company would reply to the union's reply to the company's answer to the original grievance. Back and forth it went until some sort of settlement was reached. "We worked as a team on grievances," he reflected, "probably more than on any other single thing we did."

At about the time Voso came to Fenton there was formed a labor-management safety committee. He is not sure who initiated the idea—it may have emerged from talks with the union—but he is warm in praise of its effectiveness. The committee was composed of two members of management, one of whom was Voso, and three members from the union. "Periodically," he said, "we would tour the plant looking for safety vi-

Joseph Voso, Jr. and Etta Marie Ritchie.

olations. When we found violations we would submit a report giving priority to the most urgent problems. Safety was advanced tremendously through the efforts of that committee. In fact, an OSHA inspector came in once and I showed him some of the minutes of our meetings. We had thought he might give us a citation or two, but when he saw the work we had done, he closed his notebook and left."

Etta Ritchie, who came to work for Fenton in February 1951, had seen a lot of people come and go in her 38 years at the factory. She had worked for the American Pottery Company in Marietta for five and one-half years, then spent a year at Marietta Osteopathic [Selby General] Hospital, and then another year in an insurance office. She was a little weary of typing insurance policies so she thought she would try something else. She had heard that Fenton's was a good place to work, so on one wintry day she crossed the bridge to Williamstown and applied for a job at the factory. She spoke with Frank Fenton and Mildred Metcalf, supervisor of the Selection Department. She got a job in that department. About a week later one of the office girls failed to report for work. Frank, who had noted from her application form that Etta had secretarial experience, went out to the Selection Department and asked her to come into the office and help out. Once in the office, she never left. Later on Frank asked why she had gone to work out in selection.

"I needed a job," was the quick reply.

Over the years she did many different tasks. She typed orders, figured invoices, and billed accounts. After about a year she went into the Payroll Department and for the next 14 or 15 years, until about 1966, she did the payroll. That year, James Pennell, who had been the personnel manager, left the company, and Etta took over personnel duties. With the arrival of Fischer in 1957 on a part-time basis and then full-time in 1962, she administered and scored tests. She helped Voso in his various activities after he joined the company in 1966.

The demands on office help were much greater in those days prior to the coming of modern electronic office machines equipment. A lot of the work was done by hand and there were long hours pounding those old manual typewriters, which did not correct errors themselves. "I remember one time," Etta chuckled, "when Kathryn Moody was sort of in charge of the billing department and I was working

with her. Frank came by and asked Kathryn how she was getting along. Her reply has become a joke with us over the years, although I don't think Frank was much impressed. She said, 'We can't seem to get any further ahead than two weeks behind.' That became one of our bywords."

Etta spent many hours as combination switchboard operator-receptionist. In the days before reconstruction, entrance to the first floor office was on Caroline Street just about where the Gift Shop entrance is now located. As one entered the building he found the switchboard operator-receptionist to his left and the tiny Gift Shop to his right. "If you can believe it," she said, "we had only two outside lines and we could have only two conversations in the plant at one time. Only four calls were possible. When we had an incoming call we had to connect to that line and ring until someone answered the call. You could not plug in and let it ring automatically as is done now." When filling in at the switchboard she was expected to carry on with some of her other duties, such as figuring out the payroll. In addition, she or whoever was at the switchboard served as the receptionist when anyone came into the building. If that was not sufficient, "I even worked in the gift shop and helped Polly Maidens. When she would get swamped, I would get someone to relieve me at the switchboard and run across the hall to help her." But it was a great place to work and Etta Ritchie would not trade her 38 years at the Fenton company for anything.

* * *

Success in the glass-making business is dependent upon many skills. No doubt the most important are skill in mixing the glass batch, skill in making the moulds, and skill in making the glass itself. The various colors are dependent on the batch, and the shapes and styles of the glass pieces are dependent upon the moulds. All the intricate designs and patterns one sees on Fenton glass—such as Hobnail, Thumbprint, Daisy and Button, Rose, or any other—have been carved into the moulds. Once the design and the shape of an item has been approved, a working model is made of it. Whether it be a one-piece, three-piece, or five-piece mould, the working model [or pattern] is a replica of what the final product will be, except that the design itself is not reproduced on the inside. This model is then sent away to a foundry for casting in iron. FAGCO sent its models to various foundries in the area—New Martinsville and Elkins, West Virginia, and Lancaster, Ohio, are the sites of several of them. In about two weeks the castings are back, "just sand-cast bits of iron," as Lynn Russi, veteran Fenton mould-maker, described them. Shaping, or milling machines, are used to polish off the surface. The mould is now ready to have the design carved into it.

Cutting the design is painstaking, slow work—with hammer and chisel. Naturally, the more complex the pattern, the longer it takes to cut it. One of the most complex patterns ever turned out by Fenton was the Jefferson Comport during the Bicentennial year. The mould shop personnel spent close to five months on that amazing piece of work. Measuring instruments and "depth guages" are used to make sure that the pattern is in perfect accord with the original drawings.

Every piece of hobnail glass is a result of the precise spotting of each hob in the mould and then the drilling of each individual one. The design on every mould is attended to with the same, meticulous care. In cutting narrow grooves, Russi said, "we tried to get the right depth, the right layout, and the right spacing, as near as sharp dividers can make it. We would be worn out at the end of the day—there were no half-hour breaks for us in the old days—but we were proud of what we did."

In going through Fenton's minutes for the third 25 years, the reader periodically reads about "production problems" with different pieces. The fact is that when a mould has been made there is no automatic guarantee that the piece of glass can be made from that mould. The molten glass gets obstreperous at times and may not "fill" the mould, particularly if it is of an unusual shape. Or, perhaps, the chemicals in the batch are such that the piece of glass may cling to the sides of the mould when it should fall freely out. "Making glass from a new mould is always an adventure," someone has said. In most cases production problems are solved one way or another and the item goes into the line. In a few instances, however, the problems cannot be resolved and the project must be abandoned. Some examples of this kind of thing will be discussed in the next chapter.

What happens to the moulds of glass companies which go out of business, one might wonder? Usually two things happen: they either rust away in silent oblivion, or another glass company which has managed to survive acquires them. Fenton, as a surviving company, purchased moulds from several defunct glass plants. The Paden City Glass Company of Paden City went out of business in 1951 and their moulds were sold to various companies up and down the river. Paden City, in addition to its regular line, had been making ashtrays and other items for Rubel and Company in New York. After Paden City closed down, Rubel asked Fenton if they would take the moulds and continue making the products for them. By 1959 FACGO had ceased making anything for Rubel and inquired how to dispose of the moulds. Rubel had no use for them either and invited Fenton to name a price for them. Frank Fenton offered $600 for all the moulds; Rubel accepted. Rubel glass went into the Fenton line in 1960 and much of it sold well for a number of years.

Verlys glass was developed in France by the Holophane Company and was only available in the United States through importation until the company opened an American branch, Holophane Company, Inc., in New York City in 1935. Moulds and designs were sent from France to the American factory. The company made some things in color, but was probably better known for its etched crystal pieces. In the late 1930s Holophane's Newark, Ohio branch acquired the Verlys moulds and unsuccessfully tried to manufacture a few items. In the early 1950s, it leased the moulds to A. H. Heisey Company, also of Newark, near its own branch plant. Heisey had no better luck with the product than Holophane. In 1958 Heisey closed down and sold all of its moulds, save those which it had on lease from Holophane, to Imperial Glass of Bellaire, Ohio. At this time Fenton carried on some correspondence with Holophane with an eye to the purchase of the Verlys moulds. Holophane, however, hesitated to sell

Mould Makers with Francis Lehew, Foreman. Left to Right—Lynn Russi, Fred Ryan, Herb Fenton, Jr., Ken Krames, Ed Cain, S. H. Bee, Dan McDermott, Francis Lehew.

19

and preferred a leasing arrangement similar to that it had with Heisey. Or if it did sell the moulds, it wanted the Verlys name used on the product. Fenton wanted to buy, but did not want to use the Verlys name, so the matter was dropped.

In 1966 when Dave Ellies was doing consulting work for FAGCO, Frank Fenton mentioned to Ellies that he had unsuccessfully tried to buy the Verlys moulds some years earlier. Ellies said he knew Kurt Franck who managed Holophane's Newark plant and that he thought he might be able to get them to sell. On his next trip to Newark he talked to Franck about the moulds and found that he was receptive to selling the moulds if the home office agreed. He consulted with headquarters in New York and found out that if Fenton did not use the Verlys name—quite a switch from a few years before—Holophane was willing to sell. Frank Fenton went to Holophane's Newark plant and looked over the 65 moulds stored there. A bargain was struck and FAGCO acquired all the moulds at $100 apiece, a total of $6500. It was another two years, 1968, before any items made from the Verlys moulds got into the line, but once they did they sold well.

The ancient United States Glass Company had two plants in Glassport, Pennsylvania and one in Tiffin, Ohio, when in 1963 a tornado wrecked the two Glassport facilities. The management decided not to rebuild and filed for bankruptcy, which left its 200 workers jobless. Frank Fenton spent some time in Glassport wading around in the basement muck of the old factory where the moulds were stored. He eventually bought some 20-25 moulds from U.S. Glass, although some of them may have belonged originally to Duncan and Miller, a Washington, Pennsylvania glass house which U.S. Glass had acquired in 1955. A number of Fenton's most popular pieces came from this collection.

FAGCO's mould shop at the beginning of the third 25 years was managed by Francis O. Lehew who came to the company in 1924. In 1948 he was named mould shop foreman. After 40 years of service, Lehew retired January 15, 1965. Succeeding him was Carnick Hamperian, who had joined the company in 1960 as a

Carnick Hamperian, Mould Shop Foreman and Herbert E. Fenton, Jr., Mould Maker and Maintenance Foreman.

draftsman. In 1969 he was advanced to an office position and Lynn Russi was named working foreman. Russi had come to Fenton in 1954 as a mould maker, left in 1961 to work at Viking in New Martinsville, and returned to Fenton in 1963. He was not happy as foreman, however, because he could not work on the moulds, so he relinquished his position in 1971 and went back to the bench. During these years workers in the mould shop included Ken Krames, Herb Fenton, Fred Ryan, Shirley Bee, Ed Cain, Dan McDermott, Dale Kernan, and Bill Ferrebee.

* * *

Having surveyed the tremendous increase in sales which Fenton experienced in the 1950s and 1960s, having discussed the numerous plant improvements that the record sales made necessary, having looked at the managers who guided the company through this period of momentous growth, and having peeked inside the mould shop, it is now time to examine the product. Just what was it that was causing all the commotion? What was the "Fenton Line?"

* * *

In 1966, Fenton acquired a steel fabricating company, Armstrong Tank Company, located in Williamstown. The name was changed to Armstrong Custom Fabricators. It was operated as a separate division and was sold in 1972 after management at Fenton decided that its contribution to earnings had been unsatisfactory and that continued operation in the steel business would not be beneficial to the glass company and its employees.

Chapter Eleven
THE LINE

"There is just something about it. You go into a gift shop and you recognize it at once; it has 'that Fenton look'." The enthusiastic comment came from Wilmer C. "Bill" Fenton, chairman of the board. Not many people in the hand glass business would disagree with him. As one enters a store which retails glassware, he will spot the Fenton colors, the Fenton designs, and the Fenton shapes. Even excluding hobnail milk glass, which has become the company's hallmark, there is still "that Fenton look." FAGCO's survival and success over the years has resulted from sound business practices. But more basic to this success has been the product—"the line." Year in and year out the company has upgraded, refined, and improved the line. It has experimented with new ideas and it has brought forth new shapes and designs. It has moved ever forward, keeping a close eye on market trends, withdrawing what has not sold and pressing hard with what has sold. Most everything has sold.

* * *

When Frank L. Fenton died in 1948, the company lost not only its "founding father," but its principal designer as well. And there was no one prepared to move into his designer shoes. Since his father had done the designing, son Frank M. concluded that he had better quickly educate himself in the art. He knew the company had done well in the 1930s and 1940s with products styled after the Victorian and early American patterns, so he began studying them. He began visiting antique shops where old glass could often be found for sale. Then as antique shows became popular he visited them. "I would schedule a trip," he said, "where I might be able to attend eight to ten shows that might be scheduled along the route of my trip. As I examined the glassware I had to school myself to stay away from Fentonware. I had to say to myself, 'no, I'm looking for new ideas.' I was looking for things made in the Victorian era, things that we might be able to do."

Many of Fenton's most familiar and successful pieces of glassware have been derived from items Frank Fenton has purchased at antique shows and stores. Such items would not be copied, but they would serve as models, or simply as ideas, from which a new, original Fenton product would be developed. To illustrate, most of the new shapes appearing in the January 1956 catalog were stimulated by pieces bought at such places. Slight changes from the originals were made in the shapes, but the colors were distinctively Fenton. The July 1956 catalog contained a large square bowl, 3929, which was based on a piece first made by Hobbs Brockunier that had been purchased at some show. It was a reproduction of the original, but differed from it in that it was in milk glass. In 1961 a few items were put in the line which were derived from an old piece that combined thumbprint and hobnail. That same year the Bubble Optic pattern, based on an antique pinch vase, first appeared. The Wild Rose with Bowknot patterns came from the McKee and Brothers Works in Jeannette, Pennsylvania, but was adapted to original Fenton pieces. The Wheat vase,

with its wrap around band, was found at an antique show in Denver and put in the Fenton line in modified form. The Vasa Murrhina treatment was suggested by a basket acquired at some forgotten antique shop. The glass itself had to be "reinvented" by company chemists, a challenging chore. The popular Rose pattern came from a tall, footed comport purchased in a similar place.

He conceded that he was not a designer himself, but that he learned about shapes and patterns and recognized things others had done, which, with modest changes, might look well in the Fenton line. He was by no means content with his own efforts, however, and from time to time brought in professional designers, the first of whom, in the early 1950s, was Stan Fistick. Fistick worked hard, as was reported in THE SECOND TWENTY-FIVE YEARS, but not much resulted from his efforts and after a time he was gone. "Every few years," Frank Fenton recalled, "I would get an outside designer to come in and do something for us. Except for a few pieces Stan Fistick made, we never made any money on anything an outside designer did for us. Their pieces either proved too hard to make or wouldn't sell in the marketplace. But we felt we had to keep trying that." It was not until the arrival of Tony Rosena in 1967 that the company found the designer it had been looking for.

Shapes and designs might be borrowed and adapted, but as for colors, they were indigenous to FAGCO. It was the main component of "that Fenton look." Fenton colors set the line apart from other companies more than anything else. And the all-time best-seller for the company, the one color which carried the heaviest load during the third 25 years—thereby making possible many experimental and innovative efforts—was milk glass. Particularly Hobnail milk glass. Hobnail milk glass did so well that just about anything produced in it moved quickly. But at the outset of the third 25 years, however, there were problems with the milk glass formula. Bill Fenton was receiving reports from the field—from reps and customers—that Fenton's milk glass was too weak and transparent. If the company was going to get into milk glass in a big way, it should develop a denser whiteness. Westmoreland's milk glass was actually superior to Fenton's at this time. In addition, Fenton's product often had a sandy appearance. Occasionally, the batch "burned out" at the bottom of the pot leaving a gray ring around the piece. Obviously something had to be done about milk glass.

To address this problem Fenton retained the services of Dr. Alexander Silverman, the noted glass chemist from the University of Pittsburgh. He came to Williamstown two times a month to work with Fenton chemists Charles Goe and Isaac Willard on the milk glass formula. Out of their efforts came a revised formula which produced a denser white and, incidentally, eliminated both the sandiness and the gray ring. The new milk glass was an important stimulus to the growing sales and popularity of Fenton milk glass.

Before describing the growth and changes in the

line, a word should be said about the coding system adopted in 1953. Professor James Measell discusses this in his introduction, but it might not be amiss to refresh our memories on the point here. No one can remember who was responsible for the new plan. Apparently it was a team effort with office manager Robert Simms playing the role of "chief initiator." At any rate, a two-page document entitled "Ware Number Plan" set forth the main points in the code:

> The Fenton Ware Number has three parts: a *design* code, an *item* code, and a *color* code. The three codes together name a finished piece of ware different from any other piece. For instance, a 7137 PC was formerly the 711 Miniature Rose Bowl basket in Case Opal with Crystal rings and Crystal handle in the Tiara pattern.

In explaining this example, the design, or pattern, code is "71," or Tiara; "37" is the item code, a Rose Bowl Basket; while "PC" is the color code, Case Opal with Crystal rings. (For the complete list of color codes see pages 145-153).

* * *

Turning to the line itself, 1956 marked the advent of the footed cakeplate in milk glass, 3913, which would become an all-time best-seller. It was also during the first year of the third 25 years that Fenton began describing its fluted-edged ware as "petticoat glass." The term had been used by dealers for some time, but it came to be most closely identified with milk glass bowls, vases, and plates with the silver crest crystal edging. The tremendous boom in milk glass Hobnail also began about this time. So successful did it become that many items which had been made in other colors were now being made in milk glass. The entire milk glass Hobnail line was selling so well that it would not be easy to select any one or two items as doing better than the others.

Few new shapes appeared in 1957, although that was the "Jamestown" year. New colors of "Jamestown Blue," "Silver Jamestown," and "Jamestown Transparent" made their debut. (See p. 75). At the same time Tear Drop milk glass pieces, inspired by a salt and pepper condiment set of the last century, was added to the line. The collection included salt and pepper, candy jar, sugar, creamer, oil bottle, cakeplate, sandwich tray, and candle holders. The following year, a number of new Hobnail pieces, in milk glass and cranberry, were added. An eleven inch cranberry vase, 1451, had sold well in Coin Dot so it was made in Hobnail milk glass. It was becoming customary to take pieces in other colors and patterns that were selling well and reissue them in Hobnail. Although most items were in milk glass, Hobnail was gradually extended to other colors. As Frank Fenton said, "We kept changing colors and adding new shapes and styles."

In 1957 FAGCO began working with Michael Lax, a contemporary designer from New York. While the company was doing very well with its traditional ware, Lax suggested that there might also be a market for contemporary pieces as well. Recognizing that he could have a point, Fenton worked out an arrangement with Lax whereby the company would pay him [1]

$500 down to begin work on his designs, [2] another $500 when his drawings were submitted, and [3] another $500 when the first of his glassware was made. The balance of Lax's payments would be in the form of a five per cent royalty on the sale of each piece of glass which had been designed by him.

Work proceeded and by 1958 Lax was ready with his glassware. It was totally different from anything Fenton had ever done and it certainly did not possess "that Fenton look." Lax was high on his work, however, and convinced that it would sell. But the problem was that the traditional line was selling better than ever and the company decided against introducing such a revolutionary style at this time. Lax accepted that decision—for the time being. He returned in 1959 urging FAGCO to put his ware in the line then. The company still demurred, saying the time was not yet ripe. This naturally troubled Lax who had invested a good bit in the project, but could realize no more gain until his material was sold. His argument was accepted and the new contemporary work was put in the line.

Twenty Lax items were advertised on the front and back covers of the July 1959 catalog supplement. (See CR 151, P. 142). It was called the "Horizon" line. The catalog observed, "Horizon is a marriage of beautiful Fenton colors, rubbed walnut wood tops, porcelain candle cups and bases, and rawhide thongs—as new as tomorrow; functional and beautiful, truly a pace setting achievement that has long been our forte—and always with you our customers in mind." The set included a number of candle holders with inserts, and hanging bowls with thongs, as well as bowls, nut dishes, sugar and creamer, and salt and pepper shakers. Despite a strong promotional effort in its behalf and despite its contemporary appeal, the Horizon line did not sell and was withdrawn.

Naturally, FAGCO was not relying only on the Horizon line for 1959. The Cactus pattern in milk glass and topaz opalescent was introduced that year. (See P. 66). The pattern originated many years earlier at the Greentown plant of Indiana Tumbler and Goblet, where it was made in chocolate glass by Jake Rosenthal. Some of the pieces were reproductions of Greentown items made from new Fenton moulds, while others were original with Fenton. The topaz opalescent did not sell as well as the milk glass and did not remain in the line. It was at this time that the new milk glass formula, providing a denser quality of white, came into use.

In 1959 Fenton also brought out new Hobnail shapes in milk glass, green opalescent, and plum opalescent. Interestingly, plum opalescent grew out of unsuccessful efforts to make pressed items in true cranberry. Whenever the gold ruby was made strong enough to work in a press it became a purplish plum color instead. So it was decided to put the items out in plum opalescent. This sold well in several Hobnail shapes. At the same time the attractive pink opaline color was developed by a special heat treatment to blown items. Several vases were produced in the Jacqueline pattern in this color as well as in blue and yellow opaline. Jacqueline, which appeared in early 1961, was named in the honor of the nation's new first lady, Mrs. John F. [Jacqueline] Kennedy.

1960 witnessed the introduction of another color

combination using the same basic plum opalescent glass to make petticoat glass in apple blossom. This was a grouping of milk glass items with a pink opaque edge. The glass was heat sensitive so the edges varied from light pink to dark red. Though an attractive color, it did not sell well and was soon withdrawn. But petticoat glass in silver crest and peach crest continued to do very well. Two free form ashtrays made from Rubel moulds were also listed in the 1960 catalog. Free form pieces were made from moulds without the restraining ring, so they could assume any shapes they wished. One ashtray, 9176, was nine inches in diameter, the other, 9175, was five inches in diameter. Both were made in transparent colors and crystal. Hobnail was stronger than ever in 1960 and several new items were added to that line.

One such piece, a small square berry dish, 3928, (see CR 49, P. 108), had an interesting history. Fenton had an inquiry from the Borden Ice Cream Company about manufacturing something in Hobnail milk glass that might be sold as a premium with a quart or so of ice cream. Borden liked the idea of the berry dish. When it came to the matter of volume, Frank Fenton suggested that a small number be produced at first and that they be test marketed to get some sense of the sales potential. The Borden buyer, however, was quite confident that he could use a large number of the dishes and ordered 6500 of them. Frank Fenton thought this was a pretty large number, too large, and he was right. "He should have ordered 650 instead of 6500 because they didn't sell very well. They were not illustrated well on the ice cream box and I wouldn't have wanted to buy one based only on the label on the box. Evidently no one else did either. It's my understanding that the buyer lost his job as a result of this particular fiasco."

The January 1961 catalog advertised five new overlay colors—apple green, powder blue, coral, honey amber, and wild rose—made in Hobnail, Bubble Optic, Jacqueline, and Wild Rose with Bowknot. (See P. 72). A novel piece was a honey jar made in milk glass and amber, 9080, requested by a beekeeper from Virginia. The gentleman wanted a honey jar that would hold exactly one comb of honey. He provided ideas for the design, but was not interested in being paid for them. All he wanted were some honey jars which could be given away as gifts. It was a successful and attractive item which sold well for many years. At this time, also, the Wheat vase first appeared. It has always sold well and is still in the line.

In 1962 the catalog noted that "Early American is in stronger demand than ever. These outstanding reproductions and adaptations of antique patterns were added to our line to help you [the buyers] meet this growing demand." A group of six reproduction goblets were introduced that year in the new colors of colonial pink, colonial amber, and colonial blue. (See P. 90). As had become customary, a number of new Hobnail milk glass pieces were added to the line, including the black and white salt and pepper shakers. Other new colors were opaque blue and plated amberina. Among the new designs were Thumbprint, Pineapple, Stippled Scroll, and Empress.

In January 1963 Fenton published its largest catalog to date, 32 pages. The growth of the company is well-reflected in the ever-increasing thickness of the catalogs. An introductory note states that "Items already in the line had to be proven sellers before they were listed in the new catalog. New pieces were added only after careful study and testing of sales appeal." Hobnail, certainly a "proven seller," occupied almost one-third of the catalog. It was mostly in milk glass, but a few items were in French and blue opalescent. Cranberry opalescent was also listed. New colors for the year included gold crest, blue crest, and flame crest. Thumbprint, which had done very well in its inaugural year, was featured on a number of additional pieces. Diamond Optic, a new pattern, came out in colonial blue, colonial amber, and orange. The tricky business of fixing Diamond Optic on a piece is described below:

> First, you blow the item in a spot mould or an optic mould which raises the diamond pattern on the outside of the glass. The piece is then taken over to the glory hole, reheated, and blown in a second mould which gives the shape to the piece. The process of blowing it in the second mould causes the extended portions of the pattern to be pushed back to the inside of the piece so that there is a light reflection that comes from the pattern being on the inside while the outside is relatively smooth.

In 1964 Fenton brought forth perhaps its most innovative color so far in the third 25 years, Vasa Murrhina. (See P. 76). The catalog outlines the history of this unique combination of colors:

> Many centuries ago glassmakers discovered a way to fuse different colors into singularly beautiful glassware. Their artistic efforts inspired an era of imaginative glass-making which reached its peak in the famed Vasa Murrhina glass of the nineteenth century.
>
> Fenton now brings back Vasa Murrhina, a glass so complicated to make that it can be produced only in limited amounts. Because of its intricate color patterns each piece is an individual creation, unlike any other.
>
> Vasa Murrhina, which means vessels of gems, is well named. The sparkling effects of ancient aventurine glass and other colors give it a jewel-like appearance and blend together in a finished tapestry of distinctive character. Because it is Fenton, it is authentic—made by hand, the only way it can be made.

Since the formula for producing Vasa Murrhina had been lost in history, Fenton chemists had to develop it anew. Charles Goe spent a long time working on the process, using as his model an antique piece Frank Fenton had picked up in an antique shop. Goe gathered a ball of opal glass, rolled it in a "frit"—small pieces of crushed glass—and then gathered a layer of crystal glass over the top of it. Next he would blow it out a little bit and stretch it almost like a swung-out vase. He would then crack this off and send it through the lehr. The green-blue Vasa Murrhina had an opal core which was rolled in the ground up pieces of glass, either in aventurine green and blue or cranberry Then this mass of glass, which already had some air blown in it, was re-heated in the glory hole, after which the clear crystal was gathered over the top of it.

Most of the shapes made for Vasa Murrhina were new to Fenton.

The company got into a minor hassle with the skilled workers union over this process, the union charging that chemist Goe had no right to make pieces of glass, even off-hand ware. Officers from the union's international headquarters in Toledo had to be summoned to the scene to mediate the dispute. At length they were able to convince the local workers that as long as the item was not either blown or pressed in a mould, Goe was free to carry on with his experiments.

Thumbprint continued to do well and came out in various colors. "These attractive new pieces," commented the catalog, "were inspired by the vigorous demand for Thumbprint in authentic colonial colors." One of the new Thumbprint items, a royal wedding bowl in colonial green, 4488, was an authentic reproduction. The original piece had been made by Bakewell Pears and Company of Pittsburgh shortly before the Civil War. All other pieces were designed by Fenton. It was in 1964, also, that the Rose pattern was introduced. It appeared on a comport, 9222, modeled after a tall, footed comport which Frank Fenton had acquired at an antique show. The comport was made in the four colonial colors, amber, blue, green, and pink.

In 1963 and 1964 Fenton became associated with a design organization in Columbus, Ohio, Dave Ellies Inc. Ellies did a number of things for FAGCO in the design area and also explored diversification prospects. As an example of the latter, it investigated the suitability of acquiring the American Bisque Company and recommended against the purchase since its products were too dissimilar to Fenton's basic line. Ellies also looked into the desirability of manufacturing outdoor playground equipment and prepared a number of designs for such equipment. The conclusion, however, was that such a line was too foreign to Fenton's product to be seriously pursued.

Ellies designed a line of decorative wrought iron hangers, which utilized Hobnail milk glass, planter and candle items. (See CR 50, P. 109). One unusual piece in this group was the Bull's Eye candle sconce [an ornamental wall bracket for holding a candle or a light], M677. The idea was that the Bull's Eye might be used in the building industry for wall dividers and in doorways. Several production problems developed in trying to produce these flat panels and when those problems were resolved, it was found that the manufacturing costs were so great that the project had to be abandoned.

1965 witnessed the introduction of over 100 new items, most of them additions to, or refinements of products which were already in the line. One new piece was a nine-inch footed bowl, 3621, based on a porcelain bowl Frank Fenton had bought somewhere, produced in Hobnail milk glass. Among the new Thumbprint pieces was a quarter-pound, oval-shaped covered butter dish, 4477, developed by the Dave Ellies people. The Rose candy box, made from a mould acquired from the defunct United States Glass Company, appeared for the first time in the January 1965 catalog. Autumn orange was a new color in the Vasa Murrhina line and several new shapes, based on pieces Frank Fenton had picked up at antique shows and shops, also came out in Vasa Murrhina. The con-

tinuing popularity of Hobnail milk glass was reflected in comments which appeared in the 1965 catalog:

> One could almost say that Fenton Hobnail milk glass has become an institution, for never has a glass pattern met with such enduring popularity. Your customers are buying more and more of this traditionally styled glassware each year . . . Fenton Hobnail has proven outstandingly successful because it is as beautiful as it is authentic in its Early American styling.

It was also noted that customers across the country were seeing Fenton glass in color in such publications as *HOUSE BEAUTIFUL, HOUSE AND GARDEN,* and *AMERICAN HOME.* (See pp. 25 and 26).

1966 signaled an important departure with the introduction of Fenton lamps. For years the company had been manufacturing lamp parts for lamp companies, but had not ventured into lamp-making until recently. Then it began to make Hobnail milk glass lamps and "test market" them in its own gift shop. (See CR 145-150, P. 139-141). They sold well so it was decided to test them more widely before adding them to the regular line. Of the 18 lamps introduced at the time, the catalog stated, "Market tests involving 37 stores, showed that these lamps sold extremely well. We suggest that you order them in limited quantity at first to see for yourself how well they sell to your particular customers." These test items were sold mostly by John Evans, Fenton's Pennsylvania rep. One of those in the 1966 catalog was a Hobnail student lamp, 3707. This was made with items that had been made for a long time for lamp manufacturers in cranberry opalescent and other opalescent colors. In addition to the Hobnail design, other lamps carried the Poppy and Antique Rose pattern. FAGCO also made some ruby overlay lamps, such as the 1408 Thumbprint student lamp. The lamp line developed to such a degree that in July 1967 the company put out a separate lamp catalog, called "Traditional Lamps." (See P. 111). This practice of issuing lamp catalogs continued for several years, but because of complex retailing problems with department stores, it was dropped in 1973.

As Hobnail pieces continued to flow from the Fenton moulds and presses, Frank Fenton confessed his amazement at the line's uninterrupted success. "It made me wonder," he reflected, "how we could ever think of something else to make in the Hobnail pattern. Yet we kept right on adding new items, and of course, new and different colors in pieces that had not been made in color before." The 1967 catalog provided ample evidence of this. Page 8, for example, illustrated six different sugar and cream sets and three covered butter dishes. (See CR 48-49, P. 108). "One of the ways we did this," he added,

> "was that whenever we saw an attractive shape that served a particular function in some other medium or pattern, we said 'why don't we do something like that in Hobnail.' So each year we brought out additional items for the Hobnail line. We used to call that 'sweetening up' the line. I believe the reason that Hobnail lasted so long was that we kept bringing in new kinds of hobs, new combinations of Hobnails and other things to go with them."

These rich, color-splashed pages will showcase Fenton Glass to an audience of millions this fall in:

- *The American Home*
- *House Beautiful*
- *House & Garden*

Traditional fashions in glass
…hand-fashioned by Fenton

basic white…always right for her home or yours

Is her decor quietly elegant? Or does she exult in color? Never mind. Fenton's lustrous white hobnail milk glass will flatter her home beautifully . . . and sincerely. Look for exquisite handcrafted Fenton glassware . . . for presents and for yourself, in white or colors . . . at fine stores and gift shops.

The Fenton Art Glass Company
Williamstown, West Virginia

Featuring: 3799 MI 10" Planter; 3845 MI Goblet; 3974 MI Candleholder; 3777 MI Oval ¼ lb. Cov'd. Butter; 3938 MI 12" Bowl; 3806 MI Salt & Pepper; 3825 MI Sherbet; 3816 MI 8" Plate; 3606 MI Cov'd Sugar & Cream; 4455 CB Bud Vase; 4438 CG 8½" Basket; 4484 CA Anniversary Bowl; 4425 OR Ftd. Comport DC.

Traditional fashions in glass
…hand-fashioned by Fenton

Fenton glass…better to give <u>and</u> to receive

Whether you wrap it for someone special . . . find it under your tree . . . or enjoy it to toast the season . . . Fenton hand-crafted glass adds a splendid luster to Christmastime. Select Fenton thumbprint, hobnail and other treasured antique patterns in color and milk glass . . . at fine stores and gift shops.

The Fenton Art Glass Company
Williamstown, West Virginia

Featuring: 4417 CG 8½" Plate; 4443 CG Sherbet; 4445 CG 10 oz. Goblet; 4444 CG 5 oz. Wine; 4453 CG Tall Bud Vase; 4477 CG Oval ¼ lb. Cov'd. Butter; 4403 CG Cov'd Sugar & Cream; 4408 CG Salt & Pepper Set; 4470 CG 4" Candleholder; 3628 MI Ftd. DC Comport; 3653 OR 5" Vase; 4484 CA Anniversary Bowl; 6437 GB Hdl. Basket 11" High; 7213 SC Ftd. Cakeplate.

Fenton national consumer advertising excerpts, circa 1965.

This campaign pinpoints a select audience of above-average-income shoppers, most of whom own their own homes, spend more for gifts and entertain more often. It should help build important brand awareness . . . thus further projecting Fenton as THE name in fine handmade glass.

Plan now to tie in. Schedule Fenton's FREE ad mats in your local newspaper. Place Fenton commercials on your local stations. And set up attractive displays . . . for your best fall season ever!

Traditional fashions in glass
. . . hand-fashioned by Fenton

give Fenton handmade glass . . . _if you can give it up_

Better not try your Fenton Christmas gift selections on your coffee table. You may not have the heart to part with them. For basic white Fenton milk glass has a way of charming a whole room! Look for hobnail, thumbprint and other Fenton patterns in white or colors at fine stores and gift shops.

The Fenton Art Glass Company
Williamstown, West Virginia

Traditional fashions in glass
. . . hand-fashioned by Fenton

the pleasure is half yours when you give Fenton

She'll be delighted! You will too, when she unwraps your gift of Fenton glass. For it's an eloquent compliment to her good taste . . . and yours. Ever since Virginia colonists fired America's first glass furnace in 1608, fine glassware has gladdened heart and hearth at Christmastime. Today this proud heritage is evident in every piece by Fenton. Look for it at better stores and gift shops.

The Fenton Art Glass Company
Williamstown, West Virginia

Featuring: 3792 MI Courting Lamp (Oil); 3734 MI 12" Basket; 3913 MI Ftd. Cakeplate; 3786 MI Oval Candy Box; 3610 MI 3 Pc. Ash Tray Set; 3692 MI Table Lighter; 3628 MI Ftd. DC Comport; 3952 CG 4" DC Vase; 3653 CB 5" Vase; 3652 OR Tall Vase; 3792 CB Courting Lamp (Oil); 3665 CG Miniature Cream; 3995 CA Slipper.

Featuring: 6456 GB 8" Vase; 7336 SC 6½" Hdl. Basket; 4429 CA Ftd. Comport; 4484 CG Anniversary Bowl; 3938 MI 12" Bowl; 4453 OR Tall Bud Vase; 4438 CG 8½" Basket; 4486 CA Oval Candy Box; 4479 CA Round Ash Tray; 9222 CG Rose Comport; 4454 CB 8" Ftd. Vase; 3580 SC Ftd. Candy Box; 3610 CA 3 Pc. Ash Tray Set.

Fenton national trade advertisements, circa 1965.

As an example, he pointed out an eight and one-half inch basket, 3638, on page 13, with a rope-like pattern going down the side of the piece at regular intervals. (See CR 45, P. 107).

The Rose pattern, introduced in 1965, was by now coming into its own. It was a fairly simple process to pick out a shape and then have the mould makers apply the embossed Rose pattern on that shape. Pages 16 and 17 of the 1967 catalog included many examples of this. Mould maker Lynn Russi played an important part in developing some of these pieces, such as the owl ring tree (see P. 87) in the bathroom set, which also included a tumbler and soap dish. The 9222 Rose comport, the new covered candy box, candleholders, and ashtrays were other handsome pieces which carried the Rose design. The four and one-half inch oval vase, 9251, was developed from a pottery piece purchased many years before. Roses were applied to the shape which was produced in many different colors.

Thumbprint was another successful pattern that was being used on more and more shapes. In 1967 a footed ice tea shape was introduced and ruby was added to the Thumbprint group of colors. Cigarette lighters and ashtrays were being developed in all the various lines, Hobnail and now Thumbprint. That same year Fenton's first bell in over 30 years was added to the line with the Hobnail dinner bell. Many more bells were to come. The catalog commented enthusiastically,

> One reason for this significant growth [the record sales of 1965 and 1966 had just been mentioned] is that we reevaluate the entire line each year and replace slower-moving items with exciting new pieces. In 1966 we added almost 100 new items and for 1967 we are introducing another 100 . . . . This is not done quickly or casually. Before any new design or pattern is accepted, several dozen possible replacements are carefully considered. We consider your [the buyer's] suggestions. We consult our designers. We run consumer tests. In this way, guesswork is all but eliminated. And, therefore, any new item is almost certain to be an outstanding seller.

Business continued to be so good in 1967 that no July catalog supplement was even issued.

1968 featured the first products made from the Verlys moulds, such as the vases in orange and opalescent. (See P. 92). As was mentioned before, production problems developed with these items and they were eventually withdrawn from the line. They have become highly-prized collectors' pieces because of their rarity as well as their charm. Numerous reproductions were also offered in 1968, such as the Daisy and Button covered candy box, which had been made originally by Hobbs Brockunier. The leaf ashtray, 1976, was a copy of an earlier piece which had not been made as an ashtray. Another reproduction was the seven and one-half inch candy jar, originally in the Northwood line. Northwood sold it as a tobacco jar, but Fenton recrafted it slightly to make it a candy jar.

FAGCO made an unsuccessful experiment with Hobnail crystal in 1968. Opinion was divided as to whether Hobnail was suited to crystal and whether the product would sell, so it was test marketed in October and November 1967 in stores in Milwaukee, Chicago, and New York. Reports came back that it had moved quite well and looked like a good seller, so it was put in the line in 1968. However, it just sat on the shelves across the country, never approaching the success of milk glass and other colored Hobnail. It was shortly withdrawn. On the other hand, the popularity of Thumbprint continued and, for the first time, Thumbprint pieces came out in ebony. This proved a popular color as was evidenced by the July 1968 catalog supplement which carried several additional items, a candle bowl, the Northwood tobacco jar, and the Empress and Mandarin vases, all in ebony.

The principal new design in 1969 was Valencia. It was developed from a piece of Moser glass made in Czechoslovakia early in the century. Frank Fenton saw it at an antique show, liked its style and the way the light played through it, and bought it. The first piece of Valencia (see P. 89) was an identical reproduction of the original piece, a covered candy box, 8380 CG. The new designer, Tony Rosena, then built an entire line of Valencia items, all inspired by the original Moser piece. Why was glassware from Czechoslovakia given a Spanish name? Frank Fenton explains: "At that time, the gift market was going strongly with what was called the 'Mediterranean' influence, so we decided to capitalize on that and gave it the name Valencia." The catalog noted that,

> . . . we are presenting a ten-piece collection in five colors. Market testing has indicated a strong acceptance for Valencia, so strong that we have begun making new moulds for pieces already designed and are continuing to design additional items.

Despite its appeal, the Valencia pattern was difficult to make. Many problems with "settle waves" developed and the cure was almost as bad as the ailment itself. To eliminate settle waves, the moulds had to "run hot." And when the moulds ran hot, other difficulties appeared. These were worked through, but not before some of the Hot Metal workers were retrained. Although Valencia glassware was made, it was not continued in the line for more than a couple of years because of the trouble in making it. Yet it was a lovely pattern and the company was very proud of it.

Meanwhile, Hobnail milk glass was selling as well as ever, as were the colored transparent items bearing the Thumbprint, Rose, and Daisy and Button patterns. Candle items were also coming along quickly. The miniature candle bowl, 3873, and the creative candle bowl both stimulated sales in 1969. The creative candle bowl, (see CR 86, P. 118), suggested by Bill Fenton and designed by Tony Rosena, became the number one best-seller for the year. The catalog was becoming thicker and more colorful, too. It began to show every piece in every color. This was an additional expense, but it promoted the line more effectively.

A number of pressed and blown pieces in Spanish Lace (see CR 60-61, P. 112), were featured on page 38 of the 1969 catalog. The Spanish Lace pattern, first introduced by Fenton in 1956 with a footed cakeplate, was borrowed from a butter dish made by Northwood at its old Indiana, Pennsylvania plant. The bottom of the butter dish, which Frank Fenton picked up at an antique show in New York City [he also picked up the cover for the dish], carried the Spanish

Lace design. Since its first appearance in the Fenton line, Spanish Lace has been used on a number of pressed and blown items, some of which appeared in this catalog. A new design in 1969 was Wild Strawberry. The idea came from an old picture frame Frank Fenton had purchased at an antique show. Tony Rosena developed the pattern for glassware and it was embossed on the 9088 candy box. The 5197 colonial amber and crystal "happiness birds," made from moulds acquired from the defunct Paden City Glass Company, were first introduced in 1968 and featured in the 1969 catalogs. In the July 1969 catalog supplement, zodiac medallions, (see CR 13-14, P. 99), researched and designed by Rosena, were displayed. Unfortunately, the zodiac craze had ebbed by this time and the medallions did not sell too well.

It might be appropriate at this time to say a word about the Olde Virginia line, which was not shown in the regular Fenton catalog. Beginning in the mid-1950s, Fenton began selling a line of glassware to some of the large catalog houses, such as General Merchandise Company, L. and C. Mayers, and Bennett Brothers. These companies published thick catalogs filled with descriptions of all sorts of merchandise which could be purchased at a discount. These were sent all over the country to manufacturers and assorted retail outlets large and small. Because some of these retailers might be located adjacent to regular Fenton accounts and thus could become potential competitors, nothing in the regular line was sold to the catalog people, except in the first year when a few line items were put out in different color treatments to test the market. This glassware was not advertised in Fenton catalogs.

The first such items were in milk glass with the Thumbprint pattern. This was before Thumbprint had been introduced into the regular line. Over the years other pieces with some of the familiar patterns, such as Daisy and Button and Fine Cut and Block, were included in this "irregular" line. (See CR 137-144, PP. 133-138). Even though the patterns might occasionally be the same as those in the regular line, they would always be in different colors, so there would never be, at the same time, the same piece, color, and design in both the regular and irregular lines. At first this glassware had no particular designation, but in 1959 it was given the name Olde Virginia. Olde Virginia glass was sold all over the country to retail stores Fenton would not normally sell to, and it sold well. The line was dropped in the 1970s when the catalog houses went into decline.

* * *

Two important additions to the Fenton team arrived in 1967 and 1968. Tony Rosena, who has already been mentioned as the new designer, and Louise Piper, an accomplished decorator, supplied new dimensions to the kinds of things which the company could now do. Their skill, imagination, and initiative provided a stimulus to exciting new departures in glass-making, a subject which will be taken up later. But first it is time to look at Fenton's highly successful sales organization which marketed the company's product.

Chapter Twelve

SELLING THE PRODUCT

No matter how good the line was, it would not have meant much if the product could not be sold. As with all successful companies, success was measured, to a large extent, by the work of its sales organization. The Fenton company had a very effective sales organization. Wilmer C. "Bill" Fenton, who was vice-president and sales manager from the time of Frank L. Fenton's death until 1978 when he became president, once said, "Other companies might have had as good a line as we did, but we had the best sales force in the field. That is why many of the other companies failed and we survived."

Bill, who was born in 1923, was Frank L's. second and youngest son. He graduated from Williamstown High School in 1940 and attended Marietta College from 1940 to 1943. He worked on the maintenance staff at the factory during the summer months. In fact, he had been working there only a few weeks when the stack collapsed in June 1940. He entered military service in the spring of 1943. Following his discharge in May 1946 he returned to the factory on a full-time basis in the sales department. Robert C. Fenton Sr., "Uncle Bob," vice-president and sales manager, had been succeeded by his son, Bob Jr., so Bill planned to work with him. However, Bob Jr. died very suddenly in June 1946 of a heart attack. Bill got some help from Uncle Bob before the latter's death two years later, but for the most part he was on his own. He will never forget his first sales trip in 1946, to Pittsburgh. He almost lost his nerve at one point, but some reassuring words from his father over the telephone and a substantial order placed by Joseph Horne restored his confidence.

Although he had a natural, easy way with people and enjoyed sales very much, it took Bill awhile to master the trade. He learned a good deal from talking and working with his Uncle Bob in the remaining months of the latter's life. "It was fun to watch him

Wilmer C. (Bill) Fenton, Vice President and Sales Manager 1948-1978; President 1978-1986; Chairman of the Board 1985-.

sell at the Pittsburgh show," he remembered. Another man who was very helpful was Ray Guyler of Bechtel, Lutz, and Jost of Reading, Pennsylvania. O. D. Bechtel, who headed the company, which was an important Fenton account, suggested to Bill that he go with the experienced Guyler on one of his trips. They met at Johnstown, Pennsylvania, on a Monday morning and spent the entire week together, parting Friday afternoon. It was a valuable learning lesson for the young salesman. "He was good," said Bill, "He was performing for me." Many years later Guyler told Bill that "that week on the road was the biggest sales week of my life."

When asked what was the most important lesson he learned about sales from people like his uncle and Guyler, plus his own early experiences, Bill remarked that cultivating the customers and taking a sincere personal interest in their affairs was fundamental. "If your relationship is based purely on the basis of business, it is not likely to be as effective as when business is combined with friendship." In addition, "one should really enjoy sales; he should have fun at the job. That way he will probably be a better salesman."

Bill Fenton loved to go out on the road. He enjoyed renewing old acquaintances and meeting new people. Up until 1975 he continued to service 14 large accounts in Ohio. "I would call on them, take in samples, and work the accounts. I think I enjoyed that part of my business life as much as anything I did." In his earlier years, when he was the only one from the home office who went into the field, he traveled his territory in the neighborhood of six weeks out of each six months. Other travels took him to the national or regional shows. He would leave Williamstown on Monday morning for Pittsburgh. After a couple of days there he went over to Youngstown. He would check in to a hotel, set up his displays, and invite the buyers, who had been previously informed that he would be in town, to come and see what he had.

After leaving Youngstown, he would travel to Akron for a day or so and then on to Cleveland and Detroit. Toledo was next and then it was south to Dayton, Cincinnati, and Louisville. Usually an itinerary such as this meant a two-week trip, although he might occasionally come home for the weekend. This kind of trip he made about four times a year. In the earlier years he set up his displays in his hotel and the buyers would come to him. Later, after the color catalogs appeared, it was no longer necessary to set up displays. Now all he had to do was to take a few samples of the different shapes and designs and call on the buyers directly. It cut down immensely on his work while on the road.

While Bill did the road work himself, except for a time in the late 1960s when he was assisted by Tom Lubbers, he says that one of the things which simplified his job was his able corps of sales representatives [reps]. And then the business was not that big in the earlier years. But as the company grew and the number of accounts increased in the 1960s, field trips became more of a problem. In 1973 Bill's son, Don, graduated from Muskingum College and began going with his father on his sales trips. In 1975 Don became assistant sales manager and in 1978, when Bill became company president, his son succeeded him as sales manager.

* * *

As Frank M. and Bill Fenton looked at the company's sales structure when they took control, they recognized that a number of things needed to be done. For one thing, they had no real idea how things were being handled in the Far West. They knew who their reps were there, but they did not really know them nor how they managed their operations. So in February of 1951 Bill, with his wife Elinor, went west to find out about these things. The first stop was in Denver and then they traveled on to San Francisco where the rep was a man named Alexander Bell. Next they flew north to Seattle where the rep was E. R. Wadlington. Wadlington, or "Wad," had represented Fenton in the Pacific Northwest since 1923 and was considered the dean of glass salesmen in the region. He would retire in the 1970s after 50 years of service for FAGCO.

The next stop was in Los Angeles where Bill met the company rep, M. G. Van Auken, and sub-rep Gordon MacLennan and his wife Irene. Talking the matter over with these people, Bill concluded that the MacLennans, an effective husband-wife combination, should be the reps for southern California. After Los Angeles, Bill went to Tucson, Arizona, and following a side trip to Mexico, he traveled on to Dallas. In all of these places, he got to know the reps and gained a

better understanding of how they managed their affairs. The trip was instrumental for Bill and Frank as they went about reorganizing the west coast operations.

The most important change in Fenton's sales structure during the early years of the new regime was the dropping of jobbers and the increased use of reps. The change came about in the early and mid-1950s when it was recognized that the company was losing control over the selling of its glassware. Reps were used along with jobbers under the old system, but they operated at a disadvantage. The company had no control over outlets jobbers might sell to—bus depots, service stations, or whatever—and often such outlets were in direct competition with gift shops or other good accounts serviced by the reps. It was embarrassing and frustrating to the reps who complained to the company. So gradually jobbers were eased out. It was not a pleasant task because it involved long-time relationships which had been developed by Uncle Bob, Bob Jr., and Frank L. Fenton.

The largest dollar-producing territory for the Fenton company during the third 25 years was the same as that for the previous quarter-century, the Upper Midwest. This was the region serviced by Martin M. Simpson and Company, based in Chicago. Martin Simpson had represented FAGCO for many years under the old regime. He died in the summer of 1949, but before his death he had taken in with him as partners, his brother Lewis, Ted Figler, and Warren Hill. Thus at the time of his passing continuity was assured. Some years later both Lew Simpson and Hill

Fenton sales representatives at National Sales Meeting in Marietta, Ohio in 1969. Back Row: Tom Lubbers, Jack Walsh, Don Figler, Alan Symmes, Howard Gibb, Ted Figler, Gordon MacLennan, Dr. Robert Fischer, Thayne McDonald, Frank Fenton. Middle Row: Joe Ehnot, R. P. Hutchison, Tony Rosena, Jim Thomas, Tom Fenton, Abe Peskin, Howard Aronow, Ed Coyne, Glenn Miller, Tony Garner, Fred Rosenkampff, John Coyne, Jay Sutton, Evans Coleman, John Evans, Jay Weikel, Bill Fenton, Jim Smart. Seated: Bob Benson, Carl Voigt, Miles Wittkamp, Sterling Bell, Helga Aronow, Bea Chan, Irene MacLennan, Ray Wadlington, Bill Moore, Bob Coffin.

also died, leaving Figler alone running the company, which retained its original name. Figler brought new people into the firm so that during the third 25 years, Fenton's dealings with Martin M. Simpson and Company were with Figler and his able staff.

Representatives of the Simpson company blanketed the states of Wisconsin, Iowa, Illinois, Indiana, Michigan, and Missouri, while extending their reach into the eastern sections of Kansas and Nebraska. Figler himself worked the metropolitan areas of Chicago and Milwaukee and his lieutenants did the rest. Thayne MacDonald operated in Iowa and Wisconsin, Jack Walsh in Michigan and Indiana, and Roger Swiatek in southern Illinois, Missouri, and eastern Kansas. The latter also had a big showroom in Kansas City, Missouri.

The next largest dollar-producing territory was in western Pennsylvania and Ohio. This was the domain of John H. Evans Company, which was centered in Beaver Falls, Pennsylvania. When Bill Fenton began his travels as sales manager, he covered Ohio, western Pennsylvania, northern Kentucky, southern Michigan, and the river towns of West Virginia. As the number of accounts increased he decided to assign part of this territory to someone else. John Evans was a salesman for Bechtel, Lutz, and Jost, working the western Pennsylvania area. Since FAGCO had done business with Bechtel, Bill had come to know Evans. In 1955 he hired him to take over most of the western Pennsylvania and Ohio market. At first Bill retained the larger accounts and Evans was given the small cities and towns. As he became more familiar with Fenton's operations he gradually moved into the big cities.

Evans was a hard worker and strengthened Fenton's presence in his territory. In time he was given more accounts in Ohio in addition to western Pennsylvania. Bill recalls an incident where he met Evans in Dayton, Ohio, where an interview between themselves and a representative for TV Stamps was scheduled in the afternoon. They had some time to spend in the morning and Evans invited Bill to come with him and see two new accounts he had just opened up. They traveled into downtown Dayton and then thru a maze of side streets, before stopping in front of a couple of rather obscure gift shops. "John, how did you even know about these accounts?" Bill inquired.

"Well," he replied, "I was in town over the weekend and when I am some place away from home over a weekend, I go street by street and crisscross the whole town to see if I am missing anything. I found these two places on Sunday when they were closed. So I came back Monday and opened accounts with them."

Bill Fenton added, "I think he knew every street in every town in his whole territory."

Evans really knew how to work his territory, as the Dayton gift shops example illustrates. He once remarked that he never drove on Interstate highways. "When you are out there," he said, "driving 60 or 70 miles an hour and thinking about the big account at the other end, you don't want to stop along U.S. Route 40 for a small account." He always went over the old highways unless there was a specific time he had to be some place. He did not want to miss anybody. This was the kind of attitude which made Evans' customers very loyal to him and loyal to Fenton.

Evans also did most of the market testing of Fenton lamps. He had urged the company to go into the lamp business in the first place and Bill agreed with him on the point. Bill gave him several samples of lamps to sell and "he went crazy selling them." The company had decided that lamps would make a nice focal point for Fenton displays in gift shops and they have remained a good-selling item since they were first made back in the late 1960s. Though they were higher-priced than other lamps they were of superior quality. As his business grew Evans brought in other people to work with him. He is now deceased, but the company carries on under his name. FAGCO has had many excellent sales reps and John Evans may top the list.

Close behind him is Carl Voigt. Voigt was a buyer for Sibley, Lindsey, and Kerr in Rochester, New York when he decided to cast his lot with Fenton. The FAGCO rep in western New York had trouble selling to department stores so Bill decided to try Voigt in department stores in the big cities—Buffalo, Rochester, Syracuse, and Erie, Pennsylvania. He had always liked Fenton glass from his days at Sibley's, and he now was doing a fine job in selling Fenton ware to department stores. Soon he was offered all of the company's accounts in upstate and western New York. He was delighted at the prospect and remained the Fenton representative there until his retirement in the 1970s. After his death a few years ago, his widow told Bill Fenton that "Fenton glass was Carl's life." Before retiring, Voigt trained a young man, Bob Benson, to carry on where he had left off. Benson must have succeeded, since he was voted Fenton's "salesman of the year" in the mid-1980s.

Voigt is an example of how reps and buyers of Fentonware were helpful in suggesting items which strengthened the line. In the late 1960s when he learned that the company had hired Louise Piper as a decorator, he suggested that painted violets on silvercrest would make a lovely item. Thus was born the very successful "Violets in the Snow." (See P. 83). Ted Figler of the Simpson organization designed a little three-piece hobnail mayonnaise set. This sold very well and was in the line for years. The company got good ideas from buyers. For example, the idea

James Allen, Fred Rathke and John H. Evans in the Columbus, Ohio Showroom, circa 1978.

for the best-selling silver crest cake plate came from a suggestion by Georgia Haught, a gift buyer at Higbee's department store in Cleveland. By "listening to the marketplace," Fenton received a number of suggestions for new pieces, as well as hard information about what pieces were not moving.

One of the company's most successful accounts in the latter part of the second 25 years and throughout the third 25 years was A. L. Randall of Chicago. Randall dealt with the florist industry, that is, it purchased from manufacturers various kinds of things which were used by florists. Bill Fenton met Jack Kaufman in January 1947 and arranged for Fred Tredup, president of Randall, to visit Frank L. Fenton that spring. This marked the beginning of the close relationship which developed between the two companies. Upon his death Tredup was succeeded by Jack Kaufman. Later Ray Western succeeded Kaufman. Kaufman and Western were close friends of Bill's and played an important part in Fenton's growth in the third 25 years. Randall had its own catalog, but Fenton put out a special catalog, with Randall's name on it, that contained illustrations of a number of items peculiar to the florist trade. Mainly, these were vases, baskets, and bowls. For many years Randall accounted for from seven to ten per cent of FAGCO's sales. Some 25 of Randall's key reps sold to florists.

As one might expect, catalogs were valuable promotional tools for the company. Usually a large catalog was issued in January of each year, or perhaps every other year, with a supplement coming out in July. As the new line arrived on the market at the beginning of the year, it was essential that prospective buyers know about it. This was done through catalogs and glass shows. When the company got off to a slow start in 1969, the reason given was the late release of the catalog.

Bill Fenton did all the catalogs for many years and worked with the photographer on the layout of each page and planned everything that was to be included. In the middle to later 1960s Fenton went to color illustrations in the catalogs. As mentioned earlier, this greatly simplified Bill's job when he was on the road, in that he no longer had to set up displays. It also made things easier for reps since buyers could now see the product in all its tints and shades. The company is proud of its lovely catalogs and claims to have been the first in the industry to print them in full color. Bob McDonough of Park Press in Parkersburg worked with Bill and Frank Fenton to accomplish the first full color catalogs.

National glass shows no longer play the key role they once did in the selling of glassware. At one time the January show in Pittsburgh was a big affair and just about everybody who was anybody was on hand. But after it was moved to Atlantic City, it became quite expensive to set up and maintain a display. Moreover, the setting was less favorable than in Pittsburgh. In the early 1960s, a number of hand glass plants, including Fenton, agreed among themselves not to attend that show any longer. Judging from FAGCO's success in the 1960s, its withdrawal from Atlantic City has had little impact on its fortunes. Later, though, one by one, the various hand glass manufacturers returned to Atlantic City. Fenton rejoined the show in January 1973. Still later it again withdrew.

As the years passed, hundreds of new accounts would be regularly added to Fenton's list. At the stockholders' meetings, Bill Fenton would announce

Mixing friendship with business, Ray Western, Don Fenton, Jack Kaufman and Bill Fenton, on the golf course at Bobolink outside of Chicago, Illinois.

32

Picture of the Fenton display at Atlantic City Convention Hall, circa 1980.

the number of new accounts opened in the previous year. Since there was a constant turnover in old accounts, with companies going out of business or people retiring, it was essential that they be replaced. Whenever a chain store was signed up all of its branches became separate accounts. Such companies had to be handled carefully, however, so that the branches would not compete unfairly with gift stores or other outlets in the same area where FAGCO products were sold. The company established a policy at the time jobbers were discontinued whereby the reps would have control over what came into their territories.

On one occasion early in the 1960's J. C. Penney's approached Bill Fenton with a proposal to buy Hobnail milk glass items and place them in their branch stores. The company agreed to do this as long as the glassware was not put in stores which would be competing with "exclusive" arrangements with certain Fenton outlets. Penney's balked at this condition at first, but after arguing the matter for a couple of years, accepted the terms.

Sears Roebuck had been buying from Fenton for many years when suddenly its buyer began to press Bill for a bigger discount on its purchases. He would not grant it, so Sears went to Westmoreland where it was able to negotiate a discount in buying its milk glass. Sears tried to play the two companies off against one another and finally stopped buying from Fenton when it refused to budge from its position. Several years later Sears was back buying the Fenton line, conceding it had misjudged the market and made a mistake in going to Westmoreland.

* * *

Each of Fenton's January catalogs carries a listing of all the sales representatives and their organizations. It is interesting to compare the list over the years to see what changes have occurred. The most important point to be noted in this is the longevity of service of the reps. Very few changes have occurred and where there have been changes it is generally due to the retirement or death of the reps. At the outset of the third 25 years, in 1956, 12 rep organizations were listed. Martin M. Simpson covered Chicago and Detroit, Horace C. Gray was in New York, Bill Moore and Jim Thomas together had Dallas, Charles E. Weaver and Jim and Jay Weikel together had Atlanta and Charlotte, Howard Gibb covered Washington, D.C., John Evans was in Cleveland, Columbus, and Pittsburgh, the MacLennans had Los Angeles and San Francisco, Alan W. Symmes was in Boston, Carl Voigt operated in Rochester and Buffalo, Edward J. Coyne of Giftwares Distributing handled Minneapolis, and E. R. Wadlington covered Seattle and Portland. Of course, the cities mentioned were merely the headquarters for the reps; their territories included much more than the cities themselves.

Moving ahead nine years to 1965, 14 organizations were listed, but most of the same names are among them. The Horace C. Gray organization in New York City had been replaced by Howard B. Aronow, who served into the fourth 25 years. Martin M. Simpson Company still operated throughout the Upper Midwest and John Evans had his old territory as did Edward Coyne, the MacLennans, Bill Moore and Jim Thomas, the Weikels, Howard Gibb, Alan Symmes, Carl Voigt, and E. R. Wadlington. The only new names were Sterling Bell in Pompano Beach, Florida, and Jay S. Sutton in Wheatridge, Colorado.

The next ten years revealed few changes, according to the January 1975-1976 catalog. Martin Simpson Company is listed with three offices,—Chicago, Detroit, and Kansas City. Aronow, Coyne, Evans, Mac-Lennan, Sutton, Symmes, Thomas and Moore, and the Weikels were still selling Fenton ware in the same places they had been a decade earlier. By now, however, Voigt had surrendered western and upstate New York to his protege Bob Benson, while Wadlington had turned over his responsibilities to Scott Williams. Among the new reps listed in 1975 were William P. Becker in Dumfries, Virginia, Douglas C. Cofiell in Medford Lakes, New Jersey, Howard Kapper in Anchorage, Alaska, and Miles Wittkamp of Fort Lauderdale, Florida. Missing from 1965 were Howard Gibb, who was deceased, and Sterling Bell. All of the reps listed in 1975-1976 were still on the job at the close of the third 25 years.

Usually, there have been one or two reps working for Fenton outside the United States. Every catalog has listed a rep operating out of Toronto, Ontario, and in the later years there was one in Vancouver, British Columbia. But the most distant rep was hired almost accidentally. One day in the early 1960s, Frank Fenton came into Bill's office and tossed a letter on his desk with the comment, "here's one you can file away," meaning it probably was not worth pursuing.

"It will only cost a nice letter and a catalog to find out," replied Bill.

So he wrote to F. R. Barlow and Sons Limited, of Melbourne, Australia. The response was quite positive and F. R. Barlow became Fenton's Australian rep. They sent some of their people to Williamstown on an annual basis for a number of years. More recently the company was sold and the successor failed, but it was a fruitful relationship while it lasted.

Fenton has never gone in much for national sales meetings. Its first one was held in 1969 and proved quite successful, but it did not become an annual event. They were held periodically at the national shows and then revived in Williamstown in 1986. The most recent was held in December 1988, just as this is being written, when 84 reps from across the country came to Williamstown. Previous to 1969 and a number of times since then, smaller groups of reps were brought in, one group at a time, toward the end of the year to plan the following year. Reps have been easier to handle this way and it was more convenient to listen to their ideas.

Sales reps are the lifeblood of the sales organization. As Bill Fenton put it, "Sales is not just me or those of us here in the office. It is all those people out in the field who leave home on Monday morning and return home Friday night. They sell the product."

Bonus Stock Dividend
Five
Preferred Shares*

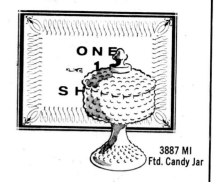

3887 MI
Ftd. Candy Jar

The Directors of Fenton Sales have voted to offer you five shares* of preferred "specials" stock. (It was hard to decide just which five shares* because all Fenton stock seems to be preferred, judging from sales in 1964.)

Here's all you need to do to cash in on this offer.

1. Check the red insert on your price list for the number of each you want.
2. Make sure your orders for these "specials" are in our hands no later than March 15, 1965, for shipment no later than March 31, 1965.
3. Order in the small minimum amount (6) for each. Naturally, larger orders will pay you even larger dividends.
4. Check to let us know if you would like a newspaper mat for local promotion. We have an attractive one.

3752 MI
11" Vase

It is requested that you not feature these "specials" at reduced prices after Mother's Day in order to protect all our dealers.

Order a well rounded display of Fenton glass. This will let the "specials" pay you extra dividends by stimulating all your Fenton sales. (Remember our big spring national advertising campaign. It will make another good reason to expect big dividends from Fenton in '65. Now is the time to buy.)

3731 MI
10" Ftd. Bowl

Sincerely,

Bill Fenton

W. C. Fenton
Vice President and
Sales Manager

AUTHENTIC
Fenton
HANDMADE

3734 MI
12" Basket

P.S. Thanks for your help in making '64 the greatest Fenton sales year yet. We greatly appreciate your business and trust the "5 specials" will make '65 even greater.

Bill

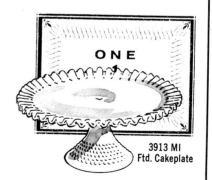

3913 MI
Ftd. Cakeplate

*SHARES - The illustrated "5 specials" at reduced prices give preferred Fenton dealers an extra share of profits.

THE FENTON ART GLASS COMPANY • WILLIAMSTOWN, WEST VIRGINIA

Letter announcing a special sales promotion in 1965.

Chapter Thirteen

THE COLLECTIBLES AND . . .

By the mid-1960s the Fenton company was enjoying the best years of its life. Both sales and earnings were at record levels, the physical plant was being enlarged, and the personnel rolls were growing. And while there were problems over at Armstrong Custom Fabricators, the future for the glass business appeared to promise only continuing prosperity. Unexpectedly, however, in 1967 and 1968 the "ship of state" ran into rough seas. There was an abrupt drop off in orders and the expanded Hot Metal Department was forced to close down some of its shops. Sliding earnings reports sent ripples of uncertainty through the factory. Then, just as unexpectedly, 1969 saw a major turn-around and the company was soon headed for an even greater success than it had yet known.

1965 was a record-breaking year and the outlook for 1966 was very good. This optimism was voiced in face of a substantial falling off in the sale of milk glass. It was hoped that new items and new colors introduced into the line in January would offset the decline in milk glass. These hopes were realized as the preliminary reports began coming in. In October 1966 the directors were told that for the first nine months of the year both sales and earnings were ahead of third quarter figures for 1965. Although no final statistics for 1966 were given in the company minutes, the tone of the discussion suggested that it had been a successful year, though it might not have been better than 1965. The trend continued in the first quarter of 1967 with sales up 12.3 per cent over the corresponding period for 1966. In reporting to the stockholders in January 1967, vice-president and sales manager Bill Fenton reviewed the growth of company sales since 1951. In 1950 the total number of accounts was 5200. Within 15 years the number had escalated to 21,400. This was divided between department stores, 3221, gift shops, 7758, hardware stores, 1045, jewelry stores, 1526, furniture stores, 1031, florists, 5880, and "other," 890.

But the beginning of a slump was apparent in the second quarter figures for 1967. It was foreshadowed by a statement appearing in the minutes of the directors' meeting of April 27. It noted that, "From every indication sales will be down substantially through the end of June." They certainly were. Sales for the second quarter dropped off 9.1 per cent compared to the same period in 1966 and were down 16.6 per cent from the first quarter of the current year. Similarly, earnings for the second quarter were off 75.8 per cent from the same period in 1966 and down 74.4 per cent from the first quarter of the current year. Combining the first two quarters of 1967, sales were up slightly over the first six months of 1966, but earnings had plunged 38.2 per cent.

In December Controller Don Alexander informed the directors that earnings for the year would probably be off 23 per cent from 1966. He was right on target for when the final figures were compiled the drop was 25.7 per cent. The 3.6 increase in sales had been unable to offset this decline. Four reasons were cited for this sudden turn-around in business: [1] catalog and advertising costs were up; [2] a greater emphasis on quality resulted in fewer salable pieces and thus a higher unit cost per piece; [3] labor and material costs had increased; and [4] the national economy had been down in the spring of the year. It was pointed out, however, that Fenton was not alone; the slump had pervaded the entire hand glass industry.

If 1967 was bad, 1968 was worse, at least the first half of it. First quarter glassware sales were down 22.6 per cent while earnings dropped a stunning 106.2 per cent, as the Glass Crafts Association reported a drop in the company's share of the market. As the unhappy statistics were flowing in, talks had already begun with the management consulting firm of Stewart, Dougall and Associates. It was hoped that the consultants would be able to advise Fenton on ways to improve its line and marketing methods. Stewart, Dougall completed its study by late July, but before any steps were taken to implement its proposals, FAGCO's business began to improve.

But second quarter data was still quite bad, although slightly better than in the first quarter. For the first six months the figures were minus 18.6 per cent for sales and minus 83.3 per cent for earnings. In spite of the gloom, however, Bill Fenton predicted in July 1968 that sales for the last six months of the year would exceed those of 1967 by 12-20 per cent. He must have known something for, indeed, the picture brightened slightly in the third quarter. Sales improved 31.4 per cent over the second quarter and were down only 8.9 per cent for the nine months, compared to 1967. Earnings for the nine months were off only 40.3 per cent. In December the projection for the year was even better yet, and this was confirmed by the final report for 1968. Sales turned out to be down only 2.7 per cent, and profits down only 26.99 per cent.

Late in the year, Frank Fenton, in reviewing capital expenditures and long range planning, told the directors that modifications in previous projections were now necessary. "For the next few years," he commented, "the physical plant is not expected to grow as it has in recent years. The long range planning program for next year should begin to include a higher proportion of monies for product development." He said that the glass and steel plants could absorb additional volume without any change in facilities. The problem now was volume of sales of the product, not the size of the plant.

He told the stockholders just what had happened in the previous four years when the hand glass industry, after attaining an all-time high, had gone into a slump. The early and middle 1960s had witnessed a seller's market, where buyers had trouble getting all the merchandise they wanted. One could well remember not too long before when Fenton did not have sufficient facilities for all the glass it could sell. This boom continued through 1966 when record sales and profits were made. But in 1967 it became a buyer's market and sales volume began to drop. This continued into 1968. The difficulty was complicated by a 100 per cent increase in the number of companies competing for the gift dollar and a substantial growth in imports.

1969 was to be the real turn-around year, although first quarter results were disappointing. In April Frank Fenton told the directors that the company had three courses it would have to follow to improve its financial condition. It must reduce costs, primarily overhead costs; it must improve its performance and solve the production problems which had developed; and it must increase its sales. At the same time it was reported that K-Mart had agreed to take the Olde Virginia line, which it was estimated, could account for 10 per cent of the company's sales volume in the fall of the year. In keeping with this last point was the fact that a number of new shops were being added and that more would probably be necessary.

The stockholders heard the good news at their annual meeting on February 26, 1970. Bill Fenton reported that 1969 sales reached $6,873,486, the highest in company history and 14.8 per cent better than in 1968, while earnings were up 20.4 per cent over the previous year. More business had come from the stamp companies, while the sale of the Olde Virginia line to the mass merchandising houses had been very successful. The turn lot business had also increased. The picture looked even better for 1970 with new items in Hobnail milk glass and Valencia, and the new colors of burmese, blue marble, and [revived] carnival leading the way. Gift shows in the early weeks of the year were the best in a number of years, while orders booked so far were already up 28.5 per cent over 1969.

*   *   *

Contributing to the return of good times was the addition of two skilled specialists, Tony Rosena, the designer, and Louise Piper, the decorator, in 1967 and 1968. Their impact was beginning to be felt in 1968 and 1969 and would continue throughout the remainder of the third 25 years. Rosena grew up in the Pittsburgh area where his father worked in the mines and then on the railroad. He received little art training in school, but later attended the Art Institute of Pittsburgh, after which he went to a place called Ad-Art, where he specialized in commercial art. With this grounding, he then studied Fine Art under Professor

Anthony Rosena, Fenton Designer

Raymond Simboli of Carnegie-Mellon University. With his formal training completed in the late 1940s, Rosena secured a job in a department store where he illustrated company ads for newspapers. They had to be ready by five o'clock each afternoon. "One day along about three o'clock," he recalled, "I got word to have illustrations of 20 television sets, in black watercolor, ready to be picked up at five. I had wondered why most of the people around there were nervous wrecks and now I knew why."

So as not to become a nervous wreck he next took a position—in the mid-1950s—with North American Aviation in Columbus. What does an artist do in an aircraft factory? Well, he becomes a "technical illustrator." When Rosena arrived at the plant he looked around and saw about 75 of these technical illustrators. He still was not sure what they did, but he found out. They made detailed drawings of the backs of instrument panels for Fury jets. "I'd go out to the plane," he said, "and pull the panel out. It looked like a mess of spaghetti to me. When we were done with our drawings, other people inked them in. From these drawings they put together their field manuals." Later on it was found that this work was too time-consuming so they began using photographs, and as Rosena commented, "probably put about 75 illustrators out of work."

He did not like that kind of work and headed home for Pittsburgh each Friday afternoon as soon as he could get away. While home he complained about the job so much he was encouraged to leave it, but he resolved to stick it out until "something better turned up." In about two years he opened his own design studio in Columbus. This was his first introduction into the glass industry. "I did a series of designs for some drinkware," he said, "and I began to see where the glass business was kind of fascinating. I was intrigued by the things you could do with a clear shape by applying colors and interior sprays, gold overlays, and all kinds of interesting things."

One job he did was for a woman who ran Gay-Fad Studios in Lancaster, Ohio. She began her business, decorating metal trays and such, in Detroit before World War II. With the war her supply of metal dried up and she turned her talents to glassware. Since she had to have her glass shipped to Detroit, she decided to relocate in Lancaster, closer to the supply. After Rosena had finished his first project for Gay-Fad, the woman asked him, "When are you going to come to work for us?" Well, this was certainly "something better" than drawing the backs of instrument panels, so he said, "right now." "I spent a lot of exciting years there," he remembered. "Designing, traveling, setting up shows; it opened up a whole new field to me."

Having been bitten by the glass bug in his years—late 1950s—at Gay-Fad, Rosena now wanted to work in a regular glass house. He took a position as a designer at the Jeannette Glass Company in Jeannette, Pennsylvania. In his post as design director, he was also responsible for all the advertising. He attended trade shows where he set up displays. The company made no new moulds, but resurrected abandoned moulds from the murky recesses of the old Jeannette plant, which had been closed down at the time of the sale. "We dug out those old moulds which hadn't been used for years, cleaned them up, and cut some new designs. That's how we built our line and were able to survive for a number of years." Money was spent on new moulds only when making products for florist companies. As for decoration, they did a lot of decorating for big retail houses like Sears Roebuck.

Rosena was at Jeannette during Fenton's long search for a full-time designer. How the company came to know about him seems to be lost in the mists of history, but whatever the circumstances, one day in 1967 he appeared in Williamstown for an interview. "I asked my wife," he recalled, "will you come and take a ride with me because I am going down to visit another broken down glass plant along the river. When we drove up to the Fenton company, we were shocked. This was no broken down glass plant; this was nothing like I anticipated; it was very impressive." In thinking back to that interview, Frank Fenton said, "Tony knew and understood glass. I told him, 'Tony, why don't you go back and design $500 worth of glass for us. Just take $500 worth of your time and see what you can develop. And then bring your drawings to us'."

Rosena returned home to his studio and drew up designs for various products which he thought might be acceptable. Incidentally, none was in Hobnail, the best-selling item of the day. He had stopped by the gift shop before leaving Williamstown to get some idea of shapes and patterns that were in the line. "Most of the things I did originally were just off the top of my head," he said. They were good ones. "We liked them," said Frank Fenton, "and put them in the works. We also hired him." Upon his permanent appointment Rosena was assigned to a little niche off the upstairs corridor. "Until they built an office for me, I sat there," he chuckled. Well, if he had not designed anything for Hobnail before, he certainly did now. "'My God,' I said to myself, 'will I ever get out of Hobnail?' But it was very profitable and allowed us to do other things."

Rosena was hired in 1967 and it was in July 1968 that the first piece made from a mould design of his reached the line. It was the Hobnail milk glass urn, 3986. It was beautiful on the drawing board, but for some reason it never sold well; apparently it was too large for the marketplace. One other item he designed, however, the creative candle bowl, 3872, was quite successful. The idea was to design a candle bowl which could accommodate three different-sized candles and allow for tapers along the outside edge—in Hobnail. The design was excellent, but it was one of those pieces which proved very difficult to make. At one point the Hot Metal people said they simply could not make the piece, that the weight distribution was wrong, that the glass would not release from the mould, or else it cracked when it did come out of the mould. By trial and error it was found that a different method of cooling and lubricating the plunger solved the problem. While the candle bowl sold well, it was not until 1970, when flower rings were added, that it became one of the "hottest" items in the line.

Rosena played an increasingly important role in design as time passed. In 1969 he developed the Valencia line from that Moser piece Frank Fenton had bought at an antique show. He also designed several Hobnail milk glass items in the same spirit as the creative candle bowl. He developed the Wild Strawberry pattern from the picture frame. The significance of his research and design work for the series of collectors plates and other commemorative pieces, which were so important to the company's well-being in the 1970s, will become apparent a bit later.

For some time the company had been thinking about getting back into the hand decorating business, which of course, was how it began back in 1905 in Martins Ferry. Fenton had continued to make hand-decorated pieces until the Depression of the 1930s compelled it to abandon the practice. Now it was ready to resume it. Feelers had been put out in a number of different directions, searching for a person or persons with the necessary skills for such work, but as yet the company had not found what it was looking for. Several people had been interviewed for the position of decorator in 1967, shortly before Rosena came to work at Fenton's. Once on the scene he became involved in these discussions. As the talks about hiring a decorator continued, Rosena told Frank Fenton, "I know someone who can hand decorate this ware and all she needs are some pieces to work with." "Well, send her some," was the reply.

Rosena had known Louise Piper and was aware of her skill as a glass decorator during his years with Jeannette Glass. Louise had once worked for Jeannette Glass and was currently employed by the Jeannette Shade and Novelty Company. Rosena packaged some Fenton pieces and took them to Jeannette where Louise decorated them. After they were fired, he brought them back to Williamstown. The company was happy with the work she had done and sent her more and more pieces to decorate. Eventually in the late winter of 1968 she was induced to come down to the factory and was hired as the chief decorator in the newly-created Decorating Department.

Louise Piper was born in Irwin, Pennsylvania, "a long time ago," and moved with her family to Jeannette when she was quite young. On her way to and from school each day she walked by the Jeannette Shade and Novelty Shop and was intrigued by the work the men—mostly Germans—were doing in the shop. "I would stick my nose in the shop periodically," she recalled, "and one day one of these gentlemen asked me if I would like to come in and look around. I said 'yes.' After I finished my looking, he asked me if I would like to learn how to do what they were doing. Again I said 'yes.' He told me to come in each day after school and they would find out what I could do. I was only 13 at the time so my mother had to approve the idea, but she did and I went to work at the shop."

This was the beginning of a life-long love affair for Louise Piper. Her fascination with glass decorating was so great that she worked steadily at Jeannette Shade and Novelty throughout her high school years and after graduation went with the company as an apprentice decorator. "I worked every night after school, on Saturdays, and even during summer vacations," she said. "I really liked it. They taught me to lay out designs, to mix colors, and other things such as what colors could be fired over the top of another color. When I came in as an apprentice—this was in the 1930s—there wasn't any opening as a decorator since all these old German men did the decorating, but they had me put the 'banding' on pieces in fine gold. These old gentlemen, in their 70s and 80s, weren't quite as steady as they once were."

In those early days Louise wanted a day off now and then, but the Germans kept after her. One would go to her home and tell her mother, "Louise is not in today." Then her mother would go after her and tell her "you wanted to get into this so now you must stay with it." While she loved the work, as a teenager, she naturally missed some of the other things. There was a lovely park in Jeannette where the young people often went swimming. Louise would go too, occasionally, but "the Germans" came after her and back to work she went.

The owners of Jeannette Shade and Novelty had a very close working relationship with Westmoreland Glass, which was located in Grapeville, just outside of Jeannette. When business was slack at one place Louise was sent to work in the other. They also had a place in Greensburg where she spent some time learning to paint on china. With the shortage of gas and soda ash in World War II, Jeannette had to let some of its people go. So Louise worked in a pottery during the war years. When the war was over one of the German workers returned to Germany, and Mr. Vaters, who managed Jeannette Shade and Novelty, invited Louise back on a permanent basis. She stayed there until she came to Fenton.

Rosena got to know Louise through Louise's sister, Mary, who worked at the Jeannette Glass Company where Rosena was the designer. Louise had painted some large plates which Mary took over to Jeannette Glass for firing. Rosena saw Mary put the plates in the lehr and asked her if they were hand painted. He was looking for someone to put designs on tableware so they could be screenprinted. So Louise began doing some work for Rosena at Jeannette Glass. Then later, after he had joined Fenton and found out they were looking for a decorator he mentioned Louise.

"He stopped by on one of his weekend visits to Pittsburgh," she said, "and asked me if I would like to paint some samples for Fenton. I said I would and the next day when I came home from work—I was staying with my sister—there were boxes upon boxes piled on the front porch of the house and she was having a fit." Louise spent that night painting some of the pieces and the next day took them to Jeannette Glass where they were fired. After work she took the packages to Greensburg and put them on the 6 o'clock Greyhound bus. Rosena picked them up at midnight when the bus reached Marietta. Within a couple of months, Louise went to work for Fenton.

Upon her arrival in April 1968, the Decorating Department was set up. Louise bought the paints and brushes and six or seven people with some art training were hired. While she was supposed to paint herself, she also had to train the novice decorators. No special facility had yet been built for the decorators, so the ware was carried down to an unoccupied space in the basement where there was a small kiln for firing. These improvised quarters served for a time until something more suitable was put up. By the time Louise was transferred upstairs and given a glass-enclosed work room along the "tour line," she had trained over 70 decorators. Not all of them remained

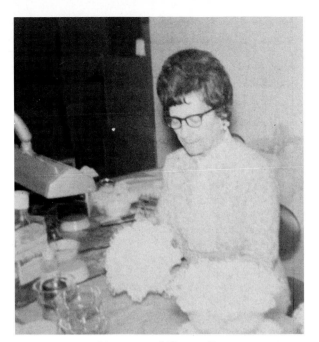

Louise Piper, noted Fenton Decorator.

with the company, although the average number in recent years has run between 35 and 40.

Louise's first decoration was called "Violets in the Snow," which appeared in the summer of 1968. The idea came from a suggestion of sales representative Carl Voigt, who served Fenton in upstate and western New York. When he learned that a decorator had been hired he proposed that violets be painted on the silver crest line. It was a happy thought and when Louise had finished her work everyone was pleased. It was tested, found to be a good thing, and was put in the line. The success of Violets in the Snow demonstrated the need for a decorating lehr to properly fire the decorated pieces. One was installed, more people—whom Louise would train—were hired, and the Decorating Department was on its way.

The success of Violets in the Snow was apparent when the January 1969 catalog appeared. The front cover featured an illustration of the new Mariner's Lamp which carried the decoration on its face. Violets in the Snow was a significant factor in the beginning of Fenton's turnaround in the latter part of 1968. In February 1969 the stockholders were told, "A decorating department was operable in June, producing 44,000 decorated items during the last six months and currently employing about 17 decorators. Other patterns are being developed for 1969." With 44,000 items, Louise and her helpers must have been awfully busy. Among the new decorations she designed for 1969 were Yellow Roses and Apple Blossoms, featured in the July catalog supplement.

* * *

Two pressures were at work which caused Fenton, in 1970, to [1] reintroduce carnival glass and [2] launch its celebrated collectors' series. Rose Presznick was responsible for the former and the developing craze for collectors editions of anything and everything was the moving force for the latter. Rose Presznick had converted an old barn near her home in Lodi, Ohio, into a carnival glass museum. She had visited FAGCO back in Frank L. Fenton's days and had learned a great deal about carnival from the early company catalogs. By now she had become an expert on the subject and had written books about it. In 1968 she decided she would like to reproduce some carnival glass and sell it at her museum as a money-making project. She came to see Frank Fenton and asked him if the company would make the moulds and manufacture the items for her exclusively. This was agreed to.

While Fenton was back into carnival it had no particular production plans in mind. Then Charley Goe thought of the plate. The company was aware of the growing popularity in this country of special Christmas plates manufactured in Europe. This popularity was enhanced no doubt by the rapid rise in value of the plates. What was purchased for $20 might within five years sell for $150. Thus in 1967 Fenton made a plate in milk glass with a little glassmaker at the center. There was no thought of developing a collectors' series. When the first plates came out of the press the reaction was negative. They simply did not look right in milk glass. The plates were put aside and forgotten by everyone—except chemist Charley Goe. When carnival was being revived for Rose Presznick, Goe thought of the plate and suggested it might look good in carnival. Carnival turned out to be the perfect medium for a collector's plate and Rosena was put to work researching and designing other plates which could go along with this first one of the glassmaker.

As the idea of a "Craftsman Series" developed, it was decided to put out one each year for 12 years and destroy the moulds at the end of every year. With all the hard work required in making these beautiful pieces it seems a shame to the uninitiated outsider that the moulds had to be destroyed. But to preserve their value for collectors it had to be done. Each catalog from 1970 through 1981, which carried photographs of the Craftsman plates, stated that the mould would be destroyed on December 31 of that year. This policy was followed with all of the other collector plate moulds. The March 5, 1971 issue of the *MARIETTA TIMES* has a photograph of Frank Fenton slicing one of these moulds in two as Bill Fenton and mould shop supervisor Carnick Hamperian observe with interest.

The first Craftsman plate, "The Glassmaker," was the only one not designed by Tony Rosena, since it was made shortly before his arrival. However, all the remaining plates in that series and in the other series as well, were his handiwork. "The Glassmaker" came out in carnival only. A few samples were made with no description on the back. Then an explanatory inscription was added to the back. It read, "The Fenton Art Glass Company commemorates with this handmade plate the earliest glass craftsman of new America . . . Jamestown—1608. Fenton No. 1 in the annual series of collector's plates by Fenton. 1970". Other plates in the Craftsman set were also issued only in carnival, but had similar inscriptions. For example, the third plate in the series, "The Blacksmith," was identified as "one James Read, who arrived with the original group of settlers in Jamestown, Virginia, May 13, 1907." Number five in the series was called "The Pioneer Cooper," who turned

Wilmer C. (Bill) Fenton and Anthony Rosena destroying the moulds for plates of the Craftsman series.

out to be the celebrated John Alden, of whom Longfellow wrote the classic lines, "Speak for yourself, John." It was noted that the barrel and cask-making skills of the cooper played an important role in the establishment of America. In number seven in the series, "The Gunsmith," Fenton honored an early American artisan, Philip Lefevre, "who operated a gunsmithery at Beaver Valley in Lancaster County, Pennsylvania, from about 1731 to 1766." Interest began to decline in the later stages of this series, which was just as well as Tony Rosena was beginning to run out of eligible craftsmen. Yet those who today have the complete set are very happy collectors. [For a complete listing of all the plates in this and the other series, (see CR 33-36, P. 104).]

Quickly upon the heels of the Craftsman set came two more series of collectors' plates. In July 1970, only six months after the Craftsman was launched, Fenton introduced "Christmas in America" [in carnival and blue marble], another series of 12 annual plates featuring famous and historic churches. As Frank Fenton explained, "Since we had started the Craftsman series it seemed desirable that we should have Christmas plates since they were highly collectible items in the marketplace at that time." These plates were sold only from July to December after which the moulds were destroyed. The first was the famous "Church in the Wildwood," or the "Little Brown Church in the Vale," which was found to still be standing out in Iowa. "We chose this famous little church," the catalog noted, "because we felt it to be particularly appropriate in depicting the feeling of 'Christmas in America'." Among other churches illustrated in this series were the "Old Brick Church" in Richmond, Virginia, the "Two-Horned Church" in Marietta, and "St. Mary's in the Mountains" in Virginia City, Nevada, also known as the "Cathedral on the Comstock." This church served as a "refuge from the frantic pace of life in what was once called the 'city of sin'." The original church was destroyed by fire in 1875 and the present structure was rebuilt in 1877 with funds collected in local saloons.

Other houses of worship honored in this series were "The Nation's Church" in Philadelphia, first organized in 1695 and later attended by George Washington, John Adams, Benjamin Franklin, and many other of the country's Founding Fathers. It was the birthplace of the Protestant Episcopal Church of America. "St. John's Church" in Richmond, Virginia, called the "Birthplace of Liberty" because Patrick Henry delivered his most famous speech, "Give me liberty or give me death," there, was the sixth plate in the series.

The January 1971 catalog announced the third collectors' series in a little over a year, the "Mother's Day" plates. There were nine in the set. Rosena employed the "Madonna" theme in all of these plates, designing figures based on paintings by the Italian Renaissance masters. "Madonna With the Sleeping Child," "Madonna of the Goldfinch," and "The Small Cowper Madonna" were the first three of these. The Mother's Day plates were sold only from January to June of each year, after which the moulds were destroyed. When Rosena was asked what he thought about all of the research he had to do in preparation

Collectors plates made for the General Federation of Women's Clubs to commemorate the Bicentennial.

for designing collectors plates, he responded like a true historian, "That's been one of the most enjoyable aspects of my job."

No series of special plates was launched in 1972, but 1973 marked a big year for collectors with the advent of the "A Portrait of Liberty Sculptured in Glass" plate series. The idea originated in 1971 with William Bright, owner of Bright of America Company of Summersville, West Virginia. Bright had a history of supplying items to women's clubs and service organizations which could be used as fund-raisers. He had discussed the idea of a plate series, tied in with the forthcoming national Bicentennial, with board members of the General Federation of Women's Clubs. They were favorable to the project. Since Fenton was just then bringing out its Craftsman and Christmas in America plate series, Bright came to Frank and Bill Fenton with his proposal. He suggested a four plate series, one each year leading up to the Bicentennial, to be made for women's clubs across the country, who would sell them exclusively through their own organizations to members and non-members alike.

Fenton liked the idea so Bright went to work organizing and promoting the project. On the eve of the release of the first plate in January 1973, Bright issued a large illustrated brochure describing the series. The introduction read as follows:

In an effort to instill a pride of country and a rekindling of the wondrous "Spirit of '76'," the General Federation of Women's Clubs has commissioned a Master American Craftsman to sculpture in glass . . . a series of four exquisite collectors plates, which will in their entirety depict a complete and moving "Portrait of Liberty." These beautiful handmade commemorative plates will be designed and produced by the prestigious Fenton Art Glass Company of Williamstown, West Virginia, who will arrange for the release of one new plate each year for four consecutive years [1973-1974-1975-1976]. Then on July 4th, 1976, a final ceremony will take place at Independence Hall, presided over by the presidents of the General Federation of Women's Clubs for the years of 1973 through 1976. At this ceremony all the moulds will be publicly destroyed, thereby creating a limited edition. This means that not only will these plates become treasured heirlooms with great personal value, but also their market value is sure to increase.

The following inscriptions on the reverse sides of the plates tell in chronological order the story of the four major movements of the American Revolution:

"The Seeds are Sown"—Plate No. 1—Issued January 1, 1973—In 1775, the people of the American Colonies were becoming convinced that they could no longer be subjected to the dictates of a foreign power. Patrick Henry echoed their convictions, when he issued the ultimate challenge . . . "GIVE ME LIBERTY OR GIVE ME DEATH."

"Independence is Declared"—Plate No. 2—Issued January 1, 1974—On July 4th, 1776, fifty-six courageous men voted their approval of a Declaration of Independence. This document, the most profound statement of democratic principles ever written,

formally announced the dramatic birth of a new nation . . . The United States of America.

"A Test of Courage"—Plate No. 3—Issued January 1, 1975—Once declared, Independence had yet to be won. At Valley Forge during the bitter cold winter of 1777 and 1778, General George Washington and his troops placed their trust in their Creator, then successfully pitted their courage against seemingly overwhelming odds.

"Liberty is Proclaimed"—Plate No. 4—Issued January 1, 1976—"Proclaim Liberty throughout all the land unto all the inhabitants thereof." Two centuries later this same proclamation still rings. The Liberty Bell with its simple inscription has become one of the most cherished and revered symbols of American freedom.

See page 41 for the front view of each of these plates.

Although the first plate was officially issued on January 1, 1973, an advance copy was available several weeks earlier. Bill and Mrs. Fenton and Bill Bright and Mrs. Bright accompanied Mrs. Kermit Haugan, president of the General Federation of Women's Clubs, to Washington for special ceremonies marking the launching of the "Portrait of Liberty" series. Mrs. Pat Nixon, wife of the president, hosted the group at dinner in the White House, after which Mrs. Haugan presented her with the first plate. The presentation was photographed and received considerable national news attention. Following the presentation, Mrs. Nixon personally conducted her guests on a tour of the Executive Mansion. "She was a lovely hostess," recalled Bill Fenton.

In general, it was a successful project and Frank Fenton gives much of the credit to Bright himself. "He was a very energetic man," he said, "who seemed to have an inexhaustible supply of the commodity. He stayed with the program and pushed it all the way along the line to make sure that it would be satisfactory to the women's clubs."

Fenton put out a Bicentennial series of its own at the same time it was producing plates for the General Federation of Women's Clubs. This began a year later than the other, in 1974, and was designed to incorporate additional items each successive year in a different color. The July 1974 catalog announced the first year's offering of three pieces, the Eagle plate, the Bicentennial bell, and the Jefferson comport, the star of the show. The original plan was to employ a lovely blue color, similar to the Favrile of Tiffany and the Blue Aurene of Steuben. However, production problems developed in making the comport in this new color, Favrene, so it was decided to go to Independence Blue, a simpler process, for the whole 1974 series. The Jefferson comport, as anyone who has examined will readily attest, was a very difficult piece to design and produce. It had front and back illustrations of Monticello, in addition to famous quotations by Jefferson. (See CR 92, P. 120). His likeness was on the stem and an eagle on the top of the lid. The comport had a limited run of 7600 pieces and no store could buy more than two for their first order. No orders were accepted for it after August 15, 1974.

In January 1975 one new piece, an eagle paperweight, was added to the original three. The color this

William Bright of Bright of America with Mrs. Haugan presenting a plate to Pat Nixon in the White House with Bill and Elinor Fenton and other women's club members, circa 1972.

year was Patriot Red. The comport was now limited to a run of 3600. It remained the only piece for which there was a limit. A Bicentennial stein was added in July of that year as well as another plate, Washington and Lafayette at Valley Forge, which was created for the Lafayette Hotel in Marietta. Both of these items were in a new color, Valley Forge White. By this time, therefore, there were six items in the Bicentennial line, The Eagle plate, Bicentennial bell, and Jefferson compote in Independence Blue and Patriot Red, the Bicentennial stein and Washington and Lafayette plate in all three colors. In 1976, one new piece was added, a planter, and one new color, chocolate, which was actually a revival of a famous old color which had not been made for many years. Thus the entire set of seven pieces were available in four colors Not surprisingly, the sale of the Bicentennial glassware dropped off after July 4, 1976. All the moulds for the set were destroyed.

One other collectors' series, although no plates were included, was issued between 1978 and 1981. It was called "Christmas Classics." (See CR 72 & 119, Pp. 115, 128). The first set included a 16-inch "hammered" colonial lamp, a fairy light, and a bell. Other pieces were added in subsequent years. An old-time scene was painted on each piece. In 1979, for example,

the "old mill stream" idea was used. This was the first of an annual limited edition collector's series of very special hand-painted artist-signed art glass originals. Each piece was dated on the back. The pieces in the set were gift-boxed and tagged with a descriptive mini-booklet.

* * *

Those were exciting times at the Fenton company. In addition to the enthusiasm generated by the series of collectors plates, other important developments were occurring with respect to the regular line's colors and shapes. Take carnival glass, for example. It appeared in many other pieces besides the Craftman series. In announcing the return of carnival (see CR 35, P. 104), the January 1970 catalog supplement stated enthusiastically that

this collectors' grouping of "Carnival Glass" was created from the original formula that Fenton used in 1907 when we introduced this unique hand glass treatment to the American public. From 1907 until 1920 carnival glass was the company's major product. Several different colors with their changing hues were created by spraying secret mixtures of metallic salts on various colors of hot glass. The most popular color proved to be the blue-green treatment reproduced in this [the "Glassmaker"] piece.

Other carnival pieces in this first year of the revival included a planter bowl, candy box, fish paperweight, and a "hen on the nest."

The new carnival glass sold well from the beginning so it was decided to add to the line. In July 1970 a swung vase, 8255, a Persian Medallion bowl, 8224, an open edge basketweave bowl, 8222, and a Leaf and Orange Tree three-toed bowl, 8223, all items which had been made in the earlier years of Fenton carnival glass, were reintroduced. In some cases it was possible to use the original moulds, although a mermaid vase and an alley cat, (see CR 82, P. 117), were made from Verlys and United States Glass Company moulds respectively. Fenton management decided to permanently mark the new Carnival pieces with the Fenton logo, *Fenton*, so collectors of early Fenton Carnival, which was unmarked, could tell the difference. The idea of using the logo on carnival proved so popular that soon there was a call for its use on everything else in the line. The company adopted this idea in 1974, thus all Fenton line items made since 1974 have the Fenton logo impressed upon them.

The January 1971 catalog, in taking up the subject of carnival glass, noted that a year earlier it had decided to experiment with ten pieces of carnival to see what the response would be. It turned out to be so great that now, in 1971, it was increasing that line to 35 pieces. Among them were a rabbit, 5174, and an owl, 5178, (see CR 88, P. 119), both made from old moulds secured from the United States Glass Company. An Atlantis vase also came from a United States Glass mould, but this may have been acquired earlier from Duncan and Miller when the latter went out of business.

An interesting item in this collection was an antique reproduction, the Grape Cluster nappy, 8225. Frank Fenton had purchased an original of it some years before at an antique shop and had been told by Rose Presznick that it was the company's Heavy Grape pattern. It was decided to recreate it, even though the original mould had been lost. Later on, while doing research at the Ohio State Historical Society, Frank learned that this pattern had been made by Imperial Glass between 1910 and 1925 and had been misidentified by an early carnival glass researcher.

Each year additional items were added to the carnival line because it was selling so well. The January 1973 catalog, which carried many new pieces, dwelt on the excitement which carnival had created throughout the industry: "Carnival glass authorities have acclaimed Fenton's reproductions of this treatment as the closest thing to the antique iridescent formula ever produced. Most people would be unable to distinguish the difference except for the Fenton hallmark which identifies each current piece."

One of the most beautiful—some might say the "most beautiful"—colors ever produced by Fenton also debuted in 1970. Somewhat overshadowed by the more famous carnival, "Burmese" caught on quickly and soon was making its own way in strong fashion. Burmese has a very unusual history, as reported in the catalog:

Burmese was created somewhat by accident by Frederick Shirley of the Mt. Washington Glass Company, New Bedford, Massachusetts. Stimulated by the tremendous popularity of Amberina in the late 1870s, Shirley began to experiment with various coloring oxides to create variations in Amberina. In 1881 he produced his first pieces with the "opaque salmon-pink shading to lemon-yellow." The introduction of these pieces caused an immediate sensation and the color combination called Burmese was patented December 15, 1885 . . .

The immediate success of this treatment evidently prompted Mr. Shirley to present several pieces to Queen Victoria. The Queen was so delighted with the gift that she immediately commissioned the company to make her a Burmese tea set and a pair of original vases. The name Burmese itself is often attributed to Queen Victoria, who was said to have exclaimed that the rich tones of blushing pink reminded her of a Burmese sunset.

Manufacturing burmese glass has proven very difficult. The Mt. Washington Glass Company itself discontinued the line in 1900. Over the years various other companies brought out a few pieces of burmese, but found that the costs and difficulties involved in making it were too great. Fenton did not have an easy time of it either. Chemist Charley Goe had devoted a number of years, off and on, toward recapturing the magic formula. One afternoon in October 1969 he came to Bill Fenton in an animated state of mind. "Bill," he said, "I really think I have it; I think I've got burmese." The two of them walked out into the factory where the first burmese items were coming off the lehr. Goe grabbed one and examined it excitedly. "This is it! This is it!"

Goe left the plant around four o'clock that afternoon and headed for the Ban Johnson Fieldhouse for his twice-weekly game of handball. Soon after the game ended, around five-thirty, he collapsed on the dressing room floor from a heart attack. He died within minutes. But as Bill Fenton observed sadly, "At least Charley's last experience at the company was a joyous one; he saw the success of his work on burmese glass. I have never seen anyone more excited and delighted than he was at what he had achieved." Bill later gave that first piece of burmese ware to Goe's widow, Caroline. With the success of these experiments, burmese entered the line in January 1970.

Sales were so good that the January 1971 catalog had great difficulty in containing its enthusiasm about burmese. (See CR 76-77-78, P. 116). "We have been extremely pleased with the reception of the Burmese treatment," it said, "both from the standpoint of sales volume and the critical acclaim accorded our Burmese by knowledgable glass collectors. To the original six items introduced last January, we have added a number of interesting new pieces and a completely new hand-painted pattern. We are confident that these Burmese additions will be as enthusiastically received by your customers." (See P. 81, CR 27, P. 102).

* * *

While the several collectors' series dominated the 1970s, a number of new—and some old—colors, patterns, shapes, and decorated ware, enriched the

44

Fenton line in the last decade of the third 25 years. Carnival and burmese, for example, were no longer new, but they continued to appear in different shapes and designs and sold well. In 1972 the Orange Tree and Cherry bowl, in carnival, was a reproduction of an early Fenton piece. New moulds had to be made for it. The following year the Heart and Vine bowl and Butterfly bonbon, also reproductions were reintroduced in carnival. In the late 1970s the company adopted a policy of making new carnival pieces on an annual basis. When a particular year ended, the line would be discontinued and a new set of carnival would be brought out the following year. It would last one year, also, and so on. Meanwhile, burmese remained a strong color throughout the period. As an example, the 21-inch, hand-painted student lamp in 1973, 7411, was very popular.

The most beautiful—and most sought-after—of the new colors were custard, rosalene, and the varieties of satin. In addition, chocolate, which had been made many years before, was revived to the great joy of collectors near and far. Custard was introduced in January 1972 and has fared very well since then. On the other hand, Rosalene, which appeared in 1976, was eventually discontinued because of production problems. Frank Fenton explains the difficulty:

Charley Goe and I had worked on this together before he died and conducted a long series of experiments. We finally got the right combination of opaque glass and gold so that the gold would strike on reheating. The glass was a very corrosive type. We had a great deal of trouble keeping it in the pots and yet that was the only place where it would work. We couldn't melt it in the day tanks; the melting conditions were wrong for it there. Sometimes the pot would last for three melts and then develop a hole because of the corrosiveness of the batch. After Dr. Subodh Gupta came with us in 1973 he carried on Charley's work and tried to make the glass less corrosive. He succeeded to a degree, but at the same time we lost the sharp dilineation of white to pink that we had in the earlier batch. The group of items we brought out in 1976 in rosalene was one of the most interesting and collectible groups that we ever made, but we finally discontinued using rosalene because it was eating up our pots too fast.

Among the items in rosalene issued that year were an ogee candy box, 9394, and a flowered footed comport. (See CR 31-32, P. 103). Rosalene pieces sold well and had the market been the only factor in the equation, they would not have been dropped.

Happily, there were no such problems with satin. This beautiful color was introduced in 1973 in three varieties, custard satin, blue satin, and lime sherbet. The pieces made in this color were not new, the same moulds being used from which milk glass items had been produced, but the effect was certainly different when they came out in the satins. In 1974 rose satin was added. (See P. 80, CR 28, P. 102). This was an attractive heat sensitive color with gold as the main coloring agent in the glass. This meant that each piece had to be blown rather than pressed, since gold based pieces could not be pressed if a pinkish hue was desired. Lavender satin first appeared in 1977.

While all the satins were winners in the marketplace, custard satin was the most successful and was constantly brightened up with new shapes and styles. Several other new colors, which were introduced in the late 1970s and which did very well, were springtime green, wisteria, and crystal velvet. (See CR 19, P. 100).

Chocolate glass was revived in time for use in the last Bicentennial pieces. The delay in reviving it was caused by the loss of the original formula, which meant that the formula had to be re-developed by trial and error. When Paul Rosenthal retired as chief glassmaker in 1949, he sold all of his formulas to the company. Frank Fenton picks up the story:

Sometime after Paul turned his records over to us I called his attention to the fact that he didn't have the Chocolate glass formula among them. He seemed surprised at the moment, but said he would get it. Several months later I asked him again about it. Finally, he came to me and said he didn't have it, that his father had sold it to the National Glass Company in 1903 and never had given it to him. So that's the reason Charley Goe tried to reinvent the chocolate glass formula.

Goe conducted many experiments, but was unable to come up with the correct formula. After Dr. Subodh Gupta arrived, he carried on where Goe had left off. He was eventually successful and Frank Fenton is satisfied that the company has really duplicated the original chocolate glass made by the Indiana Tumbler and Goblet Works in Greentown, Indiana, and by FAGCO back in the early days. "It is a heat sensitive glass," Frank remarked,

which becomes darker or lighter depending upon the heat treatment that is given to it. Most of the pieces that we made in Chocolate glass were not warmed in and reheated, so that when they came out of the mould, it was just the heat from the glass sitting in the mould that caused whatever the final effect might be. For example, if you will notice the Jefferson comport, where the glass was thickest in the stem, the molten glass would actually re-strike the glass and cause it to be lighter in color. The Patriot's bell, (see P. 94), 8467, was warmed in the glory hole to get it to be flared out the way it was. That caused the color to be much lighter out on the edges than it is in the handle. This is typical of chocolate glass.

With respect to design, Valencia was down to only two items by 1973, but a number of new patterns were ready to more than pick up the slack. Of, course, Hobnail continued to show its amazing strength, if anyone was wondering about that. The Lovebird vase, made from a modified Verlys mould, came out in January 1974. Whereas the original vase had a plain surface above the birds, Rosena designed a leaf and flower pattern which was applied to that section of the vase, which greatly enhanced the beauty of the piece. It became a good-selling item. Pink Blossom appeared at the same time on decorated pieces. (See CR 25-26, P. 102, CR 70-71, P. 114). The design was done with a fine frosting of little particles of glass. Pink Blossom became a long-time staple. Waterlily, developed from an old English bowl picked up at an antique show, was introduced on a number of items in 1975. The Hanging Heart, developed from Robert Barber's work, came out in turquoise and custard in 1976. As Frank Fenton pointed out, "It took as many as 27 persons on a shop to make a single Hanging Heart basket. (See CR 21-22, P. 101). The intertwined vines and hanging hearts must be skillfully hand inlaid while the very hot glass is being finished."

Lily of the Valley was introduced in 1978 in two items, a basket and a bell. The pattern was inspired by a Lalique bowl purchased sometime before. The bowl had lilies of the valley around the top and leaves around the bottom. (See CR 20, P. 100). Tony Rosena developed the bell and the basket, but he used the lilies of the valley in a different way than in the Lalique bowl. At the same time a Scroll and Eye nut dish, 8248, a reproduction of an old Jefferson Glass Company jelly dish, went into the line. In 1980 a new Strawberry pattern appeared in crystal velvet. This was inspired by cut glass pieces that were done in an intaglio cutting early in the century. In the last years of the third 25 years Fenton went heavily into Roses. The Rose pattern was not new, but a number of the colors in which it appeared were. Perhaps the fact that 1979 had been designated by the Rose Growers' Association to be "The Year of the Rose" accentuated the trend. At any rate, in 1978 there was Blue Roses on blue satin which was followed in 1979 by Chocolate Roses on cameo satin. In addition, the regular Roses on custard and ruby, also helped honor "The Year of the Rose."

To celebrate the company's 75th anniversary in 1980, the Velva Rose treatment was revived. (See CR 125, P. 129). A number of pieces were made, including the Dolphin candy box, the 7526 six-inch bowl, the 7572 candleholder, all of which were reproductions of items made by Fenton in the 1920s. Among the new pieces were a bell, fairy light, and epergne. Everything in this Velva Rose anniversary line not only carried the company logo, but also a "75th" along with it. These pieces sold beautifully and were limited to the six months from July to December 1980.

A number of new Hobnail pieces came from the presses in the last ten years, although it was becoming increasingly difficult to find something that had not already been made in Hobnail. In the early 1970s milk glass was still the favorite color, and in 1971 a fan vase, 3852, a covered slipper, 3700, and a covered jam dish, 3600, in Hobnail milk glass, went into the line. (See CR 132, P. 131). The first two were inspired by things bought at antique shows, while the jam dish was a Fenton original. Lynn Russi cut the mould, which was designed for a dish that would snugly hold a glass of Smucker's jelly. While the company was happy with it, Smucker's was uninterested. That same year a new Hobnail milk glass lamp, 3807, (see cover photo), was made in the Melon pattern. As the years went by more and more Hobnail pieces were made in colors other than milk glass. In the January 1975-1976 catalog 235 separate Hobnail items, all colors, were pictured. There was little question that Hobnail, particularly Hobnail milk glass, was Fenton's all-time best-selling product. (See CR 51-52-53, P. 109).

The most successful of the new shapes were the bells. Actually, bells were not new, but they did not really come into their own until the 1970s. First, a little history on bell-making by Fenton. The first two bells the company made were the BPOE Elk bell [1911] and the Daisy Cut bell [1914]. The first, which had "Atlantic City" inscribed on it, was simply a souvenir. The latter, which appeared in the 1914 catalog may actually have been made before that in carnival. The Daisy Cut bell was still in the line in the mid-1930s. Another early one, a three-dimensional rendition of the Bell Telephone symbol, came out in the late 1920s or early 1930s. However between 1937 and 1967 Fenton made no bells.

In January 1967, however, the Hobnail bell in colonial colors and milk glass went into the line. In 1970 a carnival Daisy and Button bell was put in the Olde Virginia line, but in 1971 it was transferred to the regular line. The Hobnail bell, 3667, and the Daisy and Button bell, 1966, were followed in 1973 by the Spanish Lace bell, in silvercrest, 3567. "We were becoming aware," said Frank Fenton, "that bells would sell, so we added one in silver crest since that was a major color combination in our line." In 1974 the Bicentennial bell in Independence blue was added and in 1975 the Madonna bell, 9467, in blue satin, white satin, and carnival, and the Medallion bell went into the line. More bells were added each year.

Small animals became quite popular in the 1970s. Originally made in crystal, they soon appeared in various colors as the demand for them continued to grow. The "crystal glass pets" included a bird, puppy dog, kitten, duck, swan, and bunny. They sold everywhere so more animals were added, such as the frog, turtle, and sunfish. (See CR 105, P. 123). The turtle was a re-doing of the turtle ring tree mould which had been in the line for some time. The sunfish was made from an old mould used back in the 1930s. A particular favorite was the "happiness bird," which was made from a mould acquired from the Paden City Glass Company after it went out of business.

The Decorating Department, headed by Louise Piper, accomplished fine things during the 1970s. In 1971 burmese pieces came out with roses painted by Louise. In 1972 White Daises on ebony items and Bluebells on Hobnail illustrated the diversity of the artists, as well as the enriching of the line made possible by hand painting. In reviewing the January 1975-1976 catalog, Frank Fenton remarked:

It's amazing to see how much diversity we had in the line when we developed the capability to do the hand decorating. We can take a group of items that are plain and sell them plain. On the other hand, we can put one decoration on those same pieces and you've got an entirely different feeling for the pieces. Then you could take a group of items such as Daisies on custard, which has been a good seller for us. It gives an entirely different feeling to the pieces compared to those made with the Pink Blossom on them. It appeals to a different group of people than those who buy the Pink Blossom.

One particular decoration which appeared in January 1980, Blue Dogwood on cameo satin, caused embarrassment in the front office of the company, although through no fault of the decorator. (See CR 114 & 117, Pp. 126, 127). The latter had simply painted a very attractive flower with five petals. No name had been given it. At length, someone who did not know a great deal about the petals of the dogwood tree flower, called it a dogwood. The name stuck and the five-petaled flower found its way into the catalog. The only difficulty with this is that the dogwood flower has only four petals. The error was not noted until the catalogs were in the hands of representatives and buyers, so nothing could be done about the matter. No great harm resulted except that it provided quite a chuckle for those who knew anything about dogwood trees. The next catalog displayed the dogwood flower with four petals.

Fenton had never gone into the lamp-making business very seriously, but for years it had been supplying lamp parts—the base and the globe—to some of the thousands of lamp manufacturers across the country. They had been discouraged from getting into lamp-making by some of these same people who said that they could not be competitive. Nevertheless, in the 1960s the company made some milk glass lamps from their own lamp parts and test marketed them in the gift shop. They sold beautifully. The company concluded that there was a big market for lamps in gift shops, as well as in department and furniture stores, where they were traditionally sold. So Fenton began making lamps designed especially for the gift shop trade. The lamp line continued to grow throughout the last part of the third 25 years. And each one practically became a collector's item overnight.

Fenton made one other group of special items, called the "Robert Barber Collection," for a brief period in the mid-1970s. Robert Barber had a degree in physics from the University of Wisconsin. He spent some time studying glass and ceramics and later joined the fine arts faculty at Ohio University. He spent two years there teaching classes in glass-blowing and ceramics. Now a man in his late 30s, he operated a small, one-person glass facility between Coolville and Athens, Ohio. His furnace was located in a barn. He had been buying his chemicals from Fenton because if he tried to purchase them from a large supplier in the small quantities he needed the price would have been too high for him. One day in the fall of 1974 the stack to Barber's furnace was blown out of plumb which set off a fire in the barn and everything in it was destroyed. When he got control of things he came to the Fenton company and asked for a job. With a daughter and an ailing wife, he needed work. He was hired.

Barber was put out in the factory with a couple of glassworkers and told to make anything he wanted to. A special furnace was built for him, something he designed and whose construction he supervised. At the end of 60 days the management people came to see what he had done, all of it offhand ware. He had made a group of vases in different colors, shapes, sizes, and treatments. Four of these items were selected and offered to dealers as the "Robert Barber Collection" in the early months of 1975. (See P. 95). The reaction appeared good so a second offering of six pieces was added. A limited number of each item was made. Since this was a special edition, Fenton offered return privileges to dealers who had taken them, something not done with regular line items. As it turned out, however, the collection did not sell. Con-

Robert Barber, artist/craftsman at work.

sequently, many items were returned and the project was discontinued. Barber stayed on, doing different things for a year or so, but at length the company was forced to let him go. He was able to secure a position with Pilgrim Glass in Huntington, West Virginia.

Aside from the disappointing results of his work, Barber's years at Fenton were troubled ones. Because of the uniqueness of his position in the Hot Metal Department he ran into overt hostility on the part of the unions. He ran his own operation, did things some of the workers did not understand, and kept rather unorthodox hours. None of this sat well with the veteran glassworkers who viewed him as an interloper. Barber's rather stubborn personality did little to ease relations. The situation reached the point in the spring of 1975 that Frank Fenton felt compelled to write a lengthy memorandum to the local union chairmen, a copy of which was sent to the international president of the AFGWU in Toledo. In it he pointed out that Barber's work was providing employment for a dozen or so skilled and industrial workers who might otherwise have to be dismissed, that the experimental glass Barber was making could very well become a good money-maker for the company, and that Barber's specialized skills and talents had been of value. He urged that a genuine effort be made so that Barber could carry on his work without any harrassment. It is hard to say how much the memorandum improved the matter. No doubt when Barber left to go to Pilgrim there was general joy in the Hot Metal Department.

*   *   *

Fenton had manufactured so many wonderful glass items in its 75-year history that it is no surprise to learn that hundreds of glass fanciers had built up sizeable collections of Fentonware. What joy it was to get together with other Fenton fans and try to determine if some early piece was really Fenton or, perhaps, Imperial. And when was it made? And what was that pattern? Well, it was time to get these Fenton collectors organized and the people who decided to do it were Otis and Ferill Jeane Rice of Appleton, Wisconsin.

"I tell you, we've got to start it," he said.

She shook her head. "I don't think we should," she responded. "Not with all the other things we are trying to do."

"I know about the other things," he went on, "but in spite of them I just know we have to start this club."

She began to waver. "Well, if you feel so strongly about it."

"Oh, I do, I do." After a moment he went on. "Why don't we ask the other people in town here and get their thinking. If they back the idea, and I am sure they will, then we'll go ahead."

The "other people" gave their support, and thus, in December 1975, was born the Fenton Art Glass Collectors of America, Inc., or FAGCA.

* * *

Otis and Ferill Jeane Rice lived in Appleton, Wisconsin and built nursing homes. They were also collectors. Otis collected lamps and had to construct a special room in the basement of the house to shelve his 400 kerosene and other old lamps. Ferill Jeane started to collect carnival ware in the 1960s and now has one of the finest collections anywhere, numbering around 300 pieces. As her interest in carnival glass grew she wanted to learn more about Jacob Rosenthal, who had developed it early in the century. This brought her and her husband to Williamstown to talk to Frank Fenton. Once he got to see the factory and the kind of products the company put out, Otis became convinced that a club of Fenton collectors should be formed.

But to backtrack for a moment. Otis Rice grew up in Tabor, Iowa, a tiny town in western Iowa, about 25 miles south of Council Bluffs. Ferill Jeane grew up in Alliance, Nebraska, a tiny town in the northwestern part of that state, about 60 miles northwest of Scottsbluff. They met in Alliance in 1942 and following Otis' service in World War II they were married and settled in Tabor. An electrician by trade, Otis went to work for a company which had contracted for some work at Fort Crook in Omaha, across the river from Council Bluffs. When the United States entered the war a number of large automobile maufacturers had stored their machinery in warehouses at Fort Crook while they converted to war work. It was now time to take this machinery out of storage and prepare it for peacetime usage. Otis' job was to get some of this machinery back in commission, electrically speaking.

In the meantime, he had been doing some electrical work on his own and had built up a sizeable clientele. When his company, which had been doing the work at Fort Crook, asked him to go to France for a job it had contracted for there, he was not sure he wanted to go. He took a three month leave of absence to decide whether to go to France or stay in Tabor with his developing business. At the end of the three months, business was so good that he decided to stay at home. He operated his own electrical business for almost 20 years. One type of work he was called on to do quite often was to wire old farmhouses which had never been electrified. He had already developed a passion for lamps and when he went into a house for a wiring job he would often give his services in exchange for an old lamp or two.

As a child Ferill Jeane had artistic talent, but no art courses were offered in the Alliance public schools. Aware of her interest and ability in art the school authorities in Tabor wanted her to get an art degree so she would be able to offer classes in the subject in Tabor. She entered the University of Omaha, now the University of Nebraska-Omaha, planning to be an art major. While at the university she became very interested in ceramics and thought she might want to become a ceramics engineer. Growing children interrupted these various plans, but in the process she became a collector of ceramic pieces, both pottery and porcelain.

For the next 15 years or so Ferill Jeane helped her husband with his business, raised two children, and added to her ceramics collection. One night in 1964 a nursing home in Tabor caught fire and among the casualties was an elderly lady who was a close friend of the Rice family. Otis had been badly upset by the accident, especially since he had been after the owners of the nursing home to rewire the facility. They had not done so. He brooded over the matter for a couple of days and then came to a decision. "We are going to build nursing homes," he said emphatically. "And they will be properly wired!" The Rices are still building nursing homes; it has become a family business which the children have carried on. They have built countless such homes for the elderly, primarily in Iowa, Wisconsin, and Indiana. This is how they got into glass.

In the fall of 1966 they were building a nursing home in Logansport, Indiana. The Rices did not know many people there, being from out of town, and there was little to do anyhow by way of entertainment. But Logansport did have a Saturday night auction and the Rices were regular auction-goers. "On this particular Saturday night," Ferill Jeane recalled,

> there were four pieces of glass. My mother collected wine glasses. Among these four pieces was a little wine glass. I told my husband that when those four pieces came up, to buy them, so I could send my mother a wine glass from Logansport. So he bought all of them. It was quite late when we got home so it was not until the next morning that I really had a chance to look at them. As I sat at the kitchen table having a cup of coffee the sunlight coming through the window just sparkled off of one of those pieces. To that point I had never had any particular interest in glass, other than thinking it was beautiful. I just fell in love with that tumbler, although I didn't know a thing about it. Then I remembered having seen a picture in a recent *FAMILY CIRCLE* magazine which just looked like this piece. I dug out the article and there it was—an article about carnival glass. The more I looked at that picture and then at that piece of glass, the more I fell in love with it.

The next Monday Ferill Jeane was in the Logansport library reading up on carnival glass. She also visited a gift shop in town which had a lot of glass for

Otis and Ferill Jeane Rice.

sale. She learned that she had a very old piece, a collector's item which was no longer available except at auctions and antique shops. She also learned that the proprietor of the store was a former glassworker. He was very friendly and willing to talk about glass so she began visiting him on a regular basis. "As long as we were in Logansport," she said, "he taught me about glassmaking."

The next stop after Logansport was Appleton, Wisconsin, where the Rices eventually settled. Ferill Jeane became a regular frequenter at auctions and antique shops where she added steadily to her carnival glass collection. She came to know one dealer in particular in a nearby town, who was also a school teacher. At the time there was a technical college in Appleton, which served the four surrounding counties. In the fall of 1967 they were trying to develop a course in antiques at the technical college and had asked the curator of a museum in Oshkosh to teach the course. One week before the course was to begin the curator backed out so the antique dealer-school teacher was asked to take the assignment. He in turn approached Ferill Jeane and asked her, if he did the main part of the course, would she do the section on glass? Yes, she would be happy to. One week into the course the antique dealer-school teacher also withdrew and Ferill Jeane was invited to handle the whole thing herself.

This was the beginning of a seven and one-half year career of teaching "Adventures in Antiques" at the technical college in Appleton. "Needless to say," Ferill Jeane chuckled, "in the first couple of years I was just about one lesson ahead of the class. I knew glass, but I didn't know much about antiques generally, so I spent a lot of time studying." There was little literature geared to such a course available at the time, since "collecting" had not quite become the obsession with so many people that it is today. "You had to rely a lot on hobbyist magazines and talking to people," she said. "Since then the whole field has developed."

She gave up regular teaching at the technical college in 1976, but continued to teach two night courses. At the time the Rices were building a nursing home in Peshtigo, 60 miles northeast of Appleton. Throughout that winter she drove the 120 miles each night, Monday through Thursday, to teach two two-hour classes in Appleton. She would not get back to Peshtigo until two o'clock in the morning. She might have stayed over some of the time, but she was needed back in Peshtigo during the day to handle nursing home business. But she enjoyed the classes. She had 200 students in the two courses.

A young man in one of Ferill Jeane's classes in Appleton decided that Wisconsin needed a magazine devoted to antiques. He came to her with the proposal that, if he published it, would she edit it? Yes, she would. The magazine, known as *YESTERYEAR,* is still being published. In her role as editor, she also prepared a number of feature articles. One of these was about Jacob Rosenthal, who invented carnival glass. But the more she read about Rosenthal, the more she realized that she was reading merely a rehash of something already written. She wanted something fresh and original. And the man who should know more about Rosenthal than anyone else was Frank Fenton. She called him on the phone one day in the summer of 1975, made an appointment, and "within hours, my husband and I were on the way to Williamstown."

During Ferill Jeane's interview with Frank Fenton, which lasted from four to five hours, Otis toured the plant. He watched the glass being taken from the pots and deposited into the moulds, where the pressers shaped the pieces. He observed the blowers and the finishers as they worked their miracles. Never having been in a glass factory before, he was greatly impressed by what he had seen. Not just in the Hot Metal Department, but throughout the whole plant. After leaving Williamstown, the Rices drove up the river stopping off at the Viking plant in New Martinsville, the Fostoria plant in Moundsville, and the Imperial plant in Bellaire, Ohio. To Otis, the Fenton factory and Fenton glass was superior to all the others. Everything about it was first-rate. After the Rices' return to Appleton, he talked about little else during the rest of the summer and fall of 1975 — Fenton, Fenton, Fenton.

As the weeks passed the thought of founding a Fenton collectors club ripened in his mind. After all, there must be hundreds of collectors out there and something should be done about bringing them together. "We've got to have a club," he insisted. Ferill Jeane discouraged the idea. "I had been involved in various organizations over the years," she said, "and I knew how much work was involved. I did not see how I had the time or resources to start any such thing and play an active role in it." But her husband would not leave her alone. "We've got to start a club."

Shortly before Christmas he made up his mind. He came into the room and announced, "This is it; I'm going to organize a club!" He phoned Frank Fenton, told him he was about to form a collectors' group, and asked permission to use the Fenton name in the title. Within a few days a letter was received officially authorizing use of the name. "Then," smiled Ferill Jeane, "I knew my work was beginning." She and her husband discussed how best to proceed. Should word go out to everyone through trade magazines, or should they start close to home and build from the ground up. Not knowing how many people would be interested in a Fenton collectors' group, they decided to try the idea out locally. There were four other couples in

Appleton, friends of the Rices, all of whom were antique collectors. They were Betty and Arvin Wolfgram, Don and Nancy Moore, Lois and Marlon Rehmer, and Sylvia and Tom Landry. They collected glass, among other things, and would gather periodically for dinner or to attend auctions. These people were contacted and all of them liked the idea very much. The organizing meeting, a brunch, was held New Year's Day morning, January 1, 1976. The group agreed to call themselves the Fenton Art Glass Collectors of America. They met monthly until April, 1977, over a year later, when the incorporation papers finally arrived from the state of Wisconsin.

"Then it was your husband who really started the club?" a curious visitor inquired of Ferill Jeane.

"Oh, yes," she replied. "He was the real founder. I tried to discourage him."

"But then, after the founding, you had to go to work?"

"Yes, she chuckled. "As many women will say, 'husbands get the ideas and we do the work'." He had the idea and kept insisting on it. Finally, when I agreed with him to form the club, I also agreed to do the work that was necessary. He had the family business and did not have time for FAGCA. I am sure if our positions had been reversed, he would have done the work. He being the breadwinner, however, I had to do the work. But then he has always supported me completely."

Once organized, it was now time to reach out and sell FAGCA to the glass collecting world. Ferill Jeane drove to Kansas City soon after incorporation to start spreading the word. ENCORE, a group of carnival glass collectors, and the Heart of America Carnival Glass Club, an old collecting group, were both holding their annual sessions in Kansas City. She explained to them about the formation of a new group of Fenton collectors and invited everyone there to become a member. "I got a much greater response than I had anticipated," she said. "I thought a handful of people might like the idea and join us, but everybody there seemed enthusiastic. I don't know how many members I came away from there with, but it was a goodly number."

The first FAGCA convention, a one-day affair, was held in Neenah, Wisconsin, a few miles south of Appleton, in August 1977. The group rented the banquet room at the Valley Inn in Neenah. The Wisconsin members brought their own glass with them which was arranged on 15 display tables. Announcements had been published in newspapers throughout northeastern Wisconsin that there would be a free display of Fenton glass, that the film about Fenton glass-making would be shown, and that the public was invited. "We thought that maybe 100 or 200 people might come," Ferill Jeane recalled. "In fact, over 1,000 people came through and signed our guest book that day."

Convinced now that FAGCA was a going, as well as a growing organization, Ferill Jeane and the other officers in the club decided to hold subsequent annual conventions at the home of Fenton glass, in the Williamstown-Marietta area. Since the Fenton company was the *raison d'etre* for FAGCA's existence, it seemed appropriate to meet at the site of the factory so members could view the facilities, watch the glass being made, and meet the Fenton people on their home ground. The plan, therefore, was to hold the 1978 session in the Lafayette Hotel in Marietta. However, at the time, the Lafayette was undergoing extensive renovations and was not available. So the convention was transferred to the Holiday Inn outside of Parkersburg. Beginning in 1979, all conventions have been held at the Lafayette.

Convention time was a happy time for Fenton collectors. The number of attendees increased steadily

A meeting of the Board of Directors of the Fenton Art Glass Collectors of America. Left to Right: Kay Darling, Betty Wolfgram, Arvin Wolfgram, Ferill J. Rice, Jon Merchant, Irene Smith, Otis Rice, Glenn Huguet, Stan Darling, Helen Warner, Ed Tell.

each year. At Neenah in 1977, 27 of 47 members were present. Figures for later years were, in 1978, 115 of 700; in 1979, 270 of 1400; in 1980, 300 of 2000; in 1982, 400 of 3600; in 1985 500 of 4000. In addition to FAGCA members, hundreds of non-members usually visited the exhibits. The main events of the conventions were displays of their collections put up by members, identifying sessions of disputed pieces, an auction, informational seminars, a banquet, and lots of socializing. The peak number of displays at any one convention was 38. Of course, bringing a valuable collection of Fenton ware many miles to the convention is not something to be lightly undertaken. One has to admire the daring of the displayers who have risked accidents at every stage of the process. Happily, no breakage of Fenton glass has occurred at any convention.

Prizes are awarded for the most original, distinctive, or clever displays. To suggest the variety of displays, the 1980 convention can serve as an example. Among those of that year were a table done in pink glass, a collection of patriotic gems in red, white, and blue, a setting of boots and shoes, a gathering of birds, a collection of fish inside a make-believe pond, with waterlily bowls and cattails, and a Green Bay Packers table, set up by the Green Bay, Wisconsin contingent, to look like a football field. In 1984 first place prizes were awarded for "Best Old Glass," "Best New Glass," "Best General Theme," and "Originality." Each of the exhibits had to have a central theme and certain types of glassware to illustrate the theme. "Best Old Glass" was won by "The Black Rose, which featured black rose, peach crest, and peach blow. "Best New Glass" was won by "Gone With the Wind," featuring ruby and ruby iridized glass. "Best General Theme" was won by "Two of a Kind," featuring cranberry and blue opalescent. "Originality" was won by "Tobacco Road," which featured tobacco jars, cigarette lighters, and ash trays. Another convention highlight is the gift of a special glass item, made by the company for that particular convention, to each member in attendance. Speakers at the convention banquets have included Frank Fenton, Bill Fenton, and Bill Heacock.

Soon after incorporation, in June 1977, FAGCA's newsletter made its appearance. Called "Butterfly Net," it was a two-page, typed publication, run off on a mimeograph machine borrowed from a nursing home. In the early days it was issued four times a year. After the first year it was decided that there were sufficient funds in the treasury to print "Butterfly Net," if a printer could be found at a reasonable cost. One of FAGCA's members happened to know someone who worked at a paper mill, but who also ran a little printing business out of his basement. He printed the newsletter for several years. In 1980 the "Butterfly Net" went to a bi-monthly schedule. From a two-page mimeographed sheet, it is now a neatly-printed, 30-plus page publication replete with all kinds of information about Fenton glass.

In searching for a name for their publication, the original Wisconsin members conducted a contest among themselves. Numerous suggestions were made, but a general consensus seemed to emerge after an extensive study of the early Fenton catalogs. It was found that the butterfly pattern had been used by

Fenton far more than by any other glass company. Obviously, it was a favorite design of Frank L. Fenton's, judging from frequency of its usage. So when the group was looking for a symbol, the butterfly was the favorite. From there it was just a step to transform the symbol into the name for the newsletter.

"Butterfly Net" is a veritable treasury of material for the Fenton collector. Whenever the fourth 25-years of the company history comes to be written, it will undoubtedly be the primary source of information. A quick perusal of the last five years reveals articles about [1] Fenton personnel, such as Louise Piper, [2] types of glass, such as Burmese and Stretch glass, and [3] Fenton collectors. There are instructions on how to start one's collection, and after it has been built up, how to inventory it. There are diagrams of Fenton pieces and technical discussions of glass-making. There are sections on "new finds" and color codes, and lists of patterns, colors, and shapes. Word games, film and slide programs available from FAGCA offices, committee reports, and pages and pages of "for sale" items, are regular features of "Butterfly Net." Except for a short period of time in the mid-1980s, Ferill Jeane Rice has edited the newsletter from her Wisconsin home or from FAGCA's office in Appleton.

To encourage young people to develop an interest in glass, FAGCA for many years sponsored a scholarship contest. Two $1,000 college scholarships were awarded annually to students majoring, principally, in the fine arts, but not confined only to them. Those majoring in physics, chemistry, and ceramic engineering, were also eligible, since those sciences were closely related to the glass-making art.

It has been expensive for the Rices to found and develop FAGCA. Expensive in time, energy, and money. "But we don't regret a single bit of it," Ferill Jeane is quick to point out. "We have enjoyed it to the fullest. We felt it was our contribution to the preserving of the historical value of a tremendous industry in the United States." More particularly, they are proud of bringing proper recognition to the Fenton company. It is their view, an opinion shared by others, that while FAGCO was always a top-notch hand glass company, for a long-time it was not recognized as such. By bringing together Fenton collectors and spreading abroad word of the works and achievements of the company, they feel they have now brought to Fenton the recognition which it always should have had as one of the finest, if not the finest, hand glass company.

* * *

Founded almost at the same time as the collectors' group, and also dedicated to the discovery and preservation of Fenton history, was the Fenton Museum. Located on the second floor of the factory, the museum was opened in the spring of 1977, just about when FAGCA received its incorporation papers. A museum had been in the mind of Frank Fenton for some time, ever since he began digging into the company's past. His visits to antique shops and shows when he was educating himself in design, whetted this interest. As he acquired an ever-increasing number of rare old pieces of glass, by Fenton as well as by other companies, he realized that there should be a special place to store and display them. In his researches for the

Art glass display in Fenton Glass Museum.

Fenton history in the 1960s he became convinced of the need for a museum.

One early idea for the museum, a separate building, had to be abandoned when land was unavailable. Another idea, to create a "West Virginia Glass Museum" in Williamstown, subsidized by the glass industry and public monies, was discarded when other companies, although favorable to the plan, were unfavorable about supplying funds for it. So the Fenton company decided to go ahead and establish a "Fenton Museum" in the factory building itself. The museum was in the company's long range plans for most of the 1960s. It was dropped from the plans at one point because of uncertainty about financing, but was restored in 1971. Still not much was accomplished until the mid-1970s, by which time Frank Fenton was able to devote considerable time to the project.

Bernard Stockwell of the Dave Ellies organization in Columbus, who had been retained earlier to redesign the gift shop, made a number of drawings for the layout of the museum, while Mock Woodworking Shop in Zanesville began building display cases. On one occasion as Frank Fenton and several others were experimenting with lighting and positioning of the cabinets, Stockwell inadvertently upset a shelf, sending a shower of ancient glass to the floor. With fear and trepidation, they inspected the damage. Incredibly, only two pieces were broken.

In organizing displays and exhibits for the museum,

it was decided to concentrate on the company's earlier years. And since it was decided to include pieces manufactured by other glass plants, which pre-dated FAGCO's founding, 1880 was picked as the starting point. Originally, the time span covered in the museum was from 1880 to 1948, which encompassed the life of Frank L. Fenton, the company's founder. However, in 1988, the period was brought up to 1980, so the displays now include representative pieces from the third 25 years. Each display case, of which there are more than 30, contains 25-30 pieces, bringing the total to around 700-800. Not everything in the collection is on display because of space limitations. The room is about 40 feet square. But the exhibits are rotated regularly so that in a given period of time everything finds its way to the shelves.

An effort has also been made to provide an early history of the hand glass industry in the Ohio Valley. Professor James Measell, compiler of the glass descriptions of this book, did the research on the other companies. "One summer," Frank Fenton said, "he traveled up and down the Upper Ohio Valley, ferreting out information from public records." Among these other companies, mostly now defunct, whose history is outlined in the museum, are Fostoria, Jefferson, Viking, Hobbs Brockunier, A. J. Beatty, Central, Northwood, Beaumont, Crystal, Imperial and Riverside. Glass encased news stories and pictures, plus photographs of three generations of Fentons who have managed the company, complete the displays. Adjacent to the display room is a small theatre where visitors may watch a 28-minute film, which shows the glassmaking process at the Fenton company.

The Gift Shop enjoyed a face-lifting in the early 1970s. In its early years the Gift Shop played a very unimportant role in the Fenton scheme of things. It was conceived of only as a place where "seconds" might be housed, and if anyone coming in off the street wanted to buy some of the ware that was fine. Etta Ritchie remembers when it was just a tiny room in the 1950s and how she used to run across from her switchboard post to help Polly Maidens when things got busy. Because people were coming in, not only from off the street, but from other places as well. So in the early 1960s the Gift Shop underwent its first

Displays of glass in the Fenton Gift Shop.

Glass displays—Fenton Gift Shop

account. It also assumed the responsibility for the factory tours and its own advertising.

One reason for the separation of the Gift Shop from the glass company was the thought that it would be the first of a number of similar outlets. This, it was felt, could be more readily handled if it was separate. Two additional gift shops were established, one in Huntington later in the 1960s and another in Florida in the 1980s. Neither lasted too long because they proved to be in the wrong locations at the wrong time and did not contribute satisfactory profits.

But the original Gift Shop continued to prosper. In 1971 it completed an even more extensive remodeling than had been undertaken earlier. Designed by Bernard Stockwell, who had been with the David Ellies organization, it now provided 6,200 square feet of display space. In addition to glassware, the enlarged facility now offered for sale gourmet items, candles, dinnerware, and framed pictures. No, no tee-shirts or bumperstickers—yet. At the same time the parking lot was also substantially increased to accommodate the ever greater number of visitors, who were now coming from all over the United States and Canada. The Gift Shop company proudly announced that the renovated Gift Shop would "create a gift and home decorative accessory center unequaled anywhere in the area."

* * *

Through the expansion of the Gift Shop in the early 1970s, and the founding of the Fenton Art Glass Collectors of America and the Fenton Museum in the late 1970s, the Fenton story has been preserved for years to come.

expansion as the company came to view it as a tourist attraction.

Recognizing its potential appeal, the the Gift Shop was organized as a separate entity, Fenton Gift Shops, Inc., in 1963. It was made completely separate from the glass company with its own set of officers and stockholders, its own budget, and its own books. The Fenton brothers, Frank and Bill, ran it, but as an independent corporation. It was required to pay a "privilege fee" as well as rent to the glass company. It bought all of its glass from the glass company and added the usual mark-up when the glass went on sale. It has become the glass company's largest single

Aerial photograph of the factory building taken in 1977. Notice that the brick stack is no longer there and that the water tank is no longer in evidence. (Compare it with page 13.)

Chapter Fifteen
LOOSE ENDS

The 1970s were good years for the Fenton company. Earnings and profits were up most of the time and at the end of the decade the best figures ever were reported, which provided the third 25 years with a lovely exit line. Still there were occasional problems during this period of affluence. Labor negotiations took place every two or three years, which led to a bad strike in 1971 and lesser walkouts later on. Energy and environmental considerations increased costs, while the price of raw materials escalated. Yet, all things considered, it was a good time.

How could it be otherwise with such distinguished sets as the craftsman and Christmas plate series, the women's club series, the Christmas classics series, and the Bicentennial series. How could Fenton miss with the return of carnival, the revival of decorated ware, and the renewal of bells? How could the line suffer with the advent of burmese, custard, rosalene, and the varieties of satin? And one should not ignore the popularity of those little animals, the "crystal glass pets," to say nothing of the continued success of Hobnail and milk glass. With other hand glass companies going broke all around it, Fenton not only stayed alive, but was breaking new frontiers.

Looking quickly at the ups and downs—mostly ups—of the final ten years, it should be quickly noted that overall figures through 1974 were somewhat compromised by the problems at Armstrong Custom Fabricators. Invariably, glass statistics were good while steel data was bad, which brought the final figures down. With the final disposition of ACF in 1974, the albatross had been cut away and glass alone now carried the company to new heights. By 1976 Fenton's share of the handmade Glass Crafts of America members' sales had risen to over 20 per cent. In 1980 the highest after-tax profits in the company's history were recorded.

On the other hand, it should not be inferred that all was "peaches and cream" during this time. Moments of concern arose periodically. Rising prices of raw materials, costly union contracts, and expensive energy and conservation measures were factors which nullified some of the gain. A hiring freeze was in force in 1975, which was followed by a four-day work week in the factory which lasted two and one-half months. More than once it was announced that sales would have to be increased if red ink was to be avoided. From 1975 on there was constant worry whether the gas supply would be cut back so as to slow down production. Stockholders were told in February 1976 that gas curtailment was due the following month, although conservation measures taken so far were sufficient to avoid a shutdown in production. The supplier, Hope Gas Company, reduced the gas supply again in January 1977, but as in the previous year it had no bearing on production.

In the winter of 1977-1978 a fuel shortage developed because of a coal strike. Frank Fenton reported in February 1978 that the work stoppage had caused the company to lose 30 per cent of its energy base. He said that they had for some time been thinking about acquiring stand-by equipment to carry them through

such emergencies. For that reason they were now buying a 700 KVA generator, which when installed, should pick up the slack created by any further energy reduction. As the company looked ahead to the next 10 or 15 years, it did not feel the energy situation would get any better. The generator, therefore, despite its cost—$90,000-$100,000—was considered a wise investment. In fact, however, energy supplies have not been a problem since that time.

Labor Relations

Relations between the the labor unions [#22, the skilled workers; #508, the miscellaneous workers] and the Fenton management had been relatively harmonious during the 1950s and 1960s. Following the 1950 strike and the withdrawal of the hand glass companies from the National Association of Manufacturers of Pressed and Blown Glassware in 1952, the hand glass companies had negotiated with the American Flint Glass Workers Union as a unit. Although the companies had no formal organization, their negotiations with the union were conducted in concert.

But the 1968 contract, which had been negotiated in Cincinnati, disappointed some union members. Workers at Fenton, in particular, with the company doing so well, felt they should have won a better wage settlement. There was even some feeling that the rank and file had been short-changed by the union leadership. They apparently resolved that when the 1971 talks took place they were going to proceed along different lines. So it was that on March 22, 1971, almost six months before the 1968 contract was to expire, locals 22 and 508 informed the Fenton company that they were withdrawing from industry-wide talks and would negotiate the new contract directly with Fenton.

Talks between the unions and the company began in August, but as the expiration date of the contract approached, little progress was made. A huge gap existed between what the unions wanted and what the company was prepared to offer. The unions believed that by negotiating separately they would win a better settlement than the other locals who were negotiating as a group with the other companies. This was a misconception. The Fenton management was determined that its contract proposals would be close to those being offered by their competitors, thus there seemed small likelihood that the Fenton locals would emerge from the talks in much better condition than if they had not abandoned the joint talks. Frank Fenton recalled that, "the rest of the industry was bargaining in a group and I was in constant contact with them by telephone. Every weekend we would have a meeting of manufacturers to review what had happened. We were not in a position where we were going to give our people a whole lot more than our competitors."

The Fenton locals rejected the company's offer on Friday, September 3, the contract expired Sunday, September 5, and the strike began the next day. About 375 people were idled by the strike, 300 belonging to #508, and the remainder to #22. Employees of Fenton Gift Shops Inc. were not on strike as they did not belong to either union, and the gift shop remained open. Pickets took up their positions along Henderson Avenue and Fourth Street Monday morning and were maintained on a 24-hour basis throughout the strike.

In the latter part of August 1971, by which time it seemed obvious that there would be a strike, feelings were intensified by information that several carloads of glassware were being shipped from the factory. It seemed to the unions that this was evidence that the company was negotiating in bad faith. The matter took on a different appearance when viewed from the company's standpoint. Fenton had a large order to be shipped to S. and H. Green Stamps during the fall of the year. This would have been impossible to carry out if there was a strike. So early in the summer the company talked to S. and H. Green Stamps about the problem. It was decided to ship the order before the end of August, ahead of any strike. In his notice to the employees on August 26, Frank Fenton said:

> When we were told that your locals would not bargain in the group, it seemed that things could be different this year . . . Prudent business judgment indicated that our major customers should be told of this. Particularly the S. and H. Green Stamp people.
>
> We have for years known that S. and H. does not continue to buy from those suppliers who fail to ship their orders. We told S. and H. that our labor contract expired in September, that the conditions seemed different from previous years and that there was a possibility of a work stoppage. They asked if we could ship our fall orders in August. We said we thought we could. The carloads of glass all went to S. and H. It was good insurance for us and for you.

It was the longest strike in Fenton company history, lasting a little over six weeks. Negotiations continued off and on during that time, but little progress was made until late in September and early October.

One unforeseen difficulty for the strikers was payment of their hospital insurance premiums. The company's contribution, by contract, was paid for man hours worked. When the unions struck it meant that no man hours were worked and that if they hoped to keep their hospital insurance funded, the workers themselves would have to pay the whole amount. In a notice to the two union chairmen on September 9, Frank Fenton spelled out exactly what would have to be paid in for both individual and family policies if the funding was to be maintained at an adequate level. September 30 was the deadline for that month's payment.

These hospital insurance payments were to be made to Etta Ritchie, the payroll officer, in the company's front office. This created a dilemma for the workers out on strike. Since they were picketing the building and urging nonstriking personnel not to enter, it troubled them to have to enter the office to pay their insurance premiums. To accommodate them, Etta Ritchie went outside the building, set up a desk on one of the picnic tables where the strikers could make their premium payments. "We would take their payments," she recalled, "and give them their receipts so they wouldn't have to go through the office doors and get yelled at."

Despite the awkwardness of the situation, the company did what it could to make things a little less uncomfortable for the pickets. The picket line had to be maintained 24 hours a day if the workers were to collect their strike benefits. The pickets were permitted to use a building on Henderson Avenue across from the company offices to get in from the cold on those chilly October nights. They were able to plug in their coffee pots there and had access to the rest rooms. Workers manning the picket lines were given a barrel of wood so they might build fires at night.

Negotiations which had come to a halt were resumed in the third week of the strike. Some progress was made, largely through the aegis of Bert Vottero, International First Vice-President of the AFGWU, who had come down from Toledo for several sessions. He had to leave after a couple of days, however, whereupon the talks again bogged down. Yet it appears doubtful if a settlement could have been reached before the unions had worn themselves out. After the strike was over Vottero told Frank Fenton, "There wasn't anything you could have offered those fellows that would have kept them from going on strike. They were so convinced that they had to get a lot of money." In fact, the skilled workers' union, #22, settled with the company early in the strike, but stayed out until an agreement was reached with the other union.

Wages and fringe benefits were the main points at issue in the dispute. On September 29 the company made its "best offer," with wage and fringe increments staggered over a three-year basis. Wages would go up 18 cents an hour the first year, 15 cents more an hour the second year, and an additional 15 cents an hour the third year. Hospital insurance payments by the company would go up the first two years. Six paid holidays went into effect the first year. The unions considered these proposals at a couple of meetings, but were not fully satisfied. On October 12 the company added two additional features to its earlier plan. One was an additional paid holiday in the second

Members of AFGWU Local #508 committee presenting a flag to Frank M. Fenton—circa 1972. Left to Right: F.M. Fenton, H. Fox, J. Voso, R. Freshwater, W. Voshel—Chr—#508, D. Fish, B.J. Ward.

year and the other was a willingness to consider anew the incentive system in the Hot Metal Department in an effort to find a plan more agreeable to the workers. These additional elements broke the deadlock and the #508 workers agreed to the terms of the revised contract.

Because of the stoppage, Fenton fell behind in its plans for the new 1972 line, but the final figures for 1971 were on the plus side. Both profits and sales were up for the glass operation, although not by very much. Steel sales for ACF were up, but profits were down. It was generally believed that about one-third of the workers at ACF were the ones most strongly opposed to settling the strike. Members of #22 had settled early and a majority of those at ACF seemed in favor of settling. It was no accident that the first effort to sell ACF was made two months after the strike ended.

When the 1971 contract expired in September 1974, there was no strike. The Armstrong operation had now been sold, and the unions settled quickly. This made sense since the new two-year contract gave the workers "the largest wage increase in the history of our company." When that contract ran out in 1976 another strike was called. This time the unions negotiated with the seven remaining companies in the hand glass consortium. This was the right decision because the workers came out of it with a three-year contract which again embraced "the highest wage settlement in company history."

Proposed New Ventures

In its continuing search for diversified activity, the Fenton company explored several interesting ideas in the early 1970s. In the fall of 1971, in conjunction with the gift shop, it began investigating the possibilities of establishing a multi-arts and crafts operation adjacent to the factory. Such a facility would bring together in Williamstown various activities in which visitors from both the United States and Europe could take an active part. George Fenton was abroad at the moment discussing the matter with people in England and Ireland. After his talks there were concluded he planned to move on to the Scandinavian countries. Meanwhile, gift shop personnel were contacting property-owners nearby with an eye to land acquisition for the new venture. George returned from Europe very enthusiastic about the idea and urged that the company buy the necessary land. "Our thought," reflected Frank Fenton, "was that we would put in a large hotel complex, a resort type of thing, where we would have people come in and learn how to make glass, do pottery, and other things; they would experience the actual processes. It was a nice idea and we did explore it. However, we found out that it was too costly for our resources."

In connection with the arts and crafts complex, Fenton subsidized a regional craft show held in the spring of 1972 at Marietta College. It provided a first-hand view of how a crafts exhibit operated. It was a good experience, but did not change the decision already made, not to diversify in that direction.

At about the same time, the idea of opening a restaurant on company premises was discussed. With an average of 80,000 visitors a year coming to the gift

Glass Chemists Charles Goe and Isaac Willard.

shop, many of whom would also take the factory tour, it was deemed worth investigating. Joe Ehnot studied the matter, but in the end it was decided not to proceed with the project. The principal reason was that it would put Fenton into competition with the other restaurants in the Marietta-Williamstown area. And, as Frank Fenton explained, those restaurants regularly recommended that their patrons visit the Fenton company if they were looking for something interesting to do. "Why should we compete with them?" he inquired rhetorically. In addition there remained the problem of health regulations, to comply with which would be both complicated and expensive.

Personnel Changes

The Fenton company suffered two important losses in its glass technology and research sections within a short space of time. Charles Goe, chemist for research and development, died on October 16, 1969 and Isaac Willard, chemist for production—successor to Paul Rosenthal—passed away on June 9, 1973. Willard had come to the company in the summer of 1950, fresh from the University of Pittsburgh where he had earned a degree in chemical engineering. Goe was a student at Marietta College in the late 1940s and early 1950s and worked at the company in the summer of 1951. Also a chemist, he took a position with American Cyanimid upon graduation. He had been there for nine years, when he learned he was to be transferred to the company's New Jersey offices. He was not happy with the proposed move, a fact he mentioned to Frank Fenton one evening after choir practice at Williamstown's United Methodist Church. Frank was choir director while Goe was a star tenor. Rather than lose one of his tenors Fenton suggested that Goe come over to the company and they would see if there was something available for him. And so it was that he went to work for Fenton on a regular basis on September 1, 1960. Since neither Willard nor Goe knew much about glass and glass-making when they first came to the company, Professor Alexander Silverman came down from Pittsburgh to assist them in learning the trade.

The deaths of these two men left a serious void. When Goe died the company decided to get along as best it could until a suitable replacement was found. Several people were interviewed for the position, but they did not meet the need. One chap who did meet the need, lived far away and was unwilling to relocate. In the interim various stop-gap measures were employed. At length, on June 1, 1971, Dr. Subodh C. Gupta was hired for the position. With Willard's death two years later, Gupta, more or less, absorbed his duties as well.

A native of India, Gupta arrived in the United States when he was in his late 'teens and attended Ohio State University. He received a bachelor of science degree in ceramic engineering and then took a position with a glass company in New York state for a period of time. He later returned to Ohio State and took his master's and Ph.D. degrees in engineering. Engineering positions at this time, the early 1970s, were not easy to secure so he took a job as a science teacher in a junior high school in Columbus. Frank Fenton learned about Gupta and went to Columbus to talk to him. Gupta would have preferred to work in a field closer to his professional training, but since there were none available and since he had experience in glassmaking, he accepted the offer to come to Fenton.

Gupta made a number of important contributions in his years at the company. He was able to re-develop the formula for chocolate glass, originally invented by Jacob Rosenthal, which Charley Goe had struggled with but had been unable to replicate. Also at a time when soda ash, one of the three basic ingredients of glass, was in short supply, he developed a method of making glass which required only negligible amounts of soda ash. Although Gupta, at times, was over-confident as to his ability to resolve stubborn glass-making problems, he served the company well for about 15 years. At length he became frustrated with what he was doing and left Fenton to establish his own business as a seller of scientific books.

An important addition to the management team was made in 1970 when Domhnall OBroin [Dun'-nell O-Brin] was hired as assistant to the general manager. A native of Waterford, Ireland, OBroin had been educated in Ireland, Sweden, and at the Edinburgh College of Art in Scotland. He had worked at glass factories in Sweden and Finland, as well as at the famous Waterford Glass Company in Ireland. He arrived in the United States in 1966. Frank Fenton learned of OBroin through Raymond Price, who ran the Industrial Service Bureau for the hand glass companies in Pittsburgh. Price had met OBroin when he was visiting the Pilgrim Glass Company, in Kenova, West Virginia, just outside Huntington, where he was employed. Price told Fenton that if he had an opening he might want to talk to OBroin.

Later, while in Huntington on other business, Frank Fenton visited OBroin at his home. After talking with him awhile he suggested that if OBroin ever considered leaving Pilgrim he might want to stop at Fenton to see if anything was available there. In about a year, OBroin notified Frank Fenton that he was planning to leave Pilgrim. After further interviews, he was hired. Although a no-nonsense, rather abrupt type, OBroin made his contributions to the company as manager of manufacturing during those booming collectors' series days. He had his disagreements with some people, such as Robert Barber, who came in 1975 to make his offhand ware. Ironically, when Barber was let go in 1976, he went to work for Pilgrim Glass, from whence

Kenneth Moore, Industrial Engineer; Subodh Gupta, Glass Chemist; Thomas Bobbitt, Plant Engineer; and Domhnall OBroin, Manager of Manufacturing.

OBroin had come.

The deaths of Goe and Willard, plus the assignment of Joe Ehnot to Armstrong in the late 1960s and early 1970s led to a number of additions and changes in the company's management structure. The hiring of Subodh Gupta and Domhnall OBroin, just mentioned, illustrate this. Ehnot had been plant manager at the time he resigned in 1972 to become President of Armstrong Custom Fabricators, so this left a vacancy in that position. Tom Fenton, the second of Frank M's. four sons, who had been assistant plant manager, was elevated to the post. Since Tom was also responsible for other duties, some of the plant managerial functions were spread among the company's engineers, Floyd Showalter, OBroin, and Tom Bobbitt.

Bobbitt, a native of southern West Virginia, graduated from West Virginia University in 1966 with a degree in mechanical engineering. He worked for a firm in Mount Gilead, Ohio for several years and in 1969 came to Marbon Corporation in Parkersburg, now Borg-Warner. Early in 1971 he learned of an opening for a project engineer at Fenton and applied for the position. He came to work for the company in February 1971. When Floyd Showalter left in January 1979, Bobbitt succeeded him as plant engineer. In his years as project engineer Bobbitt worked on a number of plant and product improvements. These included the modernizing of pot-setting procedures, whereby the use of a forklift truck reduced the number of men required to change pots from 20 to six. He developed a pneumatic bulk unloading system for raw materials, which largely eliminated the diffusion of soda ash throughout the Williamstown atmosphere. He designed an original furnace-blaster to facilitate loading the glass batch into the furnace and an automatic sand-blaster for glassware etching.

The New 12-Pot Furnace

Those familiar with Fenton's long history readily recall that tragic day, late in June 1940 when the stack of the furnace collapsed killing one person and wrecking the Hot Metal works. By 1970 the "new" stack, which had replaced the fallen one, was already 30 years old, approaching the age-limit of such a chimney. In a routine inspection of the stack in 1971 it was found that cracks were developing in the piers and furnace walls. Consultants were brought in to advise the company on what should be done. They said that while there was no immediate danger, the stack would have to be replaced within a few years. With the tragedy of 1940 still fresh in their minds, Frank and Bill Fenton decided to take no chances. It was determined that a one-piece six-ton steel stack should be put up in place of the 25 ton brick stack which was now showing its age. The Armstrong division made the new steel stack and an outside company was brought in to tear down the old and put up the new. No changes were made in the pots or the manner in which the furnace functioned.

The following year a furnace design committee was organized for the purpose of planning a new furnace to replace the present one. Among its members were Floyd Showalter, Ike Willard, Domhnall OBroin, Subodh Gupta, and Tom Bobbitt. The committee was asked to [1] examine the furnace design itself and all related matters, [2] propose construction maintenance and furnace heat-up procedures, [3] establish and review furnace operating practices, and [4] search for furnace design and operating information which might be compared with Fenton's current methods. While

New 12 pot furnace under construction

New 12 pot furnace completed and ready for the fires to be lighted—1976.

economy of fuel consumption was an important consideration in planning a new furnace, that issue did not assume critical importance until the energy shortage of the mid-1970s developed. It was now necessary to push ahead with the new furnace.

In a memorandum to plant manager Tom Fenton, dated January 9, 1976, from process engineer Glen Brooks, it was noted that the furnace design committee had met and discussed the possibility of obtaining a cost estimate on the construction of a new recuperative 12-pot furnace. The committee also discussed the matter of converting six day tanks to recuperative heating. Recuperative heating requires a massive "recuperator." It was nothing new on the market, but its value had increased immensely during the energy crisis. It is a piece of equipment which picks up heat from the top of the furnace and re-channels it back below to pre-heat the furnace air. "If you pre-heat your air with waste heat," explained Frank Fenton, "then you don't have to use gas to heat that air."

OBroin was asked to inquire of Sismey and Linforth Limited of Birmingham, England, for a price quotation on the construction of a recuperative multi-pot furnace. OBroin was acquainted with Mr. Linforth from his experience in England before he came to the United States. Sismey and Linforth had special expertise in the design and construction of recuperators. OBroin had also been conducting experiments with a Sismey and Linforth recuperator on one of Fenton's day tanks. It appeared to work well. But installing the recuperator and the new pots was a big job because it involved excavating the basement under the furnace—where recuperators are located. After considerable discussion and correspondence with the Sismey-Linforth people, Fenton decided to proceed with the new furnace and recuperator. Begun in 1976, work was completed in 1977. The final cost was $339,000. The investment proved a good one, paying instant dividends. The new recuperated furnace reduced fuel costs by 40 per cent annually, sufficient to pay off its price in three years' time.

Other Plant Improvements

The spring and summer of 1972 was a fruitful period of planning future plant improvements. As an example, the furnace design committee was formed at this time. A number of other projects were discussed then, some of which were completed within a year or so, while others were not undertaken until later on. A new hot metal counter system was installed in July 1972 while eight doors, to replace the selected walls in the hot metal department, were in place a month later. A study was begun of the materials handling system with the purpose of designing a long range development plan. This involved the construction of new silos and unloading and materials handling facilities. An addition to the mould storage building was planned and built. A set of portable glory holes were experimented with, but were not in every day use until the 1980s. Another warehouse shipping building also went up during these years.

Next to the construction of the recuperated furnace, perhaps the most important new facility was a 200,000 gallon water tank built in 1973 at a cost of $106,000. The company had an old 35,000 gallon water tank elevated on a large steel frame. Its purpose was to provide fire protection, but it was beginning to go bad. The company was also aware that there was no back-up water supply for the city of Williamstown. In the discussions of replacing the old water tank it was suggested that the new tank be designed in such a way that it could be readily linked with the city water supply in the event of a water emergency. This was agreed upon. The excavation was made on the east side of Caroline Avenue where the employees' parking lot is now located. A well was dug and the huge tanks were placed in the ground. A diesel pump was hooked up to the well to pump the water into the tanks, while other pumps forced the water into the fire lines. Tanks and pumps were so arranged that with the insertion of a short section of pipe the water from the tanks could be emptied into the city's water lines. Space was allotted for a chlorinator to purify the water in the event it was needed by the city. Happily, there has been no occasion to use the water either for the Fenton company or the city. But residents of Williamstown rest more easily knowing the back-up supply is there.

Private Mould Work

In the present context, "private mould work" means glass that has been made for a specific individual or company, which does not carry the Fenton name. Such companies own their moulds and bring them to Fenton where the glass is made for them. The most important private mould account Fenton has had over the years has been the L. G. Wright Glass Company of New Martinsville, West Virginia. L. G. "Si" Wright as a young man, came to Frank L. Fenton in the mid-1930s with some moulds he had acquired from the Diamond Glassware Company of Indiana, Pennsylvania. Fenton made some items for him, including a cranberry Hobnail barber bottle and cruet and a few little Daisy and Button novelties. It was the barber bottle which got the company launched into the very successful Hobnail business. Wright took the glass made for him by Fenton, put it in the back of his station wagon and began selling it to small dealers in the Mideast and Southeast. With a good business head and an accomplished selling technique, he gradually built up a thriving trade.

From the 1930s until the 1970s L. G. Wright remained a very important account for the Fenton company. He bought large quantities of glass from it, which he sold to gift shops and department stores throughout the country. A "shrewd marketer," he would come to Fenton in the spring of the year, normally a slow time for the company, and persuade Frank L. Fenton to make items for him at unusually low prices. He could do this because he supplied the moulds and carried the glass away in his own truck, and because there were no commissions to pay and it was a slack time for production. He followed this *modus operandi* in later years. As Frank M. Fenton put it, "He deserved to be able to buy at reduced prices." To suggest the importance of Wright's account, the following figures list the dollar amount of glass purchased by him: 1959—$139,000; 1960—$109,000; 1969—$99,000; 1962—$89,000; 1963—$80,000; 1964—$75,326.

To illustrate the nature of Wright's orders, in 1965 he purchased 125 different items in pressed ware and

Some of the glass pieces made by Fenton for the L. G. Wright Glass Company.

140 items in blown ware. The pressed ware list included about 25 Daisy and Button patterned pieces, and a large number of covered animal dishes which were made in plain colors and purple slag. Assorted goblets and comports were also made in plain colors. The blown ware list included lamp founts and lamp shades in ruby overlay and various opalescent colors. Among other pieces made for Wright were large pitchers, milk pitchers, pickle jars, lamp bases, tobacco jars, barber bottles, cruets and large numbers of different lamp shades in a Rose embossed pattern and in opalescent colors. Mr. Wright died in 1969, but his company has continued in business to the present time under the direction of Mrs. Wright.

Lamp Parts

The Fenton company did a substantial amount of business in lamp parts during the 1950s and 1960s before it decided to manufacture lamps itself. (See CR 145-150, Pp. 139, 140, 141). Its best customers were on the East and West coasts. Important purchasers of lamp parts in New York were Julie Art Lamp Company, Ruby Company, Pitlow Lamp Company, J. F. Marr, Philip J. Greenspan Inc., Kayess Lamp Company, Roselle Lamp Company, Brite-Lite Lamp Company, and Geringer and Sons Manufacturing Company. Out west the major purchasers were Richards Manufacturing Company, Atlas Lighting Company, E. A. Dixon Company, Louis Lamp Company, Suchard's Lamp Manufacturing Company, and Nova of California. In addition, The B. and P. Lamp Supply Company in McMinnville, Tennessee, was a substantial purchaser of Fenton lamp parts during the 1950s and 1960s. Much of the output for this concern was made from moulds it supplied, so this was private mould work as well.

The following sales figures indicate the size of the lamp part business to Fenton's overall production picture: 1961 — $133,000; 1962 — $229,000; 1963 — $252,000; 1964 — $246,000. In 1965 the figure dropped substantially to $69,000. Whatever the reason for this fall off, it was no doubt a factor in the

company's decision within the next year or so to make its own lamps. As noted earlier, the first separate lamp catalog was issued in 1967.

Glass Baskets and Handlers' Marks

In the early 1930s Fenton made several glass baskets with either wicker, silver-plated, or nickel-plated handles. With the exception of a short period of time in 1917 [see footnote on page 135 of "The First Twenty-Five Years], there is no record of glass handled baskets being made until 1938. In 1937 the company brought out a line of Daisy and Button items — hats, ashtrays, slippers, and so forth. This was the number 1900 line. By 1938 hat moulds were being used to make basket shapes with glass handles, hand-formed, in two sizes. They were made in ruby and in the other colors that were being produced in the Daisy and Button pattern. This is the first record that can be found showing a glass handled basket.

The first handler was Frank Meyers, who had worked for several years as a finisher. He also put handles on jugs and made a number of different types of offhand pieces for his own personal satisfaction. Before he came to work for Fenton in 1932, he worked for the Diamond Glassware Company in Indiana, Pennsylvania. Diamond made handled baskets in carnival glass, and it is presumed that Meyers learned that handling skill while he was there.

The glass baskets sold so well in 1938 and 1939 that it was decided to increase production of them. The problem was that the presser and finisher in a shop could make basket-shaped hats faster than one handler could put handles on them. Hence a second handler was added to the shop. The veteran glass-worker Pete Raymond, who had worked at the factory the day it opened in January 1907, became the second handler. He already was a skilled finisher and ringer.

At some point early in the "handling" days, handlers began using small metal stamps to press the end of the handles firmly into the glass article while everything was still molten. Each handler used a different stamp so his work could be quickly recognized. Other handlers were added in the 1940s and

1950s as the number of handled baskets put into the line increased substantially. John Haddix and Charles Hummel became new handlers in the 1940s.

While the first handled baskets were in the Daisy and Button pattern, in 1939 Peach Crest, Ivory Crest, Peach Blow and the Blue Ridge treatments were added. They were made from the same moulds that produced the blown glass hats. Hats numbered 1920, 1921, 1922, 1923, and 1924 were made into baskets carrying the same numbers as the hats. As Hobnail pieces entered the line in 1940 and 1941, Hobnail baskets were also made and have remained in the line until the present day.

During the third 25 years, in addition to Meyers and Raymond, the handlers have been Floyd Duff, Junior Thompson, Don Badgley, Ron Bayles, Fred Bruce, Delmar Stowasser, Robert F. Oliver Sr., Pete Dallison, and Edwin Junior "June" Garber. The 1973 catalog contained a section describing Fenton baskets and the handlers' marks. In sales tips to dealers, the catalog observed that

> an interesting selling point is the individual handler's mark which each basket bears. A highly skilled handler attaches a glowing gob of molten glass to the piece and deftly works it into a graceful arch. The stamp with which he attaches the handle bears his personal mark. The design of the mark is his alone. Thus, each Fenton basket is personally signatured by a craftsman, who in doing so, says with pride, "This basket is right."

The accompanying sketches show the various handle marks that have been identified for individual handlers and the years of employment at Fenton for each handler using that mark.

HANDLER'S MARKS

Peter K. Raymond
1907 - 1913
1921 - 2-28-64

Frank O. Meyers
2-1-32   1-3-62

D. Austin (Pete) Dallison
7-20-33   3-31-82

Fred Bruce
2-27-53   Still handling

Donald Badgley
5-19-56   1978

Ron Bayles
9-10-56   Still handling

Junior Thompson
3-18-57   4-15-77

Robert Oliver
4-29-57   Still handling

Edwin Junior Garber
9-23-57   7-16-68

Floyd Duff
10-18-62   4-28-78

Delmer Stowasser
5-17-65   Still handling

Energy and Ecology

Among the several factors adding zest to life for the Fenton company in the 1970s were growing concerns over energy and ecology. As has already been mentioned, threats of gas curtailment, plus a couple of actual reductions, troubled production from time to time. Thus conservation of energy became very important. A number of steps were taken which minimized the effect of potential or actual cut-backs. In the fall of 1975 when the prospect of a gas shortage loomed ahead, Fenton began experimenting with Number 6 fuel oil. "The idea," commented Frank Fenton, "was to develop enough oil capacity here at the factory, so that we could use number six fuel oil and would not have to shut down. A 30 per cent cut-back would have forced us to shut down. With this oil reserve we might have to cut back a bit, but we would not have to shut down." Instead, the company installed a standby oil system using No. 2 fuel oil. Of course, the biggest savings in energy came in 1977 with the installation of the recuperator when the new furnace was built.

In the area of ecology, the Fenton company had problems with both air and water pollution, which it was ordered to correct. Air pollution was caused by the corrosive chlorides used in the iridizing process in the Hot Metal Department. This was going up the stack and into the atmosphere. Frank Fenton explained how the problem was solved:

> We put in a washing system to wash the pollution out of the air. When we did that we had to drill wells to have the water to wash the air. We ran it through some coils first and it cooled the air in the factory. So it goes through the coils, then it goes through the air and in so doing, gets rid of the effluent.

With respect to water pollution the trouble stemmed from the hydrofluoric acid used for etching. Since the waste was entering the river, it had to be cleaned up before it got that far, or else no further use of the acid would be allowed. To deal with this problem, settling ponds were dug which were filled with clean water. The waste water then went into these pools, where it was neutralized, after which it was released into the river. "Actually" recalled Frank Fenton, "we were putting such good water into the river that it became an excellent bass fishing area. There was more oxygen in the water there than anywhere else. The fish gathered around the outlet." Of course, as with all industrial concerns that produce pollutants, it was quite costly for Fenton to comply with the numerous anti-pollutant regulations.

Delbert Ward

In concluding the third 25 years, perhaps mention should be made of the current employee, who except for Frank M. and Bill Fenton, has the longest record of service at the Fenton company. Delbert Ward, still active well into the fourth 25 years, came to work at the age of 14 in the summer of 1944. He really was not supposed to be working in a factory at that age, but he managed to get away with it, working after school, at nights, and during summer vacations. Two years later, when he became 16, there was no longer a problem with his age and he went full-time. He worked at various tasks in the early years, but finally became

Winford O. Hamilton, Hot Metal Superintendent — 1967; Delbert D. Ward, Jr., Hot Metal Superintendent — 1976.

Lawrence L. Badgley, Factory Manager — 1949 to 1967. "Badge," as he was known, was an important part of the management team during the growth of Fenton Art Glass in the first half of the third 25 years.

a finisher. In 1964 he was promoted to shift foreman. He was elevated to the post of Hot Metal Superintendent in 1976. Outside of 21 months of military service during the Korean War, Ward has spent all of his adolescent and adult life at the Fenton company.

The Second "Old Order" Changeth

Chapter eight of the Fenton company history, which appears in "The Second Twenty-Five Years" [pages 20-24, 145], is entitled "The Old Order Changeth." It describes the deaths of Frank L. Fenton and Robert C. Fenton, founding fathers of the company, within months of one another in 1948. Control of the company passed into the relatively inexperienced hands of Frank L's. two sons, Frank M., aged 32, and Wilmer C., aged 25. The success of Frank M. and Bill in carrying the company on to greater heights than ever, has been the subject of this book on the third 25 years. Now as the third quarter century of Fenton history draws to a close, the second generation of Fentons has served its time and is about to "pass the torch" to the third generation. While this is mostly a story for the fourth 25 years, something should be said of the matter here.

All eight of the children of Frank M. and Bill Fenton, except one went to work for the glass factory. The only "defector" was Frank's eldest son, Frank R., who pursued a very successful career as a doctor of animal husbandry. Frank's other three sons, Thomas K., Michael D., and George W, are now all part of the management team, as is George's wife, Nancy. Of Bill's

four children, Don Alan, Randall, Shelley Ann, and Christine, both Don and Shelley are in management, while Randy helps manage and serves as treasurer of Fenton Gift Shops Inc. He played basketball at Williamstown High School and graduated from Marietta College, where he captained the golf team in 1975. Christine works in customer service in the company offices. Practically all of them began working at the company on a part-time basis during their high school and college vacations.

Frank Fenton's second eldest son Tom, born in 1942, graduated from Marietta High School in 1960 and from Ohio Wesleyan University in 1964. He did graduate work at Ohio University the following year. He started in at the plant during high school and continued to work there in various capacities during summer vacations for seven years. He was a clerk in the mixing department, he "carried-in" in the Hot Metal Department, and he served as a tour guide. Following his graduate work at Ohio University, he went full time with the company in 1965. Since then he has held a number of positions, He became plant manager with Ehnot's departure in 1972 and in 1978 was named vice-president, retaining his post as plant manager.

Mike, born in 1945, attended Williamstown High School where, in 1963, he was a starter on the only state basketball championship team the school has ever had. As did the others, he worked summers at the company. He attended Wooster College after which he spent over four years, 1967-1971, in the United States Navy. While in naval service he had two tours of duty in the western Pacific during the Vietnam War. After the navy he attended Marietta College and, in 1973, went to the company full-time as purchasing agent. In 1985 he became purchasing manager and safety director.

George, born in 1949, also went to Williamstown High School, where he starred in football and basketball. He entered Wesleyan University at Middletown, Connecticut in 1967, and graduated in 1971 with a bachelor's degree in physics and astronomy. He had worked at the company every summer since 1967 and went full-time in 1972. George was sent on fact-finding missions for Fenton in his first few years and in 1976 became foreman of the Decorating Department. From 1979 to 1985 he was manager of manufacturing and represented the company in labor negotiations. In 1985 he was designated executive vice-president. In January 1986 when Bill Fenton moved up from the presidency to board chairman, George succeeded him as company president.

At about the same time George came to work for the company on a regular basis, he married Nancy Gollinger, a Williamstown girl and a neighbor of the Fenton family. A graduate of Denison University with post-graduate studies in business and marketing, Nancy had worked on various part-time projects at the company when, in 1982, she went full-time in the sales department. In 1985 she became product development manager for Fenton Art Glass and Fenton's Christine Victoria operation.

Don, Bill's eldest son, after graduating from Williamstown High School in 1969, attended Muskingum College. He played basketball in high school

The third generation. Front Row—Left to Right: Nancy G. Fenton, Christine L. Fenton, Shelley A. Fenton. Back Row—Left to Right: Don A. Fenton, Michael D. Fenton, Thomas K. Fenton, George W. Fenton, Randall R. Fenton.

and captained the golf team in college. He began working summers at the company in 1968, which he continued to do through his college years. He was a stock boy in the Gift Shop, a tour guide, and then served in the shipping and order departments in the factory. Upon his graduation from Muskingum in 1973 with a B.S. degree in mathematics, he joined Fenton full-time working with his father in sales. Bill took Don with him on a number of business trips and in 1975 Don became assistant sales manager. In 1978, when Bill advanced to the presidency, he was named national sales manager. In 1985 he moved up to vice-president-sales. Don is a six-handicap golfer, but notes that "I still have trouble beating my Dad."

Shelley, Bill's youngest daughter, also attended Williamstown High School and graduated from West Virginia University in 1981 with a degree in marketing. In her high school and college summers, she worked as a tour guide in the Gift Shop and in the order department in the factory. In February 1982 she went full-time in the sales department. There she worked with the manufacturer's representatives, attended gift shows, and helped prepare the catalogs. In 1985 she became assistant sales manager, in addition to being responsible for the layout and design of all printed materials.

* * *

After 30 years at the company's helm, Frank M. Fenton decided to step down from the presidency in 1978. He stayed on as chairman of the board. Bill, who had been vice-president, sales manager, and executive vice-president, replaced him as president. In 1985 Frank gave up the chairmanship, which was also assumed by Bill. In February 1986 Bill surrendered the presidency to George, while remaining board chairman. The third generation is now firmly in place as the fourth 25 years nears the end of its first decade. But the second generation is still on hand and is frequently called upon for advice and counsel by the third. This is a luxury which Frank M. and Bill never enjoyed when they were suddenly catapulted to the top in 1948. Despite several difficult years in the mid-1980s, the Fenton company—one of the few survivors in a highly competitive industry—weathered the storm and now appears to be in good shape to move ahead while maintaining its reputation as a distinguished manufacturer of artistic glassware.

Fenton Glass in Color
1956-1980

Fenton Glass
IN COLOR
(1956-80)

A   B   C   D   E

F   G   H   I   J   K   L   M

N   O   P   Q   R   S

This page offers just a few examples from the wide variety of Fenton colors.

A — No. 7237 CW (Cardinals in Winter handpainted decoration) 7″ basket, 1977-79.

B — No. 7237 ST (Silver Turquoise) 7″ basket, 1956-59.

C — No. 7308 AB (Apple Blossom) epergne, 1960-61. The intensity of the Apple Blossom color edges varies from light pink to nearly red.

D-E — No. 7237 BC (Black Crest) 7″ basket and No. 7451 BC 6″ melon rib vase, probably sold through the Fenton Gift Shop, circa 1970.

F — No. 9198 CG (Colonial Green) cigarette lighter, 1966-68.

G — No. 2473 JT (Jamestown Blue Transparent) cruet, 1958-59.

H — No. 2473 RO (Ruby Overlay) cruet, 1956-66.

I — No. 3869 CR (Cranberry) Hobnail oil bottle, with crystal "stuck" handle, 1956-64. Whenever the Fenton term "Cranberry" is used, it refers to this cranberry opalescent color. The "Country Cranberry" color marketed in the 1980s is the same as Fenton's Ruby Overlay from the 1940s-50s (no opalescence).

J — No. 6455 Aventurine Green and White on Crystal 5½″ vase, 1964 (this is a sample piece; compare with the colors in the lines illustrated on p. 76).

K-L — No. 6058 LC (Cased Lilac) 6½″ vase, and No. 6068 LC 6½″ handled jug, both 1955-56.

M — No. 6056 SJ (Silver Jamestown) 6″ vase, 1957-59.

N — No. 3883 CR (Cranberry) candy jar, 1954-58; note that cover is French opalescent, not cranberry opalescent.

O — Old Hobbs, Brockunier No. 323 covered butterdish in ruby opalescent (ca. 1886) for comparative purposes.

P — No. 3955 WT (Wisteria) slipper in rare Wisteria color, 1977-78.

Q — No. 1939 CA (Colonial Amber) oval basket, 1965-72.

R — No. 6209 MI (Milk Glass) tray with No. 6206 JT shakers and No. 6289 JT mustard, 1958-59. This sample set was probably sold only in the Fenton Gift Shop, since the No. 6289 JT mustard was not in the line. These articles were in the line in MI (milk glass), and the No. 6206 JT shakers are on Fenton price lists.

S — No. 2461 JT creamer, 1958-59.

Cactus
IN TOPAZ OPALESCENT

All these items were produced in TO (Topaz Opalescent) and milk glass (MI) during 1959-60. By July, 1960, only three TO items remained in the line: No. 3428 (footed nut dish; No. 3435 (handled bonbon); and No. 3445 (goblet). Most items continued in MI until January 1, 1961 when only a few articles were in the price list. Except for the No. 3450 MI 8″ bud vase, all were discontinued by January, 1963, and the bud vase was listed through July, 1964.

1—No. 3439 TO 9″ basket
2—No. 3452 TO tall vase
3—No. 3401 TO epergne
4—No. 3461 TO medium vase
5—No. 3454 TO 5″ vase
6—No. 3422 TO footed bowl (compote)

7—No. 3445 TO goblet (also listed in CA, CB, and CP in January, 1962).
8—No. 3428 TO footed nut dish (made from goblet)
9—No. 3474 TO candleholder
10—No. 3437 TO 7″ basket
11—No. 3459 TO 6″ fan vase (made from No. 3480 cracker jar base)
12—No. 3406 TO salt shaker
13—No. 3463 TO cruet with stopper
14—No. 3425 TO banana bowl
15—No. 3435 TO handled bonbon
16-17—No. 3408 TO set—covered sugar and creamer (also made without sugar lid as No. 3404 TO set)
18—No. 3477 TO ¼ lb. covered butterdish

Coin Dot
IN
TOPAZ & CRANBERRY OPALESCENT

19   20   21   22   23   24

25   26   27   28   29   30

31   32   33   34   35   36

A copy of a Victorian pattern (Polka Dot), Fenton's Coin Dot was first made in 1947 in Cranberry Red, French Opalescent and Blue Opalescent (see the index in Fenton Book II and the catalogue pages from 1947 and 1953-54 on pp. 104-106 and 128, respectively). Most of the shapes shown here were introduced in Cranberry (remember, Fenton's CR refers to cranberry opalescent) between 1956 and 1964, with Topaz Opalescent (TO) making its debut in 1959. By early 1961, only one TO item in Coin Dot remained in the line, the 1427 7″ bowl. Some shapes in CR were discontinued at various times between 1959 and 1962. The vases, basket and 7″ bowl are in Fenton price lists through July, 1964. The vases were made in Blue Opalescent (BO) in 1960-61. Some Coin Dot items were made in Lime Opalescent (LO) between 1952-54 (see items 50-51 on the next page).

19 — No. 1442 TO 10″ vase, 1959.

20 — No. 1459 CR 8″ vase, 1948-58.

21 — No. 1477 CR 8″ vase, 1960-61.

22 — No. 1440 CR 6″ vase, 1958-59.

23 — No. 1438 CR 8½″ bowl, 1957-58.

24 — Hurricane globe in CR made from old No. 170 Spiral (see Fenton, Book 2, figs, 393-4), circa 1952, not in the line.

25 — No. 1458 TO 8″ vase, 1959.

26 — No. 1441 TO 7″ vase, 1959.

27 — No. 1456 CR 6″ vase, 1948-64.

28 — No. 1454 CR 4½″ vase, 1948-64.

29 — No. 1425 CR 4″ rose bowl, 1960-61.

30 — No. 1437 CR 7″ basket, 1947-64 (some were also made for the FAGCA convention in 1978).

31 — No. 1448 TO Ivy vase, 1959.

32 — No. 1466 TO 6″ vase, 1959-60.

33 — No. 1473 TO cruet, 1959-60.

34 — No. 1425 TO 4″ rose bowl, 1960.

35 — No. 1454 TO 4½″ vase, 1959.

36 — No. 1457 TO 7½″ vase, 1959-60.

Hobnail & Coin Dot

IN CRANBERRY & GREEN OPALESCENT

37 — No. 3759 GO tall vase, 1959-60.

38 — No. 3637 CR 7″ deep basket, 1963

39 — No. 3947 CR 12 oz. tumbler, 1952-67

40 — No. 3664 CR 70 oz. ice lip jug, 1964-65.

41 — No. 3870 CR candleholder; first made about 1953, this remained in the line until 1977.

42 — No. 1477 CR 8″ vase, 1956-64 (see item 21 on the previous page).

43 — No. 189 10″ vase in Cranberry (this was introduced in 1947 and was out of the line by 1951).

44 — No. 3728 GO comport, 1959-61.

45 — No. 3974 GO candleholder, 1959-61.

46 — No. 3801 GO miniature epergne set, 1959-61.

47 — No. 3887 GO footed candy jar, 1959-61.

48 — No. 3727 GO comport or crimped footed bowl, 1960-61.

49 — No. 3756 GO 8″ bud vase, 1959-60.

50-51 — These Lime Opalescent (LO) items No. 1456 6″ vase and No. 1454 4½″ vase were made in 1952-54. Note the difference in the green color.

52 — No. 1448 CR Ivy vase, 1956-64.

53 — No. 1450 CR 5″ vase, 1952-64.

54 — No. 1440 CR 6″ vase, 1958-64. (cf. item 22)

Hobnail
IN
PLUM OPALESCENT

55   56   57   58   59   60   61   62

63   64   65   66   67   68   69

70   71   72   73

Plum Opalescent, introduced in July, 1959, and continued in the Fenton price lists until mid-1962, so the items shown here are from this relatively narrow time frame. These Hobnail shapes shown can be found in Milk Glass (MI), as well as some other colors (see p. 70-71 and CR 37-49 pgs. 105-108).

55 – No. 3760 PO pitcher vase.
56 – No. 3843 PO wine glass.
57 – No. 3761 PO handled wine decanter.
58 – No. 3839 PO 12″ oval basket.
59 – No. 3762 PO 12 oz. syrup jug.
60 – No. 3750 PO 6″ vase.
61 – No. 3758 PO medium vase.

62 – No. 3759 PO tall vase.
63 – No. 3731 PO 10″ footed bowl.
64 – No. 3974 PO candleholder.
65 – No. 3887 PO footed candy jar.
66 – No. 3756 PO 8″ bud vase.
67 – No. 3837 PO 7″ basket.
68 – No. 3728 PO comport.
69 – No. 3755 PO 9″ vase.
70 – No. 3801 PO 4-piece epergne set.
71 – No. 3771 PO candlebowl.
72 – No. 3771 PO candlebowl, tilted to show interior.
73 – No. 3924 PO 9″ crimped bowl.

Assorted Hobnail Colors

74 75 76 77 78 79 80

81 82 83 84 85 86

87 88 89 90

Fenton's popular Hobnail line was made in a wide variety of colors over a considerable period of time. This page shows a variety of green hues as well as the Topaz Opalescent (made in 1959-60), the unusual Black, and Colonial Blue.

Colonial Amber (CA), Colonial Blue (CB) and Colonial Pink (CP) began in 1962 and Colonial Green (CG) was added in 1963 (and discontinued in 1976), but Hobnail items did not appear in these colors until the mid-1960s. Colonial Amber was still in production in 1980, but Colonial Blue had been discontinued a year earlier. Colonial Pink was in production from 1962-68.

For Hobnail in colors made prior to 1956, see the index to Fenton Book 2.

74 — No. 3784 CG footed candy box, 1966-70.

75 — No. 3668 GT (Springtime Green) candy box, 1977-78.

76 — No. 3692 CG table lighter, 1965-68.

77 — No. 3952 CG 4″ vase, 1965-76.

78 — No. 3873 CG miniature candlebowl, 1969-72.

79 — No. 3995 GO (Green Opalescent) slipper, 1960-61.

80 — No. 3920 TO footed comport, 1959-60.

81 — No. 3730 TO ribbon candy bowl, 1959-60.

82 — No. 3726 TO Ivy bowl, 1959-60.

83 — No. 3850 TO 5″ vase, 1959-60.

84 — No. 3974 TO candleholder, 1959-60.

85 — No. 3995 TO slipper, 1959-62.

86 — No. 3771 TO candle bowl, 1959-60.

87-88 — No. 3799 BK (Black) 10″ planter and No. 3697 BK 8½″ planter. These were made in 1970 especially for the A. L. Randall Company, a jobber who specialized in florist's fixtures, and were not in the Fenton line.

89 — No. 3608 CB (Colonial Blue) fairy light, 1969-79.

90 — No. 3633 CB oval nut dish, 1964-68.

Colonial Amber (CA), which seems to have replaced Antique Amber (AR), appeared in a few Hobnail pieces in 1964 and continued on price lists through 1980. Ruby (RU) Hobnail commenced about 1972 and was still in the line in 1984. Orange (OR) Hobnail was last mentioned in a Fenton price list in 1977.

91—No. 3774 AR 10″ candleholder, 1959.

92—No. 3689 CA apothecary jar, 1964-69.

93—No. 3837 CA 7″ basket, 1967-80.

94—No. 3628 RU footed comport, 1972-84.

95—No. 3667 RU bell, 1972-84.

96—No. 3734 RU 12″ basket, 1972-80.

97—No. 3802 CA covered butter bowl, 1979-80.

98—No. 3965 AR squat jug, 1959.

99—No. 3654 CA 7″ vase, 1978 (not in the line).

100—No. 3804 CA 3-pc. fairy light, 1975-80.

101—No. 3650 CA nut/ice cream dish, 1967-68.

102—No. 3724 AR 8½″ three-toed bowl, 1959.

103-104—No. 3648 RU ball ash tray and No. 3665 OR miniature creamer. These offer a good study in glass color control. The ball ash tray is listed in RU in 1977-78. The OR miniature creamer dates from 1965-68. The heat-sensitive OR glass will vary in color, sometimes appearing more ruby than orange!

105-106-107—No. 3610 RU 3 pc. ash tray set, 1976-78.

108—No. 3837 RU 7″ basket, 1972-84.

109—No. 3992 RU boot, circa 1975 (not in the line).

Both of these colors are cased glass (note the opal and white inner layer). Fenton's Wild Rose (WR) was introduced in 1961 (along with Powder Blue, Honey Amber, Apple Green and Coral; for the latter two, see next page) and continued through 1962.

Opaque Blue (OB), made by gathering Colonial Blue over opal, debuted in 1962 (along with Plated Amberina; see pp. 77, 79) and was short lived; a few items were on the 1963 price lists, and only one, the No. 1359 OB vase, was listed in 1964. Some lamps in OB were made in 1967 and 1971.

110-114 — Hobnail items in Wild Rose are No. 3752 WR 11″ vase, No. 3858 WR 8″ vase, No. 3856 WR 6″ vase, No. 3656 WR 5½″ vase, and No. 3762 WR 12 oz. syrup jug.

115 — No. 1359 WR Bubble Optic 11½″ vase.

116-117 — Wild Rose with Bowknot pattern No. 2857 WR 7½″ vase and No. 2855 WR 5″ vase (don't confuse the pattern name with the color; they are separate terms). The Wild Rose with Bowknot pattern was first introduced by the McKee and Brothers firm of Jeannette, PA about 1900.

118 — No. 9156 WR Jacqueline pattern 6″ vase.

119 — No. 5858 WR vase (this design was based upon a Czech vase; this article in another color was still in the Fenton line in 1988 as the Wheat vase).

120-121 — Bubble Optic No. 1350 WR 5″ vase and No. 1356 WR 7½″ vase.

122 — No. 6080 WR covered candy box. This article was inspired by Frank M. Fenton's purchase of an antique Wave Crest jewel box; for similar items, see K, L and M on page 65.

123-126 — Hobnail items in Opaque Blue (OB) are No. 3850 OB 5½″ vase, the three-piece No. 3867 OB lavabo set and the No. 3762 OB 12 oz. syrup jug. All of these were first listed in January, 1962, but all were out of production by 1964.

Assorted Overlay Colors

127   128   129   130   131   132

133   134   135   136   137   138

139   140   141   142   143   144   145

Like Wild Rose and Opaque Blue, these are "overlay" or "cased" pieces. Apple Green (AG) and Coral (CL) appeared only in 1961, but Honey Amber (HA) was listed 1961 through 1968, although the last 3-4 years were lamps only.

127—No. 1358 HA pinch vase, 1961-62.

128—No. 3850 HA Hobnail 5″ vase, 1961-62.

129—No. 3762 HA Hobnail 12 oz. syrup jug, 1961-63.

130—No. 2857 CL Wild Rose with Bowknot 7½″ vase.

131—No. 6080 CL covered candy box (see item 122).

132—No. 1359 CL bubble optic 11½″ vase.

133-135—Hobnail items: No. 3850 CL 5″ vase, No. 3762 CL 12 oz. syrup jug and No. 3856 CL 6″ vase.

136—No. 5858 AG vase (see item 119).

137—No. 2857 AG Wild Rose with Bowknot 7½″ vase.

138—No. 9166 AG Jacqueline 48 oz. pitcher.

139-140—These items (No. 1352 GV 8½″ vase and No. 1357 GV 7½″ vase) were made in the early 1950s in Green Overlay (GV). Note the difference between this color and the Apple Green (AG) items on this page. A January 1, 1952 Fenton price list also mentions the color Honeycomb Green; this became Green Overlay under the new ware number system which became effective July 1, 1952. Fenton Book 2 shows the No. 1721 8½″ pinch vase with a six-point crimp (p. 120); this became the No. 1352 vase in the new system.

141-143—Jacqueline No. 9100 AG sugar/creamer set and No. 9106 AG salt/pepper.

144—No. 1350 AG Bubble Optic 5½″ vase.

145—No. 3762 AG Hobnail 12 oz. syrup jug.

Assorted Opaque Colors/Crests

146   147   148   149   150

151   152   153   154   155   156

157   158   159   160   159

These illustrate the relationship between opaque colors and the "crest" treatment given to them. Turquoise (TU) and Rose Pastel (RP) were made individually and as the "crests," Silver Turquoise (ST) and Silver Rose (SR), respectively. Turquoise was first listed in January, 1955, and ST was added a year later. Rose Pastel items were first listed in 1954, and SR appeared with Silver Turquoise in January, 1956. Turquoise also was the basis of Cased Lilac (LC), which was made in 1955-56. A few pieces of Green Pastel are shown, since these are sometimes confused with Turquoise.

146-148—Three items in Silver Turquoise: No. 7330 ST footed bowl; No. 7271 ST candleholder and No. 7237 ST 7" basket. Note the crystal glass edge. Compare with the other crests shown on pp. 84-85.

149—No. 3264 TU Turquoise 11½" vase, circa 1955-57; not in Fenton price lists. Note the *absence* of the "crest" edge.

150-154—Five items in Silver Rose (SR), a Fenton "crest," made from Rose Pastel (RP) by applying the crystal edge: No. 7213 SR footed cakeplate, No. 7237 SR 7" basket, No. 7333 SR handled relish, No. 7227 7" bowl, and No. 7225 SR 5½" bonbon.

155—No. 7290 ST hurricane lamp.

156—No. 7264 LC (Cased Lilac) 9" handled jug, circa 1955-56.

157-158—No. 7228 ST footed comport and No. 7225 ST 5½" bonbon.

159-160—These Hobnail items in Green Pastel (GP), No. 3974 GP candleholder and No. 3924 GP 9" crimped bowl, were made about 1954-55. Compare Green Pastel with Turquoise and with the green hues on the previous page.

Goldenrod

161 **162** **163** **164** **165**

Jamestown Blue,

166 **167** **168** **169** **170** **171**

Silver Jamestown

172 **173** **174** **175** **176**

The trio of Jamestown Blue (JB), Jamestown Blue Transparent (JT) and Silver Jamestown (SJ) debuted in January, 1957. JB was out of the line by late 1958, but JT and SJ were listed throughout 1959. Goldenrod (GD), listed only in July, 1956, was difficult to make and the yellow color varies from item to item.

161-164—Articles in Goldenrod (GD): No. 7223 GD 13″ bowl, No. 7272 GD candleholder, No. 7265 GD 12″ vase and No. 6909 condiment set. Note that yellow is on the outside of the vase but on the inside of the bowl and candleholder; both are called Goldenrod, however.

165—No. 7262 SJ 12″ vase.

166-169—Jamestown Blue (JB) items: No. 7338 JB 8½″ bowl; No. 7456 JB 6″ vase; No. 9055 JB 5″ vase, ribbed pillar pattern; and No. 7471 JB barber bottle.

170-171—Jamestown Blue transparent No. 2471 JT barber bottle (both items 170 and 171 are made with a polka dot optic mould) and No. 6080 JT candy box (see items 122 and 131).

172—No. 1021 JM (Jamestown Blue Transparent with Milk) footed Ivy ball. The JM code applies only to the dot optic Ivy ball with its milk glass base.

173-176—Silver Jamestown (SJ) items: No. 7227 SJ 7″ bowl; No. 6058 SJ 6½″ vase; No. 7237 SJ 7″ basket; and No. 7250 SJ 8″ tulip vase.

Vasa Murrhina

177   178   179   180   181   182

183   184   185   186   187   188

189   190   191   192   193   194

Vasa Murrhina, a beautiful glass with a lengthy history dating to ancient times, was reborn when Frank M. Fenton, inspired by an old Vasa Murrhina basket, directed Charlie Goe to develop this glass for the Fenton line.

Some of Fenton's Vasa Murrhina begins with opal glass which is rolled in varied-colored frit and covered with crystal before blowing. The resulting pieces have an opal glass lining which can be seen through the crystal exterior. This technique was used for Autumn Orange (AO), Aventurine Green with Blue (GB), and Rose with Aventurine Green (RG). For Rose Mist (RM) and Blue Mist (BM), the first gathering is crystal. This is rolled in the frit, and subsequently covered with more crystal before blowing.

BM, GB, RG and RM are first mentioned in January, 1964. AO appeared a year later in 1965, but BM had been dropped entirely from the line. Articles in GB and RG were listed as late as 1968, but the others were out of the line a year or two earlier.

177 — No. 6458 AO 11″ vase, 1965-67.
178 — No. 6437 AO 11″ handled basket, 1965-67.

179 — No. 6458 GB 11″ vase, 1964-68.
180 — No. 6465 RG pitcher, 1965.
181 — No. 6452 RM 7″ square vase, 1965.
182 — No. 6459 RM 14″ vase, 1964-65.
183 — No. 6457 AO 7″ fan vase, 1965-66.
184 — No. 6435 AO 7″ basket, 1965-67.
185 — No. 6435 GB 7″ basket, 1964-68.
186 — No. 6456 RG 8″ vase, 1964-66.
187 — No. 6450 RG 9″ pinch vase, 1965.
188 — No. 6437 RG 11″ basket, 1964-68.
189 — No. 6454 GB 4″ vase, 1964-68.
190 — No. 6464 GB cream pitcher, 1964-66.
191 — No. 6454 BM 4″ vase, 1964.
192 — No. 6464 BM cream pitcher, 1964.
193 — No. 6455 RM 5½″ vase, 1964.
194 — No. 6455 RG 5½″ vase, 1964.

Ruby Overlay was very popular over several decades, and collectors may find many other items than those illustrated here. Another overlay color was Plated Amberina (PA), made in 1962-63 by gathering ruby glass over opal; this is not like the gold-based Plated Amberina made famous by Joseph Locke. Plated Amberina was a contemporary of Opaque Blue (OB); see page 72.

In addition to the Yellow Opaline (YN) and Pink Opaline (PN) shown here, Blue Opaline (BN) was listed in 1960, the only year for these three colors.

195 — No. 1691 PA courting lamp, electric, 1962.

196 — No. S6458 & CC 11″ vase in Cranberry Mist Crest 1965; see No. 202.

197 — No. 7361 RO 12″ vase, 1956.

198 — No. 1650 OB 10½″ vase, 1962; see page 72.

199 — No. 1650 PA 10½″ vase, 1962-63.

200 — No. 1790 OR courting lamp, oil, 1963-65.

201 — No. S6464 CM cream pitcher was made in Cranberry Mist, 1965; see No. 202.

202 — This 6″ vase with double ring neck (specially designated No. S-6466 CC) was made in Cranberry Mist Crest in 1965 for Sears as part of their Vincent Price National Treasures series.

203 — No. 1637 OB 7″ deep basket, 1962-63; see page 72.

204 — No. 1680 PA with satin finish covered candy jar, 1962; these satin finish pieces were sold only in the Fenton Gift Shop.

205 — No. 1637 PA 7″ deep basket, 1962-63.

206 — No. 2458 RO 7″ vase, 1956-57.

207-209 — Three items in Jacqueline (all 1960): No. 9152 PN 7″ tulip vase, No. 9156 PN 6″ vase and No. 9152 YN 7″ tulip vase.

210-212 — Ruby Overlay items: No. 6006 RO salt/pepper shakers, 1956-59; No. 2461 RO creamer, 1956-68; and No. 2454 RO 6″ vase, 1958-62.

Blue Marble

213   214   215   216   217   218

219   220   221   222   223

224   225   226   227   228

This interesting opaque glass, called Blue Marble (MB), was introduced in 1970 and remained in the line through 1973. The color was produced by adding opal into a pot of opaque blue glass to produce the distinctive swirls of white.

213-218 — Rose items (all from 1970-73): No. 9235 MB 9″ basket, No. 9224 MB 7″ bowl, No. 9284 MB covered candy box, No. 9254 MB handkerchief vase, No. 9256 MB 8″ bud vase and No. 9222 MB comport.

219 — No. 9188 MB Grape & Cable with thumbprint tobacco jar, 1971. This was made from the same mould (less the special bottom plate) used for Rose Presznick's carnival glass reproduction made in 1968. This was Fenton's first carnival glass since the early 1930s.

220-225 — Hobnail items (all from 1970-73): No. 3736 MB 6½″ basket, No. 3628 MB footed comport, No. 3706 MB handled bonbon with metal handle, No. 3731 MB 10″ footed bowl, No. 3872 MB candlebowl, and No. 3886 MB candy box.

226 — No. 5182 MB large hen on nest, 1971-73.

227 — No. 3995 MB slipper, 1970-73.

228 — No. 3700 MB Hobnail covered slipper, 1971-73.

Powder Blue (BV), an overlay glass with light blue exterior and opal interior, dates from 1961. The Blue Satin (BA) items on this page date from 1971 through 1980 (the 5197 BA is in the price list for 1/71 and most of the other items appear within a few years). They should not be confused with Fenton's earlier Blue Satin (also color coded BA), which was made in 1952-54 (see Fenton Book 2, pp. 61, 123).

229-232 — BV items (all from 1961): No. 1358 BV 8″ pinch vase, No. 2857 BV Wild Rose with Bowknot 7½″ vase, No. 3762 BV Hobnail syrup jug, and No. 3856 BV Hobnail 6″ vase.

233 — No. 8424 BA Water Lily 9″ bowl, 1975-80.

234 — No. 9155 BA 8″ vase, 1974-80.

235 — No. 9188 BA Grape & Cable with thumbprint tobacco jar, 1974 (see #219 on previous page).

236 — No. 8280 BA Christmas in America plate, 1980. This depicts Christ Church in Alexandria, VA.

237 — No. 9484 BA Madonna candy box, circa 1977 (not in line).

238 — No. 8223 BA Leaf & Orange Tree three-toed bowl, 1973-77.

239 — No. 5107 BA Madonna candlelight vase, 1978-80.

240 — No. 9467 BA Madonna bell, 1975-80.

241 — No. 5165 BA cat, 1979-81.

242 — No. 5125 BA donkey and No. 5124 BA cart, both 1972. These moulds were purchased by Fenton from the United States Glass Co. (see also items 490, 494 and 498), but their history goes back even further to the Duncan and Miller Glass Co., which had been purchased by the U.S. Glass Co. in 1955.

243 — No. 5197 BA happiness bird, 1971-80. The mould for this piece was purchased by Fenton from the Paden City Glass Co. about 1950.

244 — No. 5193 BA fish paperweight, 1972.

245 — No. 5162 BA bunny, 1978-80.

246 — No. 5108 BA owl fairy light, 1975-81.

247 — No. 5170 BA butterfly, 1972.

Rose, Lime & Lavender Satin

248   249   250   251   252   253

254   255   256   257

258   259   260   261   262   263   264

These colors are from the 1970's Fenton lines of satin treatments. These are similar to the Blue Satin (BA) pieces illustrated on the previous page and to Fenton's Custard Satin (CU), which was the largest selling satin glass color (see p. 102). Almost every shape made in the various satin colors was also made in Custard Satin.

Lime Sherbet (LS) was added to the line in 1973, and Rose Satin in 1974. Lavender Satin (LN) first appeared in 1977. Rose Satin was out of the line by 1978. LN was discontinued a year later, and LS was last listed in June, 1979. These should not be confused with colors from 1952-54: Green Satin (GA), Lime Satin (LA), Peach Satin (PA), Rose Satin (RA) and French Opalescent Satin (FA).

248—No. 7434 RS 11″ basket, 1974.

249—No. 7464 RS small pitcher, melon ribbed, 1974-76.

250—No. 9155 RS 8″ vase, scroll embossed pattern in mould, 1974-77.

251—No. 3984 LS Hobnail covered candy box, 1974-75.

252—No. 8427 LS oval Pinwheel comport, 1974-75.

253—No. 8257 LS 8″ Peacock vase, 1973-76.

254—No. 8431 LS Water Lily comport, crimped, 1977.

255—No. 8472 LS Orange Tree 6″ candleholders, 1974-75.

256—No. 8242 LS Three Fruits handled comport, 1973-75.

257—No. 8233 LS Orange Tree & Cherry bowl, crimped, 1973-76.

258-264—Lavender Satin items (all 1977-78 unless indicated): No. 8456 LN Water Lily bud vase; No. 5108 LN owl fairy lamp; No. 8480 LN Water Lily footed candy box; No. 8222 LN open edge basketweave bowl; No. 9388 LN Baroque candy box (1978 only); and No. 5100 LN Praying Boy and Girl.

80

Plain & Decorated Burmese

265 266 267 268 269

270 271 272 273 274 275 276

277 278 279 280 281

Plain Burmese (BR) was introduced in 1970, as was a decorated motif called Leaf Decorated Burmese (BD), which consisted of leaf decals applied by hand and fired for permanence. BD items were out of the line by the end of 1972. The first handpainted decoration (developed by Louise Piper) on Burmese was Rose Burmese (RB) in 1971. Decorated Burmese (DB), featuring the handpainted outdoor scene, was added in 1973. The details in each scene vary slightly due to the size of the piece and the interpretation of the artist. BR, RB and DB were all still in the line in 1980.

265 — No. 7251 RB 11″ vase, 1973-76.

266 — No. 7253 RB 7″ vase, 1971-75.

267 — No. 7238 RB 7″ deep basket, 1973-75. The tag on this piece mentions Fenton's Charlie Goe, who developed the color shortly before his death in 1969 (see page 44).

268 — No. 7284 RB covered candy box, 1973-74.

269 — No. 7255 RB tulip vase, 1977-80.

270 — No. 7462 RB cruet vase, 1971-74.

271 — No. 7460 RB 6½″ vase, 1979-80.

272 — No. 7348 RB bud vase, 1979-80.

273 — No. 7437 RB medium basket, 1971-80.

274-276 — Scenic Decorated (DB) items No. 7492 DB 2 pc. fairy light, 1974-77; No. 7457 DB 5″ vase, 1975-79; and No. 7468 DB cruet with stopper (this cruet was not in the line).

277-278 — Plain Burmese items No. 7424 BR rose bowl, tight crimp, 1970-71, and No. 7437 BR medium basket, 1970-72.

279-281 — Leaf decorated Burmese (BD) items: No. 7424 BD rose bowl, 1970-72; No. 7392 BD fairy light, 1970-71; and No. 7461 BD pitcher, 1970-72.

Decorated Satin Glass

282   283   284   285   286   287   288

289   290   291   292   293   294   295   296   297

298   299   300   301   302   303   304   305

Fenton's handpainted decorated wares (particularly on custard glass) were quite popular during the 1970s. Several motifs are shown here: Daisies on Custard (DC, 1975-still in line until 1981); Old Mill on Custard (OM, 1979-1980); Christmas Morn CV, 1978; Blue Roses on Blue Satin (BL, 1978-82); Log Cabin on Custard (LC, 1976-still in the line in 1988); Bluebirds on Custard (BC, 1977-79); and Chocolate Roses on Cameo Satin (DR, 1979-82).

282-284—Daisies on Custard No. 7408 DC 10″ hurricane lamp (electric), No. 7380 DC footed candy box, and No. 7252 DC 7″ vase.

285—No. 7362 OM bell, Old Mill handpainted decoration.

286-288—Handpainted Christmas Morn CV items: No. 7466 CV bell; No. 7300 CV fairy light; and No. 7204 CV 16″ hammered Colonial lamp. All are circa 1978.

289-292—Handpainted Daisies on Custard (DC) items: No. 5125

DC donkey, 1978-80; No. 5197 DC happiness bird, 1975-80; No. 5166 DC frog, 1979-80; and No. 5169 DC duckling, 1981 only.

293-297—Handpainted Blue Roses on Blue Satin (BL); note that this is lighter than the Blue Satin described earlier (p. 79): No. 5140 BL egg, 1981-82; No. 7484 BL candy box; No. 5169 BL duckling; No. 7288 BL three-piece ginger jar; and No. 9056 BL bud vase.

298-300—Handpainted Log Cabin on Custard (LC) items: No. 7288 LC three-piece ginger jar, 1978-80; No. 7488 LC temple jar, 1979-83 and No. 7300 LC fairy light, 1976-84.

301-302—Handpainted Bluebirds on Custard (BC) items: No. 7437 BC basket and No. 8267 BC bell.

303-305—Handpainted Chocolate Roses on Cameo Satin (DR) items: No. 5163 DR small bird, No. 8267 DR bell and No. 5197 DR happiness bird.

Violets in the Snow

Bluebells

Decorated Violets (DV), better known as Violets in the Snow to most Fenton collectors, is found on Silver Crest items, except for the No. 8267 bell shown below. Violets in the Snow, developed by Louise Piper soon after her employment at Fenton, was introduced in July, 1968, the first significant handpainted decoration in Fenton's third twenty-five years. Interestingly, the Violets motif was the suggestion of Carl Voigt, a Fenton sales representative in upper New York state. DV was still in the line in 1980. Another hand-painted decoration, Bluebells on Hobnail (BB), also developed by Louise Piper, was short-lived, dating circa 1971-72.

306 — No. 7252 DV 7" vase, 1969-70.
307 — No. 7436 DV small basket, 1968-80.
308 — No. 8267 DV bell, 1978-80.
309 — No. 7336 DV 6½" basket, 1968-77.

310 — No. 7474 DV 6" candleholder, 1968-71.
311 — No. 7429 DV footed comport, 1968-83.
312 — No. 7474 DV 6" candleholder, 1968-71.
313 — No. 3567 DV bell in Spanish Lace, 1974-84.
314 — No. 7254 DV 4½" vase, 1975-84.
315 — No. 3554 DV 4" vase in Spanish Lace, 1974-80.
316 — No. 7292 DV 5" top hat, 1968-69.
317 — No. 7377 DV ash tray, 1970.
318 — No. 7498 DV bonbon w/metal handle, 1968-77.
319 — No. 3920 BB footed comport, 1971-72.
320 — No. 3926 BB 6" bonbon, 1971-72.
321 — No. 3839 BB 12" oval basket, 1971-72.
322 — 3706 BB bonbon w/metal handle, 1971.

Assorted Crests & Decorated Milk Glass

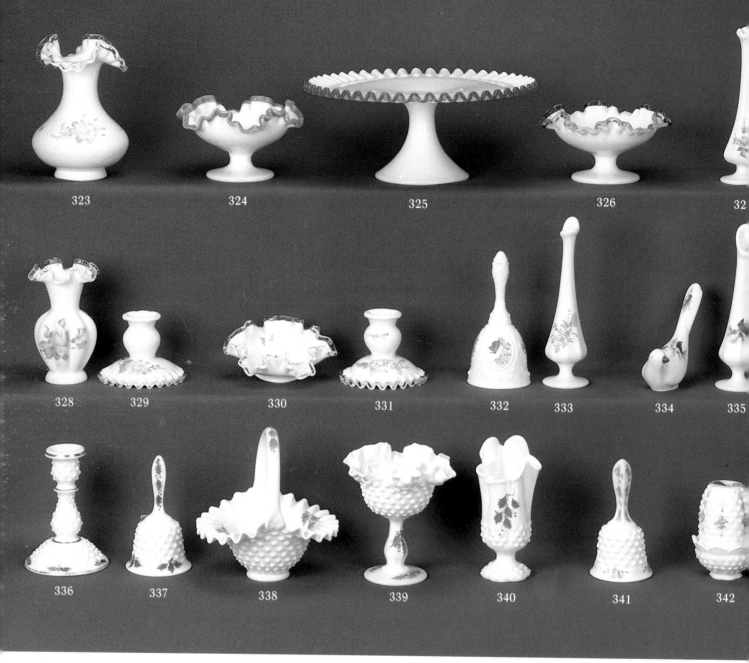

323   324   325   326   32...

328   329   330   331   332   333   334   335

336   337   338   339   340   341   342

Compare the crests shown here with those on the next page. The decorated milk glass items were made at different times, as the captions indicate.

323 — No. 7252 SC 7″ vase, decorated with a handpainted motif as a sample.

324 — No. 7329 AB (Apple Blossom) low footed comport, 1960-61 (compare with item C on p. 65). A dozen shapes were shown in the 1960 catalog. Remember, this is Apple Blossom crest; don't confuse it with Apple Blossom decorated ware, which is pink flowers on Silver Crest items.

325 — No. 7213 FC (Flame Crest) footed cakeplate, 1963.

326 — No. 7329 GC (Gold Crest) low footed comport, 1963-64.

327 — No. 9056 LW (handpainted "Love" Rose on White) bud vase, 1979-80.

328 — No. 7451 YR (handpainted Yellow Rose) vase.

329 — No. 7271 YR candleholder, 1969-70; note that these are Silver Crest items.

330 — No. 7225 AB (handpainted Apple Blossom) 5½″ bonbon and 331 No. 7271 AB candleholder, 1969-70; note that these are Silver Crest items.

332 — No. 8267 BY (handpainted Butterflies on Milk) bell.

333 — No. 9056 BY bud vase, 1977-78.

334 — No. 5197 CW (handpainted Cardinals in Winter) happiness bird, 1977-79.

335 — No. 9056 CW bud vase, 1977-79.

336-340 — Handpainted Holly on Milk (DH) items: No. 3674 DH candleholder, No. 3667 DH bell, No. 3837 DH basket, No. 3628 DH footed comport and No. 3951 DH handkerchief vase, all 1974-75.

341 — No. 3667 BB (handpainted Blue Bell on Milk) bell, 1971-72.

342 — No. 3608 RW (handpainted Roses on Milk) fairy light, 1974-75.

Assorted Crests

343   344   345   346   347

348   349   350   351   352   353

354   355   356   357

The crest edges in various colors are among Fenton's most distinctive glassware products.

343-344 — Apple Blossom Crest No. 7336 AB basket and No. 7377 ash tray, 1960-61 (compare with item 324 and item C on p. 65).

345-347 — Peach Crest No. 7200 PC epergne, No. 7272 PC candleholder, and No. 6059 PC 8½″ vase. Peach Crest goes back to 1940 (see Fenton Book 2, pp. 48, 72, 103, 113 and 126). The three PC articles here were made from 1956 to mid-1959; they were relatively high-priced and did not sell particularly well, so collectors will see few on the market today. Peach Crest consists of opal cased with gold ruby glass before final shaping by blowing; then a crystal crest edge is added. The pink color will vary in intensity.

348-349 — Black Crest No. 7333 handled bonbon and No. 7357 fan vase. These items were sold only in the Fenton Gift Shop, circa 1970.

350-351 — Blue Crest No. 7228 BC footed comport and No. 7329 BC low footed comport, 1963. Blue Crest was made using Fenton's Colonial Blue glass for the crest edge (compare these to Aqua Crest in Fenton Book 2, pp. 47, 61).

352-353 — Silver Crest No. 7206 SC salt/pepper shaker, 1956-59, and No. 7339 SC divided basket, 1958-59. Silver Crest is another line, like Peach Crest, which goes back to the 1940s (see Fenton Book 2, p. 49, 116-117).

354-357 — Flame Crest No. 7474 FC candleholders, top or bottom to the No. 7294 FC two-tier tidbit set with metal handle, No. 7429 FC footed comport, and No. 7321 FC 11½″ double crimped bowl, all 1963. The crest on the last two articles appears slightly orange, due to variations in the heat sensitive ruby glass used; some collectors refer to this as "orange crest," but no such name appears in the Fenton color codes. Compare with the Flame Crest item (325) shown on the previous page.

Thumbprint in Colonial Pink

358   359   360   361   362

363   364   365   366   367   368   369   370

372

371   373   374   375   376   377

The 4400-series Thumbprint line made its debut in July, 1962, six months after the color Colonial Pink (and Colonial Amber and Colonial Blue) had been introduced with the No. 4445 goblet and other items. The Thumbprint line grew, as more items and more colors were added (Colonial Green in 1963; Orange shortly thereafter, as well as Ruby in 1966 and Black in 1968). Several dozen articles were listed in 1965-68, then the size of the line decreased steadily, although several different colors were always available. By 1974, just four shapes were being offered. The last article in the line was the No. 4438 basket, still listed in RU as late as 1980.

358 — No. 4484 CP anniversary bowl, 1963-66. This item (and the 4445 CP goblet below in #360) is a reproduction of Argus, an early American pattern made at Bakewell, Pears in Pittsburgh in the 1800s.

359 — No. 4427 CP 12" bowl, 1963-68.

360 — No. 4445 CP goblet, 1962-68.

361 — No. 4465 CP 34 oz. jug, 1965-66.

362 — No. 4411 CP footed cakeplate, 1964-66.

363 — No. 4438 CP 8½" basket, 1963-68.

364 — No. 4408 CP salt/pepper shaker, 1963-67.

365 — No. 4470 CP candleholder, 1964-68.

366 — No. 4443 CP sherbet, 1963-67.

367 — No. 4444 CP wine, 1963-67.

368 — No. 4448 CP 8" chalice, 1965-66.

369 — No. 4429 CP footed comport, 1962-68.

370 — No. 4486 CP oval candy box, 1963-66.

371 — No. 4495 CP cigarette lighter and No. 4469 CP 6½" round ash tray, both circa 1967, but not in the line in CP.

372 — No. 4417 CP 8½" plate, 1963-67.

373 — No. 4476 CP oval ash tray, 1963-66.

374 — No. 4477 CP butter, 1965-66.

375-376 — No. 4403 CP covered sugar and creamer set, 1963-67.

377 — No. 4454 CP 8" footed vase, 1964-68.

The Fenton Rose pattern line began in 1964 with the No. 9222 comport. This article, a reproduction of an item originally made by the United States Glass Co., stayed in the line, in various colors, through 1976, and the other Rose pattern pieces came and went during this twelve year period (see items 417-418 on the next page). Lamps were still in the line in 1988.

378 — No. 4484 MI covered compote, 1956. Although this is the same piece as the anniversary bowl in CP on the previous page, it was called a covered compote when Thumbprint was made in MI as part of Fenton's Olde Virginia Glass line (see CR 137 and 139 pp. 133, 135)

379 — No. 4438 BK 8½″ basket, 1968-76.

380 — No. 4425 OR footed comport, 1971-73.

381 — No. 4442 CB 12 oz. tumbler, 1962-68.

382 — No. 4445 RU 10 oz. goblet, 1966-73.

383 — No. 4449 CA 13 oz. ice tea, 1966-71.

384 — No. 4453 OR tall bud vase, swung 1963-73.

385 — No. 4416 CG divided relish, 1966-67.

386 — No. 9246 CB Rose goblet, 1967-68.

387 — No. 9299 CG owl ring tree, 1967-68.

388 — No. 9284 CG Rose footed candy box, 1967-74.

389 — No. 9222 CG Rose comport, 1964-73.

390 — No. 9282 CP Rose candy box, 1965-66; made in a mould purchased from the United States Glass Co.

391 — No. 9223 OR Rose comport, double crimped, 1966-74.

392 — No. 9270 CB Rose candleholder, 1967-68.

393 — No. 9251 CB Rose 4½″ oval vase, 1967-68.

394 — No. 9271 CP Rose ash tray, 1966-68.

395 — No. 9272 CB Rose individual ash tray, 1968.

396 — No. 9216 CB Rose soap dish, 1967-68.

397 — No. 9210 CB Rose set of four individual ash trays (9272 CB) with rack, 1968.

398-399 — No. 9203 MI Rose covered sugar and creamer set, 1967-73.

Thumbprint & Miscellaneous

400 — No. 4464 CB 2 qt. ice lip jug, 1964-66.

401 — No. 4409 CB salt/pepper shakers, footed, 1968.

402 — No. 4488 CB royal wedding bowl (reproduction of Argus 7″ bowl and cover), 1964-66.

403 — No. 4401 CB 4 pc. epergne set, 1964-67.

404 — No. 4441 CB small sherbet or wine, 1962-64.

405 — No. 4443 CG sherbet, 1963-70.

406 — No. 9102 CG Fine Cut and Block 2 pc. fairy light; this was in the Olde Virginia line, 1970-76 (see CR143-144).

407 — No. 9176 CG swirl ash tray, 1965. This article and the No. 9156 were made in other colors and crystal after Fenton bought the moulds in 1960 from Rubel & Co. of New York City. Both ash trays had been made by Fenton for Rubel in the early 1950s (see Fenton Book 2, p. 150).

408 — Fine Cut and Block sample piece (not in line) in CG, circa 1974.

409 — No. 1994 CG Daisy and Button bootee, Olde Virginia line, circa 1969-72 (see CR 142).

410 — No. 5173 CB bird ashtray, Olde Virginia line, 1969 (CR 141).

411 — No. 9180 OR Fine Cut and Block candy box, Olde Virginia line, 1969-75.

412 — No. 8399 OR Valencia pattern lighter, 1969-71 (see item 421 on the next page).

413 — No. 5106 RU Santa Claus fairy light, 1969-79.

414 — No. 1939 OR oval English basket, 1967-69.

415 — No. 9195 OR high button shoe, 1965.

416 — No. 1990 CO Daisy and Button boot, 1971-73.

417 — No. 9242 CA Rose bathroom tumbler, 1967-68.

418 — No. 9206 CA Rose salt/pepper shakers, 1967-68.

Valencia Pattern

419   420   421   422   423

424   425   426   427   428   429   430

431   432   433   434   435   436

The Valencia pattern, designed by Fenton's Tony Rosena, made its appearance in 1969. Frank M. Fenton recalls that a Moser piece was reproduced as the No. 8380 candy box (item 431 on this page), ultimately inspiring the rest of the line. In 1969, a variety of CA, CB, CG and OR articles were listed, along with crystal. The line was cut back considerably in 1972-73, and only two items (Nos. 8356 and 8380) remained through 1974.

419—No. 8320 CG flared bowl, footed, 1969-71.

420—No. 8359 CG handkerchief vase, 1969-72.

421—Cigarette lighter in CG made from No. 8344 wine, not in the line, circa 1970.

422—No. 8386 CG footed candy box, 1969-71.

423—No. 8374 CG candleholder, 1970-71.

424—No. 8398 CG cigarette box, 1969-72.

425-426—No. 8306 CG sugar and cream set, 1970-71.

427—No. 8338 OR 8″ basket, 1970-72.

428—No. 8343 CA sherbet, 1970-71.

429—No. 8356 CA bud vase, 1969-74.

430—No. 8352 CB tall vase, 1969-72.

431—No. 8380 CA candy box, 1969-74.

432—No. 8377 CA ash tray, 1969-72.

433—No. 8328 OR 8″ bowl, 1970-71.

434—No. 8344 CA wine, 1970-71.

435—No. 8345 CA goblet, 1970-71.

436—No. 8349 CB footed ice tea, not in line in CB, circa 1970.

Assorted Colors

437   438   439   440   441   442

443   444   445   446   447   448

449   450   451   452   453   454

Springtime Green (GT) and a light orchid color called Wisteria (WT) were both unveiled in January, 1977, and both remained in the line until the end of 1978. Wisteria was made by using Neodymium as the coloring material; this same ingredient was used in Fenton's opaque Lavender Satin (see p. 80). The items shown in the top two rows were all made in Colonial Amber, Colonial Blue, Springtime Green and Wisteria (see CR 19).

The Colonial Pink (CP) goblets in the bottom row were put in the line in January, 1962; the Thumbprint (No. 4445) continued to be listed in CP as late as 1968, but the others were discontinued in CP four years earlier.

437 — No. 9385 GT Knobby Bull's Eye candy box, 1977-78.

438 — No. 8406 GT Heart fairy light, 1977-78.

439 — No. 8435 GT Threaded Diamond Optic basket, 1977-78.

440 — No. 8465 GT Threaded Diamond Optic bell, 1977.

441 — No. 9322 GT Tree of Life comport, 1977-78.

442 — No. 8488 GT Colonial candy box, 1977-78.

443 — No. 8455 CB Threaded Diamond Optic 7″ vase, 1977.

444 — No. 8425 CB Threaded Diamond Optic 6½″ bowl, 1977-78.

445 — No. 7075 CB 5½″ freeflow ash tray (made in various colors between 1960-70 as No. 9175), 1977.

446 — No. 8465 WT Threaded Diamond optic bell, 1977.

447 — No. 8425 WT Threaded Diamond Optic 6½″ bowl, 1977-78.

448 — No. 8488 WT Colonial candy box, 1977-78.

449 — No. 9045 CP Pineapple goblet, 1962-64.

450 — No. 6345 CP Flower Band goblet, 1962-64.

451 — No. 3445 CP Cactus goblet, 1962.

452 — No. 9145 CP Stippled Scroll goblet, 1962-64.

453 — No. 4445 CP Thumbprint 10 oz. goblet, 1962-68.

454 — No. 9229 CP Empress footed comport, 1962-64.

Ebony
(BLACK)

455   456   457   458   459   460

461   462   463   464   465   466

467   468   469   470   471   472   473

Black glass was re-introduced in 1968 and remained in the line through 1976, so most of the pieces shown here are from this period. For information on Fenton's earlier black glass, see Fenton Book 2, pp. 28, 62.

Frank M. Fenton reports that the last of a batch of black glass would frequently be "worked out" by making small items (such as 467 and 470 below), which were later sold only through the Fenton Gift Shop.

455 — No. 9222 BK Rose compote, not in line (probably made for A. L. Randall; see items 87 and 88), circa 1979.

456 — No. 4425 BK Thumbprint footed comport, 1968-74.

457 — No. 4454 WD 8″ footed vase, White Daisies on Black decoration, 1972-76.

458 — No. 7380 BK footed candy box, not in line in BK; usually found with White Daisies decoration, 1973-75.

459 — No. 8252 BK Empress vase, 1968-69.

460 — No. 8251 BK Mandarin vase, 1968-69.

461 — No. 4429 BK footed comport, 1968-75.

462 — No. 7488 BK temple jar, 1981; these were also decorated with silver poppies in 1981-82.

463 — No. 5180 BK Wise Owl decision maker, 1969-72.

464 — No. 4495 BK Thumbprint cigarette lighter, 1968-69.

465 — No. 4438 BK Thumbprint 8½″ basket, 1968-76.

466 — No. 9188 BK Grape & Cable tobacco jar, 1968-69.

467 — No. 8294 KB Panelled Daisy toothpick, not in the line, circa 1982 for Fenton Gift Shop.

468 — No. 5140 WD egg (White Daisies on Black decoration), 1973.

469 — No. 4469 BK Thumbprint 6½″ ash tray, 1968-69.

470 — No. 3795 BK Hobnail toothpick, not in the line, circa 1974 for Fenton Gift Shop.

471 — No. 3602 BK Hobnail kitchen salt (these were paired with another in MI and sold with the color code BW, Black and White), 1962-65.

472 — No. 3633 BK Hobnail oval nut dish, not in the line, circa 1974 for Fenton Gift Shop.

473 — No. 3872 BK candlebowl, 1968-74.

Fenton from Verlys Molds

474   475   476   477   478   479

480   481   482   483   484

485   486   487   488

Verlys glass originated in France in 1931 as part of the Societe Anonyme Holophane Les Andelys. In 1935, the Holophane Lighting Company of Newark, Ohio, established a wholly-owned subsidiary called Verlys of America, which purchased moulds from Holophane Francaise, a French company. The Newark venture was discontinued about 1951, and Holophane leased the moulds about four years later to the nearby Heisey firm, which, in turn, produced its own Verlys of America line for a short time.

Fenton purchased the moulds from Holophane about 1966, agreeing that the Verlys name would no longer appear. In 1968, the Mandarin and Empress vases were pressed. Incidentally, "Empress" is Fenton's term for the Verlys vase called Kuan Yin (Goddess), designed by Ted Mehrer. In 1977, the Empress and Mandarin moulds were changed so that Fenton could produce blown ware with them (see pp. 19 and 20).

474 — No. 8251 MI Mandarin vase, 1968-69.

475 — No. 8252 MI Empress vase, 1968-69.
476 — No. 8252 BR Empress vase, 1977.
477 — No. 8251 FO Mandarin vase, 1968.
478 — No. 8252 FO Empress vase, 1968.
479 — No. 8252 OR Mandarin vase, 1968.
480 — No. 8258 LS Love Bird vase, 1974-75.
481 — No. 8253 OR Vessel of Gems vase, 1968.
482 — No. 8226 RE hexagonal bowl, 1976-77.
483 — No. 8226 CN hexagonal bowl, 1970-73.
484 — No. 8258 CN Love Bird vase, 1974.
485 — No. 5102 WS Girl & Fawn book ends, 1972.
486 — No. 8226 MI hexagonal bowl, 1968-69.
487 — No. 8221 MI nut dish, 1969.
488 — No. 8299 MI planter, 1969.

Assorted Carnival Glass

(1970-80)

489 490 491 492 493 494 495

496 497 498 499 500 501

502 503 504 505 506 507 508

Carnival (CN) was introduced in 1970, Orange Carnival (CO) in 1972, and a cobalt blue carnival treatment, called Independence Blue (IB), was produced in 1975-76 as one of the Bicentennial colors. Orange Carnival lasted just two years, 1972-73, as did Ruby Iridescent (RN, 1976-77), but CN, often called "amethyst carnival" by collectors, remained in the line through 1983.

489 — No. 8254 CN Mermaid planter/vase, 1970-72 (made from a modified Verlys mould).

490 — No. 5150 CN Atlantis vase, 1971-72 (made with a mould purchased from the United States Glass Co.).

491 — No. 8240 CN Butterfly & Berry tumbler, 1972-73.

492 — No. 8466 CN Faberge bell, 1977-78.

493 — No. 9179 CN "The Cabinetmaker" plate, No. 10 in the Craftsman plate series, 1979.

494 — No. 5177 CN 10½″ Alley Cat, 1970-72 (made with a mould purchased from the United States Glass Co., originally designed by Reuben Haley for Duncan and Miller).

495 — No. 5172 CN Swan candleholder, 1971-73.

496-497 — No. 9173 CN Orange Tree 8″ candle bowl, 1973, and No. 8230 CN Butterfly handled bonbon, 1973-74. These may have been iridized with a slightly different spray than the CN items above, so the resulting color is not identical.

498 — No. 8227 RN Pinwheel comport, 1976-77 (made with a mould purchased from the United States Glass Co.).

499 — No. 8234 RN Persian Medallion comport, 1976-77.

500 — No. 8223 RN Leaf & Orange tree nut bowl, 1976-77 (often called Fenton Flowers by collectors).

501 — No. 8407 RN Chou Ting ceremonial light, 1977.

502 — No. 8228 CN Hearts & Flowers flared bowl, 1971-73.

503 — No. 9199 CN Turtle ring tree, 1973.

504-505 — No. 5170 CN Butterflies. Note that 505 is plain, while 504 has some pattern on the wings. The plain ones are ca. 1970, and the others date from about 1971, when the pattern was added to the mould.

506 — No. 5170 CO Butterfly, not in line, circa 1971.

507 — No. 5193 CN Fish paperweight, 1970-72.

508 — No. 8428 RN Butterfly & Berry bowl with peacock tail interior, 1976-77.

93

Bicentennial Glass

509 510 511 512 513

514 515 516 517 518

519 520 521 522 523

As the 1976 American Bicentennial approached, Fenton made plans to produce new items and special colors. The natural choices were red, white and blue, of course, but Fenton also added Chocolate (CK) glass, because, said Frank M. Fenton, "it's an exotic color and was associated with Fenton's history. We first made it here in 1907." Charlie Goe had experimented with Chocolate, but color chemist Subodh Gupta developed the best color in Chocolate glass. The opal glass was called Valley Forge white (VW, introduced in 1975), while the others were Independence Blue carnival (IB, introduced in 1974) and Patriot Red (PR, introduced in 1975), an opaque, slag-like color reminiscent of Fenton's Mandarin Red of the 1930s (see Fenton Book 2, pp. 26, 67).

509-511—No. 8476 Jefferson covered comports in CK, PR and IB. The CK and PR were limited to 3600 each, and IB to 7600 (stores were limited to two in their first orders). Initially, Fenton planned to make the Jefferson comport in "Favrene" an iridescent blue similar to Tiffany's Favrile and Steuben's Blue Aurene; production problems were encountered, and Independence Blue was made instead by iridizing a slightly lighter cobalt blue (see the cover for the Favrene color).

512-513—No. 8446 stein in CK and PR.

514-516—No. 8467 Patriot's (also called Bicentennial) bells in CK, PR and IB.

517-518—No. 9418 Eagle plates in CK and PR.

519-521—No. 8470 Eagle paperweights in CK, PR and IB.

522-523—No. 8499 Patriot planters in VW and IB.

Robert Barber Collection

524   525   526   527   528

529   530   531   532   533

Art Glass Eggs

534   535   536   537   538   539

Studio glass craftsman Robert Barber was "glass-artist in residence" at Fenton in 1975. Four limited edition articles (ware numbers 0001 through 0004) were offered for sale in late April, 1975, and six additional items (0005-0010) came shortly thereafter in the same year (see p. 47).

524 — No. 0001 HF Hyacinth Feather Vase, 12½" tall (limited to 450).

525 — No. 0005 ST Summer Tapestry Vase, 11" tall (limited to 550).

526 — No. 0007 CI Hanging Heart Vase, 10" tall, custard iridescent (limited to 600).

527 — No. 0008 TH Hanging Heart Vase, 10" tall, turquoise iridescent (limited to 600).

528 — No. 0002 TH Turquoise Iridescent Vase, Hanging Heart pattern, 11" tall (limited to 600).

529 — No. 0009 LA Labyrinth Vase, 9" tall, in amethyst and white (limited to 700).

530 — No. 0003 BH Bittersweet Vase, Hanging Heart pattern, 7½" tall (limited to 750).

531 — No. 0006 CV Cascade Vase, 7½" tall (limited to 700).

532 — No. 0004 BF Blue Feather Vase, 7½" tall (limited to 1,000).

533 — No. 0010 LB Labyrinth Vase, 9" tall, in blue and white (limited to 700).

Note: dimensions given for items 524-533 are approximate.

534-539 — These six Robert Barber Eggs are mentioned only in the July, 1976, catalog supplement and accompanying price list.

534 — No. 5005 EG reddish-orange egg.

535 — No. 5002 EG dark blue egg.

536 — No. 5008 EG multi-color egg.

537 — No. 5001 EG pink egg.

538 — No. 5007 EG green egg.

539 — No. 5004 EG light blue egg.

540   541   542   543   544

545   546   547   548   549   550

551   552   553   554   555

In the late 1960s, Fenton contemplated a "revival" of Pekin (note the spelling) Blue (see Fenton Book 2, pp. 41, 68) and the addition of a vibrant Jonquil Yellow to the line. Sample items were made, and some were photographed at the factory for Alan Linn's *The Fenton Story of Glass Making* (see Plate IX). Plans for these colors were dropped, but Fenton later unveiled a similar shade called Peking (note the spelling) Blue in their January, 1980 catalog supplement as "a reintroduction of a popular color. . . ." Some 19 articles appeared in the January, 1980, price list, but Peking Blue was quickly dropped from the line and did not appear in the May 15, 1980 price list. The articles shown on this page were probably all made in 1968-69. In 1968, the color code assigned to Jonquil Yellow was JO, and "Pekin Blue II" was designated BJ (for Blue Jade).

540-544—Items in Jonquil Yellow: No. 9222 JO Rose comport.
541—No. 1980 JO Daisy and Button candy box.
542—No. 8252 JO Empress vase.

543—No. 7458 JO 11″ melon vase.
544-550—Items in Pekin Blue II: No. 3837 BJ Hobnail basket.
545—No. 3731 BJ Hobnail 10″ footed bowl.
546—No. 3886 BJ Hobnail candy box.
547—No. 1990 BJ Daisy and Button boot.
548—No. 1980 BJ Daisy and Button candy box.
549—No. 3736 BJ Hobnail basket.
550—No. 5180 BJ Wise Owl decision maker.
551-552—Jonquil Yellow No. 5178 JO Pelican ash tray (from a Verlys mould; see items 474-488) and No. 3608 JO Hobnail fairy light.
553—No. 3974 BJ candleholders.
554—No. 3974 JO candleholders.
555—No. 1990 JO Daisy and Button boot.

CR 1—January 1971

CR 2—January 1971

CR 3—January 1971

CR 1-2-3-4-5-6   These lamps are from the January, 1971, lamp supplement, although many were in the line in 1966 and were shown in the first lamp supplement printed in 1967. Fenton had returned to making lamps under its own name in 1966, although they had manufactured private mould lamp parts for others for over thirty years and had sold some Hobnail lamps through the Gift Shop. Fenton decided to separate the lamps from the lines shown in the regular catalogs, so lamp supplements were issued periodically; this practice was discontinued in 1973, and lamps were featured in the regular Fenton catalog.

The Blue Overlay and Burmese colors were first produced in 1971, and the massive brass bases for the double ball Gone with the Wind lamps were also new at that time.

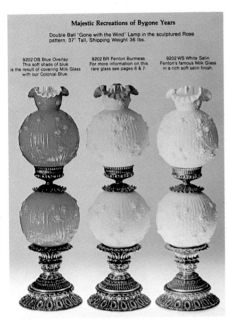

CR 4—January 1971

CR 5—January 1971

CR 6—January 1971

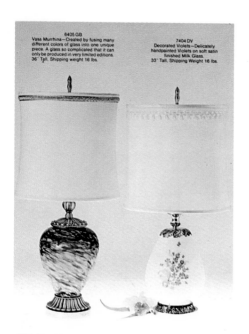

6405 GB
Vasa Murrhina—Created by fusing many different colors of glass into one unique piece. A glass so complicated that it can only be produced in very limited editions. 36" Tall, Shipping weight 16 lbs.

7404 DV
Decorated Violets—Delicately handpainted Violets on soft satin finished Milk Glass. 33" Tall, Shipping Weight 16 lbs.

CR 7—January 1971

Fenton Lamps

We guarantee complete satisfaction with each Fenton lamp. Only the finest materials have been used in their construction. Each lamp bears the Underwriters' Laboratory Seal attesting to the high standard of construction and the quality of materials used.

All glass parts are hand blown in the fine Fenton Tradition of Handmade Glass. The color of the glass shades is inherent in the colors of the various glasses used to make the shade. None are sprayed or doped to achieve coloring. The handpainted Violets have been ceramic fired in the glass for permanence and will not fade or chip off.

We have tried to provide you with a unique line of table lamps which cannot be duplicated. We think your customers will find them to be delightful decorative accents as well as useful lamps.

Double Ball Rose Lamp
8" Ball, 22" Tall
Shipping Weight 11 lbs.
9207 MI
Milk Glass

CR 8—January 1971

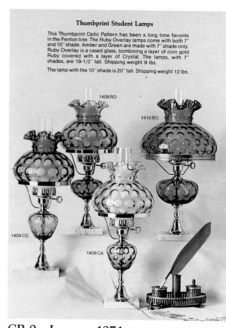

Thumbprint Student Lamps

This Thumbprint Optic Pattern has been a long time favorite in the Fenton line. The Ruby Overlay lamps come with both 7" and 10" shade. Amber and Green are made with 7" shade only. Ruby Overlay is a cased glass, combining a layer of coin gold Ruby covered with a layer of Crystal. The lamps, with 7" shades, are 19-1/2" tall. Shipping weight 9 lbs.

The lamp with the 10" shade is 20" tall. Shipping weight 12 lbs.

1408 RO
1410 RO
1408 CG
1408 CA

CR 9—January 1971

CR 7-8-9-10-11-12   These lamps are also from the January, 1971, lamp supplement. The Thumbprint and Poppy lamps had been in the line since 1966, and the Rose lamps are easily recognized as extension of the Fenton Rose pattern. There were 18 lamps in the 1966 line and 29 in 1967.

The lamps with cloth shades were a totally new venture, aimed at the lamp department of furniture and department stores. Few were made and they did not sell well, so today's collectors will not find them readily. By 1972, Fenton management had determined that all of their lamps sold best in shops which displayed the rest of the Fenton line, so attempts to market lamps to furniture and department stores were halted.

Three of Fenton's loveliest glass treatments: Burmese, Vasa Murrhina and Hand Painted Violets make these lamps truly unusual decorative accents.

The cloth shades are fine antique shantung and satin; are preshrunk and of the "no hug" construction.

7405 RB
Hand Painted Roses on Fenton Burmese
33" Tall, Shipping Weight 16 lbs.

7410 RB
Hand Painted Roses on Fenton Burmese
21" Tall, Shipping Weight 12 lbs.

7492 RB
Burmese Fairy Light

Burmese was created somewhat by accident by Frederick Shirley of the Mt. Washington Glass Company, New Bedford, Massachusetts. Stimulated by the tremendous popularity of Amberina in the late 1870's, Shirley began to experiment with various coloring oxides to create variations of Amberina. In 1881 he produced his first pieces with the opaque salmon-pink shading to lemon-yellow. The introduction of these pieces caused an immediate sensation and the color combination called Burmese was patented December 15, 1885.

As the formula for this ware contains an unusually exotic and corrosive mixture of ingredients, Burmese proved too costly to produce and by 1900 Mt. Washington had discontinued its line of Burmese. Periodically over the years other glassmakers have attempted to bring out a few Burmese pieces. However, the degree of difficulty and the cost of making Burmese inevitably defeated them. Fenton is proud to offer this unique glass treatment to the American public.

CR 10—January 1971

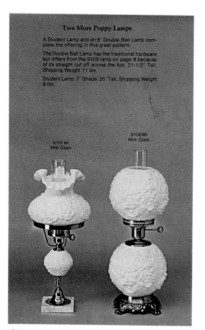

Two More Poppy Lamps

A Student Lamp and an 8" Double Ball Lamp complete the offering in this great pattern.

The Double Ball Lamp has the traditional hardware but differs from the 9109 lamp on page 8 because of its straight cut off across the top. 21-1/2" Tall, Shipping Weight 11 lbs.

Student Lamp 7" Shade, 20" Tall, Shipping Weight 9 lbs.

9107 MI
Milk Glass

9108 MI
Milk Glass

CR 11—January 1971

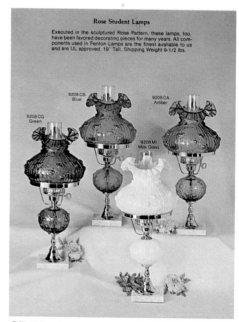

Rose Student Lamps

Executed in the sculptured Rose Pattern, these lamps, too, have been favored decorating pieces for many years. All components used in Fenton Lamps are the finest available to us and are UL approved. 19" Tall, Shipping Weight 9-1/2 lbs.

9208 CB Blue
9208 CA Amber
9208 CG Green
9208 MI Milk Glass

CR 12—January 1971

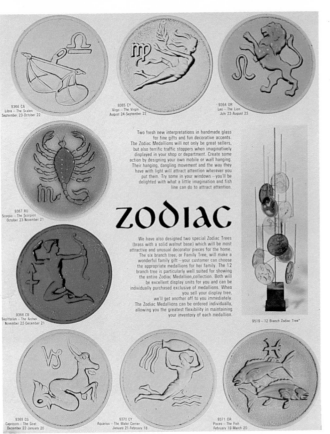

CR 13-14   These Zodiac items, designed by Fenton's Tony Rosena, were featured in the July, 1969, catalog supplement shown here. The items were in the line from July, 1969 to December, 1970. The pieces sold well at first, but dealers had problems in retailing all of the pieces and were left with inventory that did not move. Re-orders were not strong in 1970, and public interest in horoscope items began to wane about the same time.

CR 15-16   The Candy Stripe lamps were made in 1976-77 from the Rosalene glass formula. This unusual color treatment was accomplished by chilling the ribs after the balls were blown in a rib mould. In hindsight, Frank M. Fenton suggests that slow sales of the Candy Stripe lamps were due to the fact that they were "a little bit too garish for most homes." Both of these pages are from the catalog issued for 1977-78 which appeared in January, 1977.

CR 17-18-19 These three pages from the 1977-78 complete catalog show some of the popular Ruby line as well as Wisteria, a new color produced in 1977-78.

CR 20 The Lily of the Valley pattern was initiated in 1978, and this page from the 1979-80 catalog shows the expansion of the line as well as the new Cameo Opalescent color, which was a revival of a hue made in the 1920s (see Fenton Book 1, p. 72). Cameo Opalescent remained in the line through 1982.

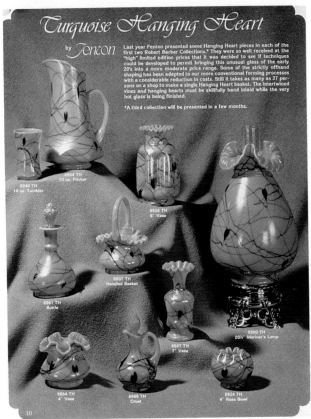

CR 21-22 These Hanging Heart lines, which appeared in the January, 1976, catalog supplement, were inspired by Robert Barber's offhand, limited edition pieces (see p. 95). The pieces shown here were mould-blown, and the many production steps and skilled hand work needed for the inlaid hearts and vines required considerable labor. They were made only in 1976.

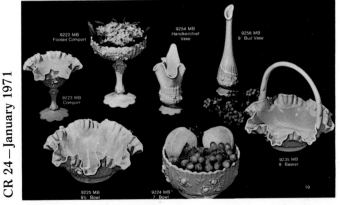

CR 23-24 Compare these articles in Blue Marble from the January, 1971, catalog with those shown on p. 78. Blue Marble began in 1970 and continued in the line through 1973.

CR 25-26   The name Pink Blossom was first used for this decoration in 1974, replacing the hard to pronounce term "Pink Anemone" which had been introduced a year earlier. These pages are from the 1977-78 catalog issued in January, 1977. The Pink Blossom decoration on Custard Satin glass was both popular and long-lived, remaining in the line from 1973 to 1986.

CR 27   Burmese items, plain and decorated, from the January, 1970, catalog supplement.

CR 28   A nice grouping of satin glass items from the 1975-76 complete catalog issued in January, 1975. Note the Custard Satin (CU) items; this popular color was introduced in 1972 and was still in the line in 1983.

CR 29-30   Rose Satin articles from the 1977-78 complete catalog issued in January, 1977. In the line from 1974-77, this color was a heat sensitive glass containing gold. Unlike the other satin glass colors, it could be made only by blowing, so there are no pressed articles in Rose Satin.

CR 31-32   Rosalene was introduced in the January, 1976, catalog supplement, from which these photos are taken. Note the sharp delineation between the white and pink colors on many of these pieces, which were made from a Rosalene mixture developed by Fenton's Charlie Goe. This mixture proved quite corrosive to the melting pots, so the formula was altered by Subodh Gupta, who succeeded Goe after his death. The later (1977 and thereafter) Rosalene is somewhat more homogeneous in tone and lacks the sharp delineations.

CR 33   Note the other plates in the American Craftsman Series, as depicted in the January, 1978, catalog supplement (see CR 93 and 118). The final plate in the series was The Housewright" in 1981.

CR 34   Note the other plates in the Christmas series (see CR 121). The final plate in the series was San Xavier del Bac in 1981.

CR 35   The January, 1970, catalog supplement re-introduced iridescent ware first made at Fenton in 1907.

CR 36   Note the other Mother's Day plates (see CR 90 and 91 for the last two of the series).

104

Hobnail

CR 37 — January 1967

CR 37-38-39-40-41-42-43-44-45-46-47-48-49

Fenton's Hobnail is one of the great success stories in the history of American pattern glass. Beginning in the late 1930s (see Fenton Book 2, pp. 9-10 and the index), Hobnail became a staple, if not the backbone, in the line for many years. Items were produced in many different colors, and new articles were being designed for inclusion in the line. In the 1975-76 catalog, over 230 Hobnail items were listed, counting articles in all the different colors separately. In reflecting on the success of Hobnail, Frank M. Fenton remarked as follows: "I sometimes wonder how we could ever think of something else to make in Hobnail, but we kept right on adding new items and new and different colors. Whenever Bill or I saw an attractive shape in some other medium or pattern, one of us would say, "Why don't we make something like this in Hobnail?" It would be impossible for this book to show every item in the Hobnail line, of course, but this page and the three which follow are from the January, 1967, catalog, and many different shapes and colors are represented. See pp. 68-74 for Hobnail items in color.

**Fenton Hobnail
Bowls and Candleholders**

Your customers know and love Fenton Hobnail for its warmth, charm and traditional beauty. Yet Hobnail seems forever fresh and new.

In milk glass and color, its simple unobtrusive appeal matches the quality of Fenton workmanship. The name, derived from the hobnails pioneer Americans wore on their shoes, is beautifully descriptive.

CR 38 — January 1967

Fenton Hobnail Vases, Planters and Epergnes

3690 MI
9½" Planter

3699 MI
Square Planter

3659 MI
9" Vase

3657 MI
7" Vase

3655 MI
5" Vase

3705 MI
Hanging Bowl

3656 MI
5½" Vase DC

3726 MI
Ivy Bowl

3701 MI
Epergne Set

3750 MI
6" Vase

3757 MI
Ftd. Ivy Vase

3652 MI
Tall Vase

3652 CA
Tall Vase

3652 OR
Tall Vase

3652 CG
Tall Vase

3652 CB
Tall Vase

3756 CA
8" Bud Vase

3756 CB
8" Bud Vase

3756 MI
8" Bud Vase

3756 CG
8" Bud Vase

3756 OR
8" Bud Vase

3753 MI
Ftd. Vase

3760 MI
Pitcher Vase

3752 MI
11" Vase

4

CR 39 — January 1967

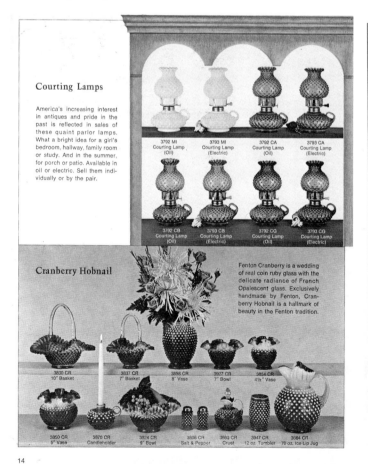

Courting Lamps

America's increasing interest in antiques and pride in the past is reflected in sales of these quaint parlor lamps. What a bright idea for a girl's bedroom, hallway, family room or study. And in the summer, for porch or patio. Available in oil or electric. Sell them individually or by the pair.

3792 MI
Courting Lamp
(Oil)

3793 MI
Courting Lamp
(Electric)

3792 CA
Courting Lamp
(Oil)

3793 CA
Courting Lamp
(Electric)

3792 CB
Courting Lamp
(Oil)

3793 CB
Courting Lamp
(Electric)

3792 CG
Courting Lamp
(Oil)

3793 CG
Courting Lamp
(Electric)

Cranberry Hobnail

Fenton Cranberry is a wedding of real coin ruby glass with the delicate radiance of French Opalescent glass. Exclusively handmade by Fenton, Cranberry Hobnail is a hallmark of beauty in the Fenton tradition.

3830 CR
10" Basket

3837 CR
7" Basket

3856 CR
8" Vase

3927 CR
7" Bowl

3854 CR
4½" Vase

3850 CR
5" Vase

3870 CR
Candleholder

3924 CR
9" Bowl

3806 CR
Salt & Pepper

3663 CR
Cruet

3947 CR
12 oz. Tumbler

3664 CR
70 oz. Ice Lip Jug

14

CR 40 — January 1967

3858 MI
8" Vase

3656 MI
5" Vase

3697 MI
8½" Planter

3799 MI
10" Planter

Emphasize that Fenton offers Hobnail in a complete line of floral accessories . . . vases for one perfect rose . . . tiny containers for pansies and violets . . . lustrous white planters for ivy.

All are extremely popular gifts. Your customers know a Fenton container makes the loveliest floral gift even lovelier. They complement any flower or floral arrangement, and continue as a lasting gift even after the flowers are gone.

3658 MI
12" 3-Toed Vase

3887 MI
Lavabo

3653 CA
5" Vase

3653 CB
5" Vase

3653 CG
5" Vase

3653 OR
5" Vase

3654 MI
3-Toed Vase

3759 MI
Tall Vase

3756 MI
Medium Vase

3764 MI
Violet Bowl

3854 MI
4½" Vase

3850 MI
5" Vase

3801 MI
Min. Epergne Set

3956 MI
6½" DC Vase

3957 MI
6¼" Fan Vase

3958 MI
8" DC Vase

3959 MI
8" Fan Vase

3994 MI
4½" Jardiniere

3996 MI
6" Jardiniere

5

CR 41 — January 1967

106

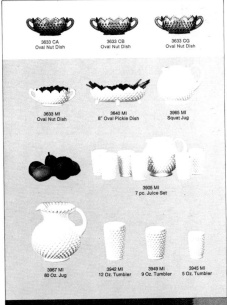

3633 CA
Oval Nut Dish

3633 CB
Oval Nut Dish

3633 CG
Oval Nut Dish

3633 MI
Oval Nut Dish

3640 MI
8" Oval Pickle Dish

3965 MI
Squat Jug

3905 MI
7 pc. Juice Set

3967 MI
80 Oz. Jug

3942 MI
12 Oz. Tumbler

3949 MI
9 Oz. Tumbler

3945 MI
5 Oz. Tumbler

Fenton accessories for dining, display, smoking

Demonstrate afresh the beauty and versatility of Fenton Hobnail.

While your sales indicate that Hobnail is becoming more and more popular in color, this is plus business because Fenton Hobnail Milk Glass continues to be the outstanding seller.

Fenton's complete line of ashtrays, lighters and smoking accessories is bold and bright . . . meant for the most masculine den, study or family room. Here are the gifts you have needed for Father's Day, Dad's Christmas present, graduation and groomsmen's gifts. A permanent display of these masculine gifts in Hobnail is also a helpful reminder for birthday and anniversary gifts.

3689 CA
Apothecary Jar

3689 CB
Apothecary Jar

3689 MI
Apothecary Jar

3689 CG
Apothecary Jar

10

CR 42 — January 1967

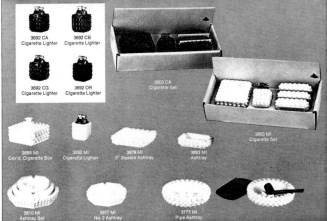

3776 MI
Round Ashtray

3973 MI
Medium Ashtray

3972 MI
Small Ashtray

3610 MI
3 Pc. Ashtray Set

3973 CA
Medium Ashtray

3972 CA
Small Ashtray

3610 CA
3 Pc. Ashtray Set

3610 CB
3 Pc. Ashtray Set

3973 CG
Medium Ashtray

3972 CG
Small Ashtray

3610 CG
3 Pc. Ashtray Set

3610 OR
3 Pc. Ashtray Set

3692 CA
Cigarette Lighter

3692 CB
Cigarette Lighter

3692 CG
Cigarette Lighter

3692 OR
Cigarette Lighter

3603 CA
Cigarette Set

3603 MI
Cigarette Set

3685 MI
Cov'd. Cigarette Box

3692 MI
Cigarette Lighter

3679 MI
5" Square Ashtray

3693 MI
Ashtray

3610 MI
Ashtray Set

3877 MI
No. 2 Ashtray

3773 MI
Pipe Ashtray

11

CR 43 — January 1967

Hobnail comports, bonbons, nut dishes and candy jars

Sweets are sweeter when they're served in Fenton ware! Besides their customary use . . . for candy, nuts, mints and fruits . . . these pieces make excellent focal points for centerpieces. Display them attractively on an uncrowded counter or shelf, adding real nuts, mints, Christmas ornaments or permanent flower arrangements for suggested uses.

3784 CA
Ftd. Candy Box

3784 OR
Ftd. Candy Box

3784 CG
Ftd. Candy Box

3784 CB
Ftd. Candy Box

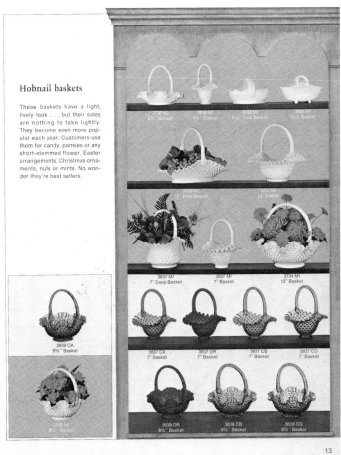

3628 MI
Ftd. CG Comport

3528 MI
Ftd. Nut Dish

3725 MI
Jelly Dish

3228 MI
Comport

3920 MI
Ftd. Comport

3637 MI
Ftd. Peanut Dish

3907 MI
7" Bonbon

3631 MI
Ftd. Nut Dish

8" Bonbon

3786 MI
Wedding Jar

Oval Candy Box

3880 MI
Candy Jar

Candy Jar

3784 MI
Ftd. Candy Box

3688 MI
Covd. Candy Jar

3980 MI
Ftd. Candy Jar

3887 MI
Ftd. Candy Jar

12

CR 44 — January 1967

Hobnail baskets

These baskets have a light, lively look . . . but their sales are nothing to take lightly. They become even more popular each year. Customers use them for candy, pansies or any short-stemmed flower, Easter arrangements, Christmas ornaments, nuts or mints. No wonder they're best sellers.

3736 MI
4½" Basket

4½" Basket

6½" Oval Basket

Oval Basket

3839 MI
12" Oval Basket

3830 MI
10" Basket

3637 MI
7" Deep Basket

3837 MI
7" Basket

3734 MI
12" Basket

3638 CA
8½" Basket

3638 MI
8½" Basket

3837 CA
7" Basket

3837 OR
7" Basket

3837 CB
7" Basket

3837 CG
7" Basket

3638 OR
8½" Basket

3638 CB
8½" Basket

3638 CG
8½" Basket

13

CR 45 — January 1967

Fenton proves expensive-looking gifts needn't cost a lot!

At right is an assortment to delight giver and receiver. Each is different . . . distinctive . . . in the bright, happy mood of an old-fashioned sampler.

To sell more, explain how the little shoes, top hat, vases and dinner bells could have graced great-grandmother's whatnot shelf.

Below are two more American favorites: the Fenton Hobnail Milk Glass footed cakeplate and serving plate. Both have pretty crimped edges, still another distinguishing mark of Fenton.

CR 46 — January 1967

Fenton Hobnail serving pieces

Show your customers how these Fenton pieces add color and personality to casual or formal china. Display them to dramatize a breakfront or corner cupboard.

The Hobnail pattern is formed by blowing or pressing the glass into a mold which has a series of carefully hand-sculpted indentations. They become the raised part, or hobnails, in the finished piece.

CR 47 — January 1967

Fenton Hobnail adds spice to a table setting

Sugars, creams, cruets, salts and peppers and butter dishes are hand-fashioned to give them a cheery warmth. Show your customers how to mix and match them with their best china or everyday dishes for decorative interest and contrast. Hobnail also makes wonderful gifts for any special day because they go so happily with any table setting.

The very strong sales appeal of this lovely glassware is due to its versatility, its beauty, and to the many practical uses that can be made of it.

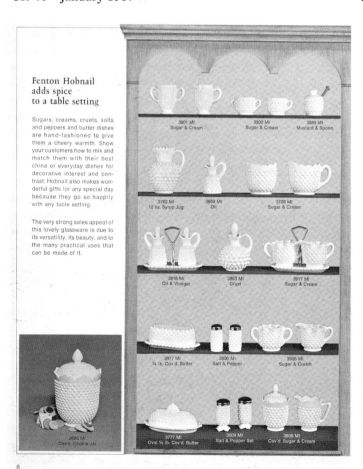

CR 48 — January 1967

Fenton Hobnail gift suggestions

Fenton's personal touch lends flair and imagination to the least expensive gift. Tell your customers to add these pieces to coffee table, hutch or cabinet for gay accents and conversation-starters . . . an inexpensive way to brighten up a room.

Recommend them for hostess, wedding and shower gifts . . . Christmas and Mother's Day, too.

CR 49 — January 1967

108

THE FENTON ART GLASS COMPANY, WILLIAMSTOWN, WEST VIRGINIA 26187

CR 50 These interesting Hobnail items are from the July, 1964 catalog supplement. The Hobnail items in Milk Glass with wrought iron hangers were in the line for only six months. Note the bullseye candle sconce.

The Centerpiece For All Seasons

A change of flower rings and candle and the whole room changes from spring to fall to Christmas. Whether used as a chip & dip, a low candle bowl, a single candle-holder or with the candle epergne, the possible combinations are unlimited.

CR 51-52-53 This page and two below show items from the January, 1975, catalog. The versatile candle pieces and the candy boxes were quite successful. For information on Shelley, see p. 130.

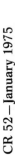

Fenton Candy Boxes Every year Fenton candy boxes are on our "best sellers" list. Carry a wide selection for your customers . . . they really do sell.

CR 54 — July 1961

CR 55 — July 1961

CR 54-55-56-57 These four pages, all from the 1961-62 catalog (issued July, 1961) show the extensive Silver Crest line. The phrase "petticoat glass" to describe the fluted edges on most Silver Crest items had been born in the mid-1950s, when Fenton learned that some of its dealers used the term. The company liked the phrase, too, and later used it to describe crimped and double crimped articles in the Hobnail and other lines.

CR 56 — July 1961

CR 57 — July 1961

Fenton Traditional Lamps

..."a thing of beauty is a joy forever."

Sales of the handsome traditional lamps we introduced in January, 1966, have far exceeded our most optimistic expectations.

Dealers throughout the country have ordered, reordered and reordered. Many tell us the lamps virtually sell themselves—especially when used as supplemental lighting for display areas. They report such lighting lends an inviting, hearthside charm that stimulates sales of other items displayed nearby. Leaving several lighted after closing time is another good selling idea. Even after you've closed the doors, they will keep your shop right on selling.

Because of their popularity, we have added several new lamps and beautiful new color combinations to the line.

If you do not already sell Fenton Traditional Lamps, you will find it profitable to do so. Why not order now?

 The complete lamp is listed by Underwriters Laboratories, Inc. and bears the coveted Good Housekeeping Seal of Approval.

Rose Student Lamps
An appealing lamp for a desk, small table or chest. Beautiful rose-patterned Fenton double-crimped shade and fount have handsome marble base. Fenton accessories are available to match.

New Rose Double Ball Lamps
This romantic style has two 8" ball shades. Three-way switch permits lighting both shades or top or bottom shade alone. Particularly attractive for bedroom, hall, living room and to light your store displays!

CR 58-59   Both of these pages are from the 1967 lamp catalog, which was titled "Traditional Lamps." The Rose line consisted of 17 different lamps, although all were made from just four different moulds: 8″ ball shade; 10″ ball shade; fount; and 7″ student shade. The idea for the Poppy pattern came from an Imperial Glass Co. vase purchased at an antique show by Frank M. Fenton. When the Poppy motif was adapted to lamps, it proved extraordinarily popular, and Poppy lamps were still in the line in 1988-89 (see also CR 1, 2, 4, 8-9, 11-12).

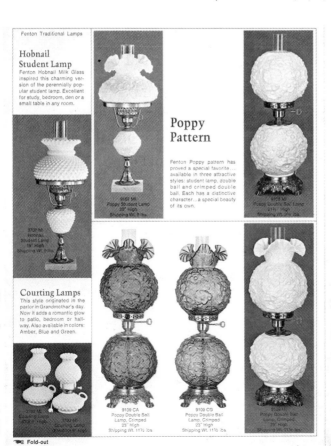

Fenton Traditional Lamps

Hobnail Student Lamp
Fenton Hobnail Milk Glass inspired this charming version of the perennially popular student lamp. Excellent for study, bedroom, den or a small table in any room.

Poppy Pattern
Fenton Poppy pattern has proved a special favorite... available in three attractive styles: student lamp, double ball and crimped double ball. Each has a distinctive character... a special beauty of its own.

Courting Lamps
This style originated in the parlor in Grandmother's day. Now it adds a romantic glow to patio, bedroom or hallway. Also available in colors: Amber, Blue and Green.

Fold-out

Fenton Traditional Lamps

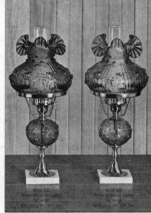

Thumbprint
In addition to our two student lamps in popular Thumbprint, a number of complementary Fenton accessories are available. When a customer purchases a lamp, you will profit from sales of these handsome Fenton pieces.

LAMP COLOR CODE:
CA—Colonial Amber   HA—Honey Amber   OG—Shelley Green Overlay
CB—Colonial Blue   MI—Milk Glass   RO—Ruby Overlay
CG—Colonial Green   OB—Colonial Blue Overlay   WR—Wild Rose

LAMP SECTION, 1967 CATALOG, THE FENTON ART GLASS COMPANY, WILLIAMSTOWN, WEST VIRGINIA 26187

111

The beauty of handmade milk glass and crystal combined with the elegance of an Old World pattern. Each piece is skillfully edged by glass artisans with a ribbon of pure crystal.

CR 60-61   The Spanish Lace pattern further enhanced the popularity of the Silver Crest line. These pages are from the 1979-80 complete catalog (issued in January, 1979).

CR 62-63   A year after its introduction, the Rosalene line was selling well. These pages are taken from the 1977-78 complete catalog issued in January, 1977 (see CR 31-32).

CR 64-65   Two pages from the 1979-80 complete catalog (issued January, 1979) showing the white "Roses on Ruby" decoration.

CR 66   Violets in the Snow on Spanish Lace and other items from the 1975-76 complete catalog (issued January, 1975).

CR 67   White Satin and Anniversary plates from the 1975-76 complete catalog.

113

Daisies on Custard

A delightful pattern of brown-eyed daisies handpainted on satin finished custard. Each petal is permanently frosted. Each piece is individually signed by the artist who paints it. These lovely florals have had an exceptional sales record their first year. Here are some new items to broaden your selection.

9308 DC
19½" Student Lamp
Shipping Weight 9½ Lbs.

7256 DC
6" Vase

8298 DC
Medallion Candy Box

9056 DC
Bud Vase

8267 DC
Medallion Bell

7480 DC
Candy or Puff Box

Fenton

HANDPAINTED
Daisies on Cameo Satin

Happy little orangey—rust daisies handpainted on new Fenton Cameo Satin glass. These rich beige art glass pieces are "naturals" for the flourishing market for earth-tone decorative accents . . . and each piece is signed by the artist.
On Order Blank—Page 3, Column 2.

7204 CD
16" HAMMERED
COLONIAL LAMP
SHIPPING WGT.—7½ LBS.

7209 CD
21" STUDENT LAMP
SHIPPING WGT.
—10 LBS.

7252 CD
7" VASE

7237 CD
7" BASKET

7429 CD
FTD. COMPORT

8267 CD
MEDALLION BELL

7254 CD
4½" VASE

5197 CD
HAPPINESS BIRD

9056 CD
BUD VASE

5163 CD
SMALL BIRD

5162 CD
BUNNY

7300 CD
FAIRY LIGHT

5161 CD
SWAN

CR 68-69-70-71   Four pages of Fenton decorations: Daisies on Custard (1976); Daisies on Cameo Satin (1978); and Pink Blossom (1974 at left, and 1973 on right). The decoration was not named in the 1973 catalog, but it was called Pink Anemone on the accompanying price list; in 1974, the name was changed to Pink Blossom.

Pink Blossom

Delicate pink flowers daintily hand painted on rich Fenton Custard glass —makes any time blossom time.

7410 PY
21" Student Lamp

7229 PY
Ftd. Nut Dish

7429 PY
Ftd. Comport

7461 PY
Pitcher

Purest satin finished custard glass with delicate hand painted pink flowers—each proudly signed by the artist.

7380 PY
Candy Box

7252 PY
7" Vase

7437 PY
Basket

7406 PY
10" Hurricane Light
and Base

7300 PY
Fairy Light

5143 PY
Egg

5197 PY
Bird

114

CR 72—July 1979

CR 73—January 1979

CR 72-73-74-75   Four pages of Fenton decorations: Nature's Christmas (July, 1979); Cardinals in Winter (January, 1979); Butterflies (January, 1977); and Bluebirds on Custard (January, 1979).

CR 74—January 1977

CR 75—January 1979

Burmese

We have been extremely pleased with the reception of our Burmese treatment, both from the standpoint of its sales volume and the critical acclaim accorded our Burmese by knowledgeable glass collectors.

To the original six items introduced last January, we have added a number of interesting new pieces and a completely new handpainted pattern. We are confident that these Burmese additions will be as enthusiastically received by your customers.

A LITTLE ROMANCE IN THE HISTORY OF BURMESE

Burmese was created somewhat by accident by Frederick Shirley of the Mt. Washington Glass Company, New Bedford, Massachusetts. Stimulated by the tremendous popularity of Amberina in the late 1870's, Shirley began to experiment with various coloring oxides to create variations of Amberina. In 1881 he produced his first pieces with the opaque salmon-pink shading to lemon-yellow. The introduction of these pieces caused an immediate sensation and the color combination called Burmese was patented December 15, 1885.

Many of the early Mt. Washington pieces were decorated by local artists. The immediate success of this treatment evidently prompted Mr. Shirley to present several pieces to Queen Victoria. The Queen was so delighted with this gift that she immediately commissioned the company to make her a Burmese tea set and a pair of original vases. The name Burmese itself is often attributed to Queen Victoria, who was said to have exclaimed that the rich tones of blushing pink reminded her of a Burmese sunset.

The Queen's enthusiasm for Burmese prompted the well known English glassmakers, Thomas Webb & Sons to apply for and receive a license to produce this treatment. Their production became known as Queen's Burmese.

Producing this ware proved to be terribly costly for both companies and by 1900, Mt. Washington had discontinued its line of Burmese. Periodically over the years other glassmakers have brought out a few Burmese pieces. However, the degree of difficulty and the cost of making Burmese inevitably defeated them. Fenton is proud to once again offer this unique glass treatment to the American public.

CR 76-77-78   Three pages of Burmese from Fenton's January, 1971, complete catalog. CR 76 is plain, undecorated Burmese; CR 77 shows Leaf Decorated Burmese, and CR 78 is Rose Burmese. See p. 81.

Carnival

A completely new grouping of items, presented for the first time in historic Fenton Carnival Treatment. Space is precious to the collector. This prompted these smaller "collectibles". These pieces will be available just for the life of this catalog.

CR 79   In the late 1970s, Fenton began to offer assortments of carnival items for a limited period of time. This page, from the January, 1977-78 complete catalog, indicates that items would "be available just for the life of this catalog." Later, assortments were offered for about one year, making this Fenton carnival a sort of "limited edition."

Carnival

Carnival

CR 80-81-82-83   Four pages of Fenton carnival: upper left and upper right are from January, 1973; lower left is from January, 1971; and lower right is from January, 1975. See p. 93.

Original Formula Carnival Glass These collector's pieces of "Carnival Glass" were created from the original formula that Fenton used in 1907 when we introduced this unique hand glass treatment to the American public.

117

Ruby Iridescent

Beautiful Ruby Glass in shimmering iridescent finish. Fenton made this exotic glass years ago (1910-1920) and today collectors pay high prices for original pieces. Ruby Iridescent Glass has proved to be popular since its reintroduction by Fenton. These are the antiques of tomorrow.

9101 RN
24" POPPY GONE WITH THE WIND LAMP
Shipping Weight 13 lbs.

8436 RN
DRAPE & TIE COMPORT

8201 RN
PAGODA CANDY BOX

8223 RN
LEAF & ORANGE TREE BOWL

5197 RN
HAPPINESS BIRD

8227 RN
PINWHEEL COMPORT

8426 RN
BUTTERFLY & BERRY BOWL

8234 RN
PERSIAN MEDALLION COMPORT

9107 RN
20" STUDENT LAMP
Shipping Weight 9½ lbs.

9155 RN
8" VASE

8407 RN
CHOU TING CEREMONIAL LIGHT

9467 RN
MADONNA BELL

8222 RN
BASKET WEAVE BOWL

8424 RN
CAROLINA DOGWOOD BOWL

8238 RN
PERSIAN MEDALLION BASKET

CR 84-85   Ruby iridescent items from January, 1977. See items 498-501, p. 93.

3872 BK
Candle Bowl

3872 M
Candle Bowl

Fenton
"the creative Candle Bowl"

3872 CA
Candle Bowl

3872 CB
Candle Bowl

3872 CG
Candle Bowl

CR 86   "Creative Candle Bowl" from January 1969.

Fenton
Orange Carnival

Orange red iridescent carnival glass in antique patterns of Early Century charm and warmth. Like all Fenton Carnival Glass, photographs cannot capture the vibrant aliveness of this glass. To see it is to want it.

9126 CO
Daisy Candy Box

8295 CO
Strawberry Toothpick Holder

1966 CO
Bell

8223 CO
Leaf & Orange Tree Bowl

8229 CO
Cupped Hearts & Flowers Bowl

9088 CO
Wild Strawberry Candy Box

Persian Medallion Bowl

8225 CO
Grape Nappy

9291 CO
Handled Ftd. Fruit Comport

9230 CO
Handled Butterfly Bonbon

Flared Bowl

8234 CO
Persian Medallion Comport

1990 CO
Boot

9227 CO
Pinwheel Comport

CR 87   Orange Carnival from Fenton's 1973 complete catalog.

Original Formula Carnival Glass

Just a year ago we decided to try a small grouping of ten items in our old Iridescent formula that Fenton was first to introduce in the early 1900's. The retail response to this treatment has been amazing. In fact, we have had to significantly increase our production capability to meet the Carnival demand. There are now 35 items to start off our second year. Many of these pieces are made from the same moulds that were used more than 60 years ago. Others are authentic antique reproduction and a few are simply items that we feel lend themselves so well to the Carnival treatment.

CR 88 — January 1971

CR 89 — January 1971

CR 88-89   More Fenton carnival, this time from the January, 1971, catalog.

CR 90 — January 1978

CR 91 — January 1979

CR 90-91   These two pages (from January, 1978, and January, 1979, respectively) show still more Fenton carnival, plus the Mother's Day plates in the line at that time. The carnival items were offered for just one year (see CR 79).

119

CR 92—January 1975

CR 92 The page at left is from the 1975-76 complete catalog, issued in January, 1975. The Jefferson comport is described, and the color Patriot Red was added. The Bicentennial bell was renamed Patriot's bell. For other Bicentennial items, see pp. 41, 42, 43 and 94.

The Jefferson comport is a massive, well-detailed item. The lid contains quotations from Thomas Jefferson. Note also the eagle finial on the lid which is similar to the paperweight and the tip of the bell handle.

Thomas Jefferson's quotes on the cover of comport

"I have sworn upon the altar of God eternal hostility against every form of tyranny over the mind of man."

"The happiest moments of my life have been the few I have passed at home in the bosom of my family."

"The tree of liberty must be refreshed from time to time with the blood of patriots and tyrants."

"My confidence in my countrymen generally leaves me without much fear for the future."

CR 93—January 1979

CR 94—January 1974

CR 93 The Craftsman plate series was in full swing, and Fenton added a stein and bell in the January, 1979, catalog.

CR 94 Mother's Day plates (in carnival, Blue Satin and White Satin) and Fenton carnival from January, 1974).

CR 95-96   Two pages of Cameo Opalescent articles from the January, 1979, offering. The Cameo Opalescent Spiral group was a revival of a color treatment used in the 1920s (see p. 100 CR 20 and Fenton Book 1, p. 72.)

CR 97-98   Blue Opalescent items from the January, 1978, catalog.

CR 99-100-101-102-103-104-105-106   Crystal Velvet was introduced in 1977, and this page and the next show selections from catalogs in 1977-80 as captioned.

Crystal Velvet.....

5107 VE
MADONNA PRAYER LIGHT

8433 VE
WATER LILY FTD. BASKET

8458 VE
WATER LILY BUD VASE

8480 VE
WATER LILY FTD. CANDY BOX

8222 VE
BASKET WEAVE BOWL

8466 VE
FABERGE BELL

5100 VE
PRAYING BOY & GIRL

8429 VE
WATER LILY ROSE BOWL

28

the unusual clarity of pattern and
elegant soft look of handcrafted glass!

8434 VE
7" WATER LILY BASKET

8464 VE
WATER LILY 36 OZ. PITCHER

8454 VE
CURTAIN BOWL

8473 VE
WATER LILY CANDLEHOLDER

9168 VE
BRIDE & GROOM BELL

8409 VE
CURRIER & IVES LIGHT

8424 VE
9" WATER LILY BOWL

29

Notice the new Craftsman Bell and Stein in Crystal
Velvet. The Craftsman Stein features a panoramic
view of early American glassmaking . . . Craftsman
Bell features a bas-relief of the glass Finisher, the
Fenton trademark. (See sketch on page 74.)

8457 VE
3 TOED GRAPE VASE

9660 VE
CRAFTSMAN BELL

9640 VE
CRAFTSMAN STEIN

8438 VE
3 TOED GRAPE BASKET

8441 VE
LOTUS NUT DISH

Velvet Accents

We've added 3 new little creatures: the Cat, Turtle
and Sunfish . . . by Fenton, of course.

5161 VE
SWAN

5163 VE
SMALL BIRD

5171 VE
BUTTERFLY
ON STAND

5162 VE
BUNNY

5197 VE
HAPPINESS BIRD

5165 VE
CAT

5164 VE
TURTLE

5166 VE
FROG

5167 VE
SUNFISH

27

Crystal Velvet...

the unusual clarity of pattern
and elegant soft look of
handcrafted glass!

Other velvet items shown on pages 26-29 in
catalog — on order blank - page 2, column 1

8427 VE
OVAL PINWHEEL
COMPORT

5168 VE
OWL

9299 VE
OWL RING TREE

"Wise" additions to our
popular figurine
grouping.

Beautiful little strawberries engraved into the glass
. . . . . each tiny facet sparkles to reflect the crafts-
manship of the master mouldmaker and glass
artisan. We're very proud of this newest pattern
from Fenton.

9427 VE
7" BOWL

9428 VE
COMPORT

9437 VE
7" BASKET

9465 VE
BELL

9407 VE
FAIRY LIGHT

9454 VE
BUD VASE

3

123

CR 107-108 Front and back cover of Fenton's catalog supplement for January, 1980, the start of the firm's 75th year. This page and the next three are from this catalog supplement.

CR 109 These bells were made from goblet moulds originally owned by the Redcliff Company, a concern which made ironstone dinnerware.

CR 110 The Topaz Opalescent color is back after about two decades (see p. 66).

124

PEKING BLUE

. . . a reintroduction of a popular color last produced by Fenton in the mid 30's. An enchanting translucent blue in characteristic Traditional and Oriental forms. Rich color and simplicity of design make these pieces highly suited for contemporary settings.

NOTE: Peking Blue, like the Jade Green, is not an homogenous glass. The interior structure of this glass lacks uniformity as is evidenced in small bubbles and irregularities in the texture—just as in the mineral Jade that is so beautiful in artistic carvings.

CR 111-112 Two new colors, Peking Blue and Jade Green, recalled the past (see pp. 96 in this book as well as Fenton Book 1, p. 69 and Fenton Book 2, pp. 29, 41, and 66). These colors are very difficult to make, and the firm discontinued them soon after the catalog supplement was released.

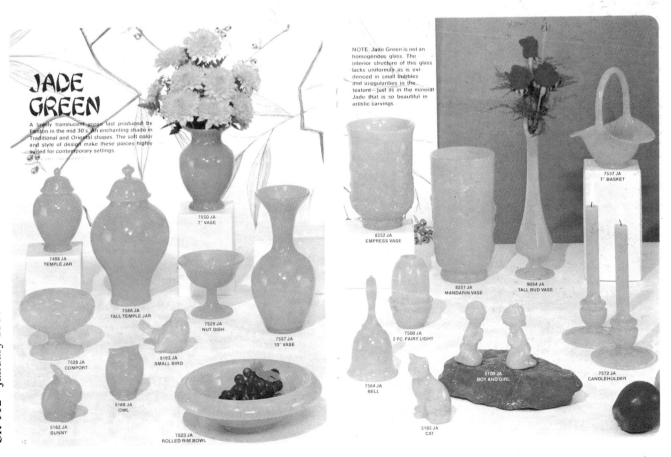

JADE GREEN

A lovely translucent green last produced by Fenton in the mid 30's. An enchanting shade in Traditional and Oriental shapes. The soft color and style of design make these pieces highly suited for contemporary settings.

NOTE: Jade Green is not an homogenous glass. The interior structure of this glass lacks uniformity as is evidenced in small bubbles and irregularities in the texture—just as in the mineral Jade that is so beautiful in artistic carvings.

"Sunset" on Cameo Satin by Fenton

a new dimension in handpainted glassware—a haunting portrayal of the sun setting behind a rustic old barn. This scene creates a gentle, nostalgic feeling. Absolutely beautiful!!!—and each piece signed by its artist.
On order blank — page 3, column 2.

7418 SS
8" PLATE

7204 SS
16" HAMMERED COLONIAL LAMP
SHIPPING WGT.—7½ lbs.

7564 SS
BELL

7254 SS
4½" VASE

7300 SS
2 PC. FAIRY LIGHT

14

7209 SS
21" STUDENT LAMP
SHIPPING WGT.—10 lbs.

7255 SS
TULIP VASE

7437 SS
BASKET

7488 SS
TEMPLE JAR

15

CR 113-114 Fenton's decorated lines remained strong in 1980 with these two lines, both on Cameo Satin. The Blue Dogwood illustrations show a flower with five petals, which is botanically incorrect, since Dogwood flowers have four petals. The decorators at Fenton changed as soon as possible, of course, but some "five petal Dogwood" items did reach the market (see p. 46).

Blue Dogwood on Cameo Satin

A beautiful new collection of handpainted, artist signed "Parlor" pieces with the comfortable feel of yesteryear.
On order blank — page 3, column 3.

7429 BD
FOOTED COMPORT

7204 BD
16" HAMMERED COLONIAL LAMP
SHIPPING WGT.—7½ lbs.

7252 BD
7" VASE

7488 BD
TEMPLE JAR

7300 BD
FAIRY LIGHT

5197 BD
HAPPINESS BIRD

5165 BD
CAT

18

7912 BD
HURRICANE LAMP
Pewter Finish

9056 BD
BUD VASE

7363 BD
BOTTLE

7229 BD
NUT DISH

5161 BD
SWAN

7484 BD
CANDY BOX

5162 BD
BUNNY

5163 BD
SMALL BIRD

CR 115-116   These crystal items (from the January, 1980, catalog supplement) in the Fine Cut and Block and Daisy and Button patterns were made in moulds formerly used for color production of Fenton's Olde Virginia line, which was discontinued in 1979.

CR 117   Compare these Blue Dogwood articles with those in CR 114 (hint: they all have five petals!). Made for only a few days in 1980, the five-petalled articles are rare collector's items now.

CR 118   The carnival Hobnail pieces were made only for 1980, continuing the Fenton plan of producing an assortment of items in carnival for one year only.

CR 119-120-121-122   These pages are from the June, 1980, catalog supplement.

Currier & Ives

Please Note: The plates in each treatment will be the first of a projected annual series of Currier & Ives Plates.
On order blank—page 2, column 1.

WINTER IN THE COUNTRY—
"The Old Grist Mill" in Antique Blue
—this bas-relief design, so artistically sculpted by the mould maker, is accented by the *hand blending* of color shades and hues.

8400 TB
11" LAMP

8461 TB
BELL

8409 TB
FAIRY LIGHT/VASE

8418 TB
8" PLATE W/STAND
1st in a series

ANTIQUE BROWN—an unusual blending of shades of brown and tan. A collector's delight.
On order blank—page 2, column 1.

8409 TN
FAIRY LIGHT/VASE

8461 TN
BELL

8418 TN
8" PLATE W/STAND
1st in a series

6

CRYSTAL VELVET—
a nostalgic pattern in a market proven treatment.
On order blank—page 2, column 1.

8400 VE
11" LAMP

8461 VE
BELL

8409 VE
FAIRY LIGHT/VASE

8418 VE
8" PLATE W/STAND
1st in a series

ANTIQUE WHITE—
a beautiful "go-with-all" color.
An extra softness has been added.
On order blank—page 2, column 1.

8418 AW
8" PLATE W/STAND
1st in a series

8409 AW
FAIRY LIGHT/VASE

8461 AW
BELL

8400 AW
11" LAMP

7

CR 123-124-125   These pages are also from the June, 1980, catalog supplement. Velva Rose was another revival of a Fenton 1920s color treatment, an iridescent stretch glass (see Fenton Book 1, p. 65). The Velva Rose pieces were made only during the last six months of 1980; below the characteristic Fenton oval logo, there is a small "75," denoting the firm's 75th anniversary.

Velva Rose

First introduced by Fenton in the 20's, this iridescent stretch glass treatment is being brought back this year to help commemorate our 75th anniversary. Some of these patterns were also first made in the 20's while some are either entirely new or adaptations of old patterns.

Please Note: This grouping in Velva Rose will be made only in 1980 and each piece will bear the mark
On order blank—page 3, column 3.

7580 VR
DOLPHIN CANDY BOX

7505 VR
5 PC. EPERGNE SET

7562 VR
BELL (STAR CRIMPED)

9056 VR
BUD VASE

7527 VR
FOOTED COMPORT

7572 VR
CANDLEHOLDER

9422 VR
PERSIAN MEDALLION
COMPORT

7551 VR
DOLPHIN FAN VASE

7536 VR
8½" BASKET

7529 VR
NUT DISH

7526 VR
6½" BOWL

8408 VR
PERSIAN MEDALLION 3 PC.
FAIRY LIGHT

7516 VR
SALVER

5

This is
Shelley's
BREAD &
BUTTER

And this is our bread and butter...

Like others, we will not be at the Atlantic City Show. Your Fenton Representative will be at all the regular shows and will call personally to share our bread and butter with you.

Incidentally, he will have 96 exciting new items to show you.

THE FENTON ART GLASS COMPANY • WILLIAMSTOWN, WEST VIRGINIA

52   CROCKERY & GLASS JOURNAL for December, 1961

CR 126—1961

Simply beautiful

FENTON MILK GLASS is so pure and so full of beauty that its usefulness may be overlooked. These vases are created for floral arrangements. But with or without flowers, an attractive display of handmade Fenton glass promotes active sales.

May we send you our catalog?

The Fenton Art Glass Company
WILLIAMSTOWN, WEST VIRGINIA

CR 127—1962

CR 126-127-128-129 These four trade advertisements from 1961-64 featured Shelley Fenton, the daughter of Wilmer C. ("Bill") Fenton. Shelley was 3½ in 1961, when her picture appeared on the cover of the January, 1962, catalog supplement; for this photo and Shelley at 16, see p. 109. In 1989, Shelley is selling Fenton glass and is responsible for all Fenton catalogs (see p. 63).

Of course Shelley is too young to court . . .

... but it really doesn't matter, for her Fenton Courting Lamps are actually lamps of many uses.

In the bedroom, in the living room, or wherever these richly colored lamps are used, they add a gentle light.

Adapted to oil or electricity, the attractive price and versatility of these handmade "early American" lamps will lead many of your customers to buy them in pairs.

Suggest Fenton Courting Lamps for the patio – They will make every party an occasion.

May we send you our catalog?

THE FENTON ART GLASS COMPANY • WILLIAMSTOWN, WEST VIRGINIA

CR 128—1963

Fenton
Glass . . .
"handled"
with care

Shelley is holding a Fenton 7237 SC 7" Basket

Each Fenton basket (like all Fenton glass) is made by hand—not just any hands but those of very skilled craftsmen. You should see them put the handles on these baskets. They really "handle" them with care—the kind of care people expect in fine things and readily find in Fenton. See the whole line—America's finest glass in color—at your regional show.

In Atlanta, Fenton has a completely *new show room*—711 Atlanta Merchandise Mart. Please come in, your orders will be handled with care.

THE FENTON ART GLASS COMPANY   •   WILLIAMSTOWN, WEST VIRGINIA
JUNE 1964   101

CR 129—1964

CR 130   This sheet was mailed to Fenton sales representatives in 1969 before the catalog was ready for distribution. It shows a variety of milk glass items, including Violets in the Snow decoration on Silver Crest (top row).

Your Hand Painted Violets Are Ready When we introduced our new Violets in the Snow last July we anticipated a lively demand for this delightfully fresh concept in handmade glass. But we never dreamed the demand would be so great as to sell out our entire Fall production in a few short weeks.

The Violets should prove to be as exciting for Spring sales as they were for Christmas. Be sure your Easter and Mother's Day orders are placed early.

We invite your inquiry.

THE FENTON ART GLASS COMPANY
Williamstown, West Virginia 26187

CR 131   This ad for Violets in the Snow items appeared in *Gifts and Decorative Accessories* for January, 1969.

CR 132   New milk glass Hobnail pieces added in January 1972; plus White Daisies handpainted on black and a new Burmese cruet.

How do you sell *Fenton* lamps? Just turn them on.

Handmade from authentic patterns, these traditional lamps by Fenton sell themselves.

Pre-sold through national advertising, all you need to do is turn them on. They do the rest.

The Fenton Art Glass Company
Williamstown, West Virginia

Lamps shown:
(A) 9205 WR, (B) 9208 MI,
(C) 9205 OG, (D) 9207 HA, (E) 9207 OB.

The complete lamp is listed by Underwriters Laboratories, Inc. and bears the Good Housekeeping Seal of Approval.

CR 133   This trade magazine ad, circa 1967, showed Fenton lamps in five colors: Opaque Blue; Honey Amber; Green Overlay; Milk Glass; and Wild Rose.

CR 134   May 1961

... and speaking of magic — Fenton glass will disappear from your shelves and large black figures will appear on your profits report. Assure your customers of having a well rounded selection of Fenton glassware all Fall — Order adequately — early.

CR 134   Ad from *Crockery and Glass Journal*, May, 1961.

CR 135 — February 1956

CR 135   Ad from *Crockery and Glass Journal*, February, 1956. The punch set in Silver Crest with its crystal ladle is very hard to find today.

CR 136 — February 1956

CR 136   This ad and one similar to it appeared in *Crockery and Glass Journal* in February, 1956, and July, 1958.

Fenton's Olde Virginia Glass

The next few pages (CR 137-144) show Fenton glass sold by various wholesalers and catalog houses. These items were not part of the regular Fenton line, and the Fenton name was generally not associated with them. Some articles, such as the compote (J) in CR 137 and the tidbit tray (J) in CR 138, were reminiscent of items in the Fenton line, but design or finishing details set them apart. In 1960, the phrase "Olde Virginia Glass" was coined, and it was associated with this merchandise until Fenton ceased making it in 1979. CR 139 and CR 140 (from 1961 and 1962, respectively) show an array of Thumbprint items, some of which bear resemblance to the regular Fenton line (see items 86-88). Compare the Thumbprint creamers and covered sugars in CR 138 and 140 to see changes in design.

AUTHENTIC AMERICAN

Milk Glass

Charming Colonial flavor . . . captured in purest white Milk Glass in the beloved Hobnail-and Thumb Print patterns . . . graciously hand-crafted by master designer into enchanting table accessories . . . smart wall decorations. Functional and beautiful . . . perfect in any surroundin

Ⓐ **LAVABO.** Captivating decorator piece authentically reproduced in luscious milk glass . . . in the lovely thumb print pattern. Basin holds plants or flowers . . . water them by turning spigot on lavabo. 13½″ high. Sh. wt. 12 lbs.

Ⓑ **HURRICANE LAMPS.** Impart a friendly nostalgic flavor . . . beautiful on a table, buffet or mantle. An impressive 10″ tall . . . fashioned in thumb print pattern milk glass. Sh. wt. 9 lbs.

Ⓒ **9-PC. BEVERAGE SET.** So pretty . . . such a delightful way to serve beverages! Versatile 80-oz. jug holds fresh flowers, too! Purest white milk glass in the hobnail pattern. Eight 12-oz. tumblers. Shipping wt. 12½ lbs.

Ⓓ **FOOTED COVERED "WEDDING" COMPOTE.** What nicer way to serve candy and nuts than in this lovely table accessory . . . beautiful thumb print milk glass. 10″ high. Sh. wt. 6 lbs.

Ⓔ **FOOTED NUT DISH.** Tasty tidbits take on added enticement when presented in this dainty milk glass compote . . . graced with authentic thumb print pattern. 5½″ high. Sh. wt. 2 lbs.

Ⓕ **EPERGNE.** This stunning table accessory leads a double life! Remove flower holders and you have a 10″ fruit or snack bowl! Executed in gleaming white milk glass in the hobnail pattern. 9″ high. Sh. wt. 6 lbs.

Ⓖ **FOOTED BANANA BOWL.** Authentic reproduction of a classic milk glass design . . . decorative and practical . . . as a centerpiece—a serving piece for candy or fruit. 6¾″ high. Sh. wt. 4½ lbs.

Ⓗ **FOOTED CAKE PLATE.** Lends added appetite appeal to any cake!-Conceived in milk glass . . . generous 13″ plate has rhythmic hand-scalloped edges, thumb print base. 5″ high. Sh. wt. 6½ lbs.

Ⓙ **LACEWORK COMPOTE.** Slender lines of pure milk glass artistically woven in a lattice-like border . . . forms a fascinating centerpiece when filled with fruit or flowers. 9″ high. Sh. wt. 5 lbs.

Ⓚ **2-PC. CHEESE DIP.** Party-time favorite! Center footed bowl holds that delectable cheese dip . . . 12″ plate takes dozens of potato chips and crackers. Versatile—each piece has several separate uses! Sh. wt. 7 lbs.

Ⓛ **PLANTER PLATE.** Your pet greenery blooming behind a chalky white milk glass plate (cleverly hiding the planter box). Fascinating on any wall! Diam. 9¼″. Plant not incl. Sh. wt. 2½ lbs.

310 L&C MAYERS CO.

CR 137   From L. & C. Mayers Co., circa 1956.

133

AUTHENTIC AMERICAN
Milk Glass HAND-MADE

*Lovely accessories flawlessly fashioned
in genuine milk glass.
Today's treasures—
heirlooms of tomorrow
graciously styled to lend
new richness to wall,
table or buffet.*

**As table accessories
or decorative accents**

A LACEWORK COMPOTE—in frosty white milk glass. As functional as it is beautiful. Daintily woven bowl border looks like exquisite lace. A lavish centerpiece, 9″ high. Sh. wt. 5 lbs.
T9020M590 . . . . Retail **$8.95**

B FOOTED CAKEPLATE—lends new grace to any table. Crafted in creamy white milk glass . . . a full 13″ in diameter. Frilly French ruffled border, thumb print base, 5″ high. Sh. wt. 6½ lbs.
4413M480 . . . . Retail **$7.50**

C COVERED CANDY DISH in coveted antique design. Truly a showpiece on table or buffet. Beautifully conceived in a thumb-print pattern. 7½″ diameter. Sh. wt. 5 lbs.
4480M430 . . . . Retail **$6.50**

D FOOTED NUT DISH. Captures the dignity of yester-year. Unsurpassed in beauty. Daintily detailed with a crisp ruffled border, thumb print pattern. 5½″ high. Sh. wt. 2 lbs.
4428M167 . . . . Retail **$2.50**

E 2-PC. CHEESE DIP SET—a party-time must . . . serves appetizers, pastries, etc. Thumb-print pattern. Footed bowl for cheese . . . 12″ plate holds your favorite "dippers." Versatile—each piece has several uses. Sh. wt. 7 lbs.
4404M497 . . . . Retail **$7.50**

F EPERGNE—this enchanting table accessory plays a dual role. Acts as candy dish without flower holders. Beautiful hob-nail pattern rendered for lifetime loveliness—matchless beauty. 9″ high. Sh. wt. 6 lbs.
4801M550 . . . . Retail **$8.50**

G LAVABO. An eye-catching decorator for hall or alcove. Lovely thumb-print pattern. Basin for flowers or plants. Water plants by turning on spigot. 13½″ high. Sh. wt. 12 lbs.
4467M1530 . . . . Retail **$24.95**

H 9-PC. BEVERAGE SET—popular hobnail design. Makes frosty drinks look even cooler. Versatile 80-oz. jug doubles as a flower vase. Eight 12-oz. tumblers. Sh. wt. 12½ lbs.
T3811M1070 . . . . Retail **$16.50**

J 2-TIER TIDBIT—a cocktail-time favorite. Makes a wonderful server or decorative centerpiece. Overall thumb-print pattern. Chromed handle. Large plate 13″ diameter, small 9″. Sh. wt. 7 lbs.
4494M690 . . . . Retail **$10.95**

*A hostess' delight!
Perfection in flawless
hand-made milk glass!*

K 15-PC. PUNCH SET—an elegant server for festive occasions. Lavishly massive—magnificently detailed in thumb-print motif. Glass dipper, 12 cups, 12 hooks for hanging cups included. Holds 4 quarts. 11″ high. Sh. wt. 29 lbs.
4406M2450 . . . . Retail **$36.95**

L 5-PC. BREAKFAST SET—a perfect accent for any table. In highly decorative, ever-popular thumb-print pattern. Salt and Pepper 4″ high, cream and sugar with cover 7″. Sh. wt. 6 lbs.
4402M497 . . . . . . Retail **$7.50**

M HURRICANE LAMPS—true colonial charm in famed authentic thumb print pattern. Beautiful on buffet, table or mantel. Each holds 1 candle. Both are an impressive 10″ tall. Sh. wt. 9 lbs.
4498M797 . . . . . . Retail Pair **$12.95**

CR 138   The punch set is rare today. Note the *absence* of "thumbprints" on the bowl, although they are clearly visible on the base.

OLDE VIRGINIA GLASS

WILLIAMSTOWN, WEST VIRGINIA

4445 MI
Goblet

4438 MI
8½″ Basket

4430 MI
6½″ Oval Basket

4429 MI
Footed Comport

4480 MI
Covered Candy Jar

4486 MI
Oval Candy Box

4405 MI
Hanging Planter

4467 MI
Lavabo

4408 MI
Salt and
Pepper Set

4437 MI
Handled Basket

4428 MI
Footed Nut Dish

4456 MI
Bud Vase
(Packed 1 pair)

4401 MI
4-pc. Epergne Set

4404 MI
Chip 'n Dip

4484 MI
Covered Compote

4427 MI
Round Bowl

4490 MI
10″ Planter

4474 MI
Low Candle Holder
(Packed 1 pair)

Olde
Virginia
Glass
HANDMADE

4413 MI
Footed Cakeplate

4473 MI
Candleholder
(Packed 1 pair)

**EARLY AMERICAN
REPRODUCTIONS
IN HANDMADE MILK GLASS**

CR 139   Catalog sheet from 1961. All the items except the goblet, footed comport, and low candle holders had been introduced a year earlier.

F-1

OLDE VIRGINIA

All genuine milk glass pieces are flawlessly hand-made in forever-enchanting "Thumb print" pattern.

A LAVABO. Captivating conversation piece authentically reproduced in Thumb print Milk Glass! Basin holds plants or flowers; 11 in. wide x 5¼ in. high. Turn spigot on 12 in. tank to water them. Wt. 10 lbs.
4467MIF1530 . . . . Retail $24.95

B OIL COURTING LAMP. Hand-made replica in authentic baby dot optic pattern glass. Fill with oil or kerosene and light wick. Glows softly to set a quiet mood. 9½ in. high. Lovely in pairs. Wt. 4 lbs.
2490CAF665 Colonial Amber . . . . Retail ea. $9.95
2490CBF665 Colonial Blue . . . . Retail ea.   9.95

C ELECTRIC COURTING LAMP. Same but electric. 110-120 volts, AC-DC—U.L. approved. Wt. 5 lbs.
2491CAF823 Colonial Amber . . . . Retail ea. $12.95
2491CAF823 Colonial Blue . . . . Retail ea.   12.95

D FOOTED CAKEPLATE. Lends party charm! Genuine Thumb print Milk Glass edged with frilly French ruffle. Use as salver or torte plate, too! 13 in. diameter, 5 in. high. Shpg. wt. 6½ lbs.
4413MIF530 . . . . Retail $7.95

E 4-PC. EPERGNE SET. Enchanting accessory leads a double life! Remove flower holders to make fruit/ snack bowl, 10 in. diameter. Flawlessly fashioned in Thumb print Milk Glass, 9 in. high. Wt. 6 lbs.
4401MIF620 . . . . Retail $9.95

F 12 IN. CRIMPED ROUND BOWL. Delicately shaped for rare elegance! So expressive in Thumb print Milk Glass. (Add candle holders for an outstanding console ensemble.) Shpg. wt. 5¾ lbs.
4427MIF397 . . . . Retail $5.95

G PAIR OF CANDLE HOLDERS. Live graciously in the soft glow of candlelight! Thumb print Milk Glass enhances the flickering glow. Each 8½ in. high. (Candles not included.) Shpg. wt. 4 lbs.
4473MIF597 . . . . Retail pr. $8.95

H 7 IN. HANDLED BASKET. Romantic Thumb print Milk Glass to grace a table heaped with fruit, to add lustre to living, to hold sweet violets! Delicately proportioned . . . swept-up ruffle edge. Wt. 2¾ lbs.
4437MIF260 . . . . Retail $3.95

J 8½ IN. HANDLED BASKET. Sumptuous server of nuts, candies, fruits . . . picturesque "background" for flowers and plants. A treasured heirloom in flawless Thumb print Milk Glass. Shpg. wt. 3 lbs.
4438MIF330 . . . . Retail $4.95

K 2-PIECE CHIP 'N' DIP. Entertaining is festive fun with this party-time Milk Glass favorite! Serve appetizers, chips from 13 in. scalloped-edge plate. Center footed bowl holds "dip". Wt. 6 lbs.
4404MIF565 . . . . Retail set $8.50

L PAIR OF BUD VASES. Stately and graceful, these 8 in. tall glistening Milk Glass vases display flowers with pride. Enchanting in any setting, any room . . . in pairs or alone. Shpg. wt. 1¾ lbs.
4456MIF330 . . . . Retail pr. $4.95

M COVERED SUGAR and CREAMER. Piquantly picturesque in rich Thumb print Milk Glass enhanced by fluted edges. Footed sugar bowl has cover. Matching creamer with handle. Shpg. wt. 2 lbs.
4403MIF272 . . . . Retail set $3.95

N SALT and PEPPER SET. Bring charming warmth to your table! Pure white Milk Glass with hand crafted Thumb print design is an elegant touch in every decor. Each 4 in. tall. Shpg. wt. 1 lb.
4408MIF190 . . . . Retail set $2.95

P FOOTED NUT DISH. Glistening server for tidbits or sweetmeats. Rich Thumb print design captured in pure white Milk Glass. A favorite of every hostess! 5½ in. high. Shpg. wt. 2 lbs.
4428MIF183 . . . . Retail $2.75

R COLONIAL VASE. Hand-made reproduction of a treasure from Early American art! Created in small polka dot optic glass. 11 in. high. Wt. 3 lbs.
2462CAF447 Colonial Amber . . . . . . Retail $6.95
2462CBF447 Colonial Blue . . . . Retail   6.95

S OVAL CANDY BOX. Tempting treasure! Exquisite Thumb print Milk Glass footed bowl with cover lends itself to many attractive and useful purposes. Shpg. wt. 2¾ lbs.
4486MIF310 . . . . Retail $4.75

T SQUARE PLANTER. Fill this sparkling Thumb print Milk Glass beauty with a nosegay of bright flowers. See how it adds gaiety to the whole room! Size: 4¼ in. square x 4 in. high. Shpg. wt. 2 lbs.
4497MIF183 . . . . Retail $2.75

U 10 IN. PLANTER. Show off your greenery the prettiest way! Right in this enchanting Thumb print Milk Glass holder. Fill with fresh or pretend plants. 10x4½x4 in. high. Wt. 4½ lbs.
4490MIF381 . . . . Retail $5.50

CR 140 Catalog sheet from 1962. The bud vases (L), 8½" basket (J), and the epergne set (E) were also offered in Topaz Opalescent by some catalog houses. The courting lamps (B and C) and the vases (R) were made in Fenton's Colonial Blue and Colonial Amber, but the optic pattern on them was different from Fenton's regular line.

136

Olde Virginia
Carnival Glass
...made from
original formula

Williamstown, West Virginia 26187

9120 CN
Console

9151 CN
Ftd. Nut Dish

1964 CN
Bootee

9180 CN
Candy Box

1992 CN
Hat

9158 CN
Swung Vase

1995 CN
Slipper

CR 142 In 1971, carnival glass was added to Olde Virginia Glass; these articles were all marked with the OVG logo.

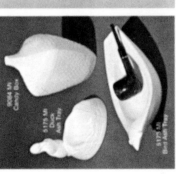

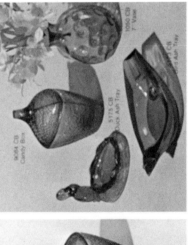

Olde
Virginia
Glass

Williamstown, W. Va. 26187

CR 141 By 1969, Olde Virginia Glass was available in Milk Glass and four other colors: Colonial Amber; Colonial Blue; Colonial Green; and Orange. These four hues were Olde Virginia staples from 1969-79. The Duck ash tray was a Verlys mould.

137

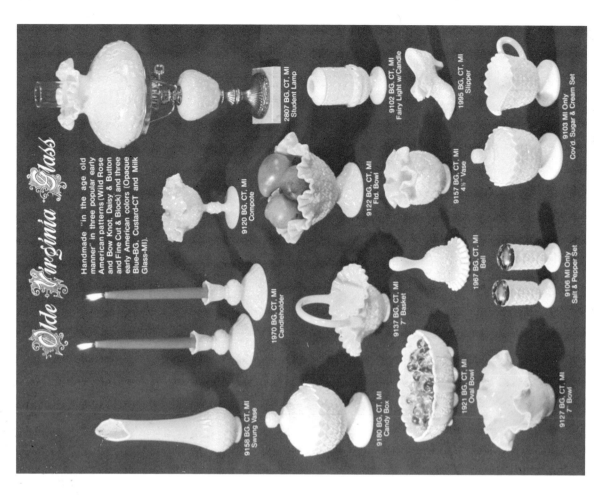

Olde Virginia Glass

Handmade "in the age old manner" in three popular early American patterns (Wild Rose and Bow Knot, Daisy & Button and Fine Cut & Block) and three early American colors (Opaque Blue-BG, Custard-CT and Milk Glass-MI).

9158 BG, CT, MI
Swung Vase

1970 BG, CT, MI
Candleholder

9120 BG, CT, MI
Compote

2807 BG, CT, MI
Student Lamp

9102 BG, CT, MI
Fairy Light w/Candle

1995 BG, CT, MI
Slipper

9103 MI Only
Cov'd. Sugar & Cream Set

9122 BG, CT, MI
Ftd. Bowl

9157 BG, CT, MI
4½" Vase

9137 BG, CT, MI
7" Basket

1967 BG, CT, MI
Bell

9106 MI Only
Salt & Pepper Set

9180 BG, CT, MI
Candy Box

1921 BG, CT, MI
Oval Bowl

9127 BG, CT, MI
7" Bowl

CR 144   Opaque Blue and Custard joined Milk Glass as part of Olde Virginia Glass production in 1976. Neither the Custard nor the Opaque Blue had the satin finish characteristic of Fenton's regular line.

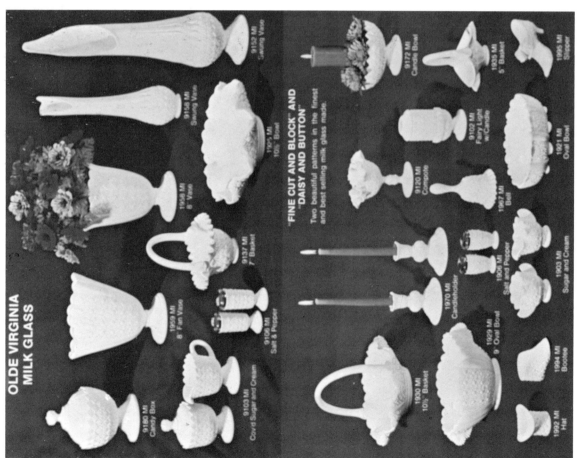

OLDE VIRGINIA MILK GLASS

9152 MI
Swung Vase

9158 MI
Swung Vase

1995 MI
10" Bowl

1958 MI
8" Vase

9137 MI
7" Basket

1959 MI
6" Fan Vase

9106 MI
Salt & Pepper

9180 MI
Candy Box

9103 MI
Cov'd Sugar and Cream

1992 MI
Hat

"FINE CUT AND BLOCK" AND "DAISY AND BUTTON"

Two beautiful patterns in the finest and best selling milk glass made.

9172 MI
Candle Bowl

1935 MI
5" Basket

1995 MI
Slipper

9120 MI
Compote

9102 MI
Fairy Light
w/Candle

1967 MI
Bell

1921 MI
Oval Bowl

1970 MI
Candleholder

1906 MI
Salt and Pepper

1903 MI
Sugar and Cream

1930 MI
10½" Basket

1909 MI
9" Oval Bowl

1904 MI
Bootee

CR 143   These items were available in Milk Glass as well as the other colors (Colonial Amber, Colonial Blue, Colonial Green, and Orange) in 1973. By this time, all Olde Virginia items were being marked with the OVG logo.

Fine Handblown Glass

LAMP PARTS

MANUFACTURED BY

The Fenton Art Glass Company

WILLIAMSTOWN, WEST VIRGINIA

COLOR CODE

AL—Amber w Opal FO—French Opalescent
AR—Amber   HS—Honeysuckle
BY—Burgundy   RL—Rose Opalescent

CR 145-146-147 In the early 1950s, Fenton made special items for manufacturers of lamps and ceiling fixtures. At first, these were offered only in large quantity lots, but a Fenton west coast representative, Richard Craven, suggested that smaller quantities be offered. These three catalog pages illustrate various lamp parts in Fenton stock between 1955 and 1966. In 1966, Fenton began to offer lamps in the regular line, and these lamp parts were phased out over the next few years.

The Burgundy (BY) color in CR 145 was different from Fenton's regular Cranberry color, which is cased. Rose Opalescent was the Burgundy color cased with French Opalescent. The Coin Dot pattern items in CR 145 were also made in Cranberry Opalescent.

CR 148-149-150   Additional lamp parts in Fenton colors.

The Hobnail parts in CR 147 were available in Cranberry Opalescent (CR) and Amber (AR). The Wild Rose with Bowknot pattern items (second row from the bottom) were available in Milk Glass, Peach Blow, and Honey Amber.

Fine Handblown Glass LAMP PARTS

G-1428 S-1
G-1428 FO
S-1424 FO
P-1454 FO
S-1455 FO
S-1471 FO

P-1425 FO
N-1424 FO
T-3720 HA
T-3866 CR

Detailed descriptions and fitter sizes are given in our current price list. The price list designates those illustrated items carried in stock, and those available in turn lot quantities only.

3832 HA
3831 HA
T-3753 HA
T-3853 HA
T-3870 HA
T-3866 CR
T-3867 CR

MANUFACTURED BY

The Fenton Art Glass Company

WILLIAMSTOWN, WEST VIRGINIA

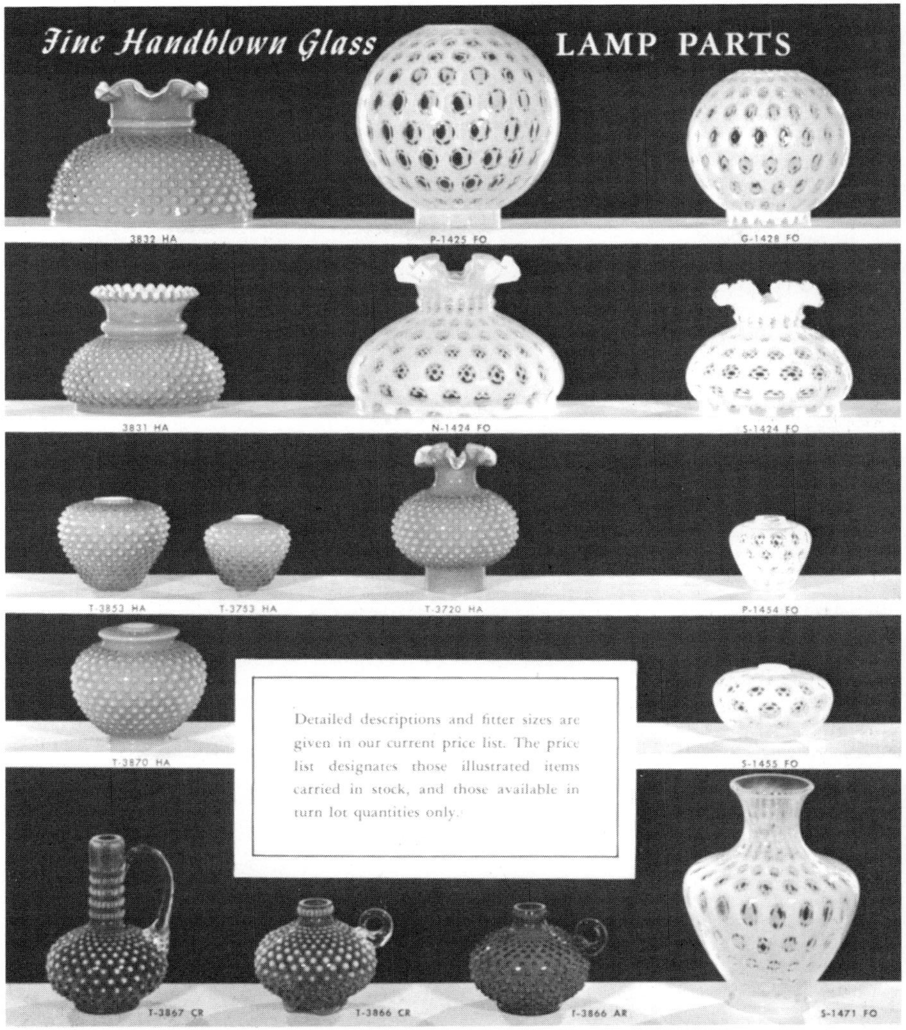

COLOR CODE

AR—Amber   FO—French Opalescent   HA—Honey Amber
CR—Cranberry   HA—Honey Amber

Fine Handblown Glass LAMP PARTS

G-1425 HS
P-1421 HS
N-1424 HD

G-1450 HS
S-1455 HD
S-1429 HS

S-9071 AR
T-9052 CG
P-1454 CG
S-1455 CG
S-1455 AR
G-3732 AR

S-9021 CG
S-1424 CG
N-1424 CG
N-1424 AR

G-1473 HS
G-1432 HS
T-1429 HS

P-1457 HS

MANUFACTURED BY

The Fenton Art Glass Company

WILLIAMSTOWN, WEST VIRGINIA

COLOR CODE

AR—Amber   HD—Honeydew
CG—Colonial Green   HS—Honeysuckle

HORIZON

designed by Michael Lax for *Fenton*

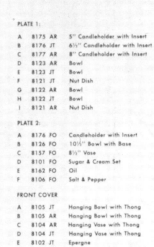

PLATE 1:

A	8175 AR	5" Candleholder with Insert
B	8176 JT	6½" Candleholder with Insert
C	8177 AR	8" Candleholder with Insert
D	8123 AR	Bowl
E	8123 JT	Bowl
F	8121 JT	Nut Dish
G	8122 AR	Bowl
H	8122 JT	Bowl
I	8121 AR	Nut Dish

PLATE 2:

A	8176 FO	Candleholder with Insert
B	8126 FO	10½" Bowl with Base
C	8157 FO	8½" Vase
D	8101 FO	Sugar & Cream Set
E	8162 FO	Oil
F	8106 FO	Salt & Pepper

FRONT COVER

A	8105 JT	Hanging Bowl with Thong
B	8105 AR	Hanging Bowl with Thong
C	8104 AR	Hanging Vase with Thong
D	8104 JT	Hanging Vase with Thong
E	8102 JT	Epergne

PLATE 2

For well over a half a century Fenton has specialized in Early American designs — and very successfully too!

However, knowing that you have a number of contemporary minded customers we have had Michael Lax, a young inspirational contemporary designer, develop the "Horizon" line as shown on the front and back covers. "Horizon" is a marriage of beautiful Fenton colors, rubbed walnut wood tops, porcelain candle cups and bases, and rawhide thongs — as new as tomorrow; functional and beautiful, truly a pace setting achievement that has long been our forte — and always with you our customers in mind.

8103 Hangers needed with 8104 & 8105

PLATE 1

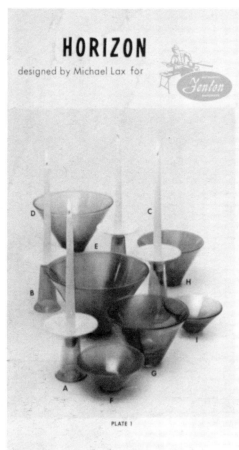

...because you ask for them-

Fenton

NEW STYLES
in
Proven Patterns
.....and Colors

For the story of this line designed by Michael Lax: see p. 22.

TEARDROP MILKGLASS

A. 6901 MI   Sugar and Cream
B. 6963 MI   Oil Cruet
C. 6929 MI   9" Bowl
D. 6983 MI   Ftd. Candy Box

JUST OUT

If you buy enough Fenton to make a good table display, you'll want one of our new distinctive Fenton counter cards. When you place your order, be sure to ask for it.

E. 6913 MI   Ftd. Cakeplate
F. 6985 MI   Candy Box
G. 6997 MI   Sandwich Tray
H. 6974 MI   Candleholder

Fenton

THE FENTON ART GLASS COMPANY, WILLIAMSTOWN, WEST VIRGINIA

New Milk Glass pieces in the Teardrop pattern — January 1957

hobnail milkglass

What more can we say about Hobnail Milk Glass? It continues to outsell every other pattern and color in our line or in any other line. Color and style trends have not affected the continuing demand for Fenton Hobnail Milk Glass.

Five versatile new service items are featured for 1970. The sixth item shown, the 3822 MI, is an old favorite which we redesigned to make even more attractive.

And for those many of you who asked, we have also designed a cute little Miniature Sugar to go with the popular Miniature Cream.

5170 RU

5170 CA

The Year of the Butterfly

You'll be delighted with these sparkling little creatures. They will add a little fun and excitement to any display ... and to your spring sales. Whether you scatter them throughout your shop or create a Butterfly table, we think your customers will be happily choosing Butterflies.

They are packed six to a carton in the assorted colors. And, by the way, an interesting sales tip for your sales people — Butterflies are the Oriental symbol for a happy marriage. Be sure you have enough to make all your customers happy.

HOBNAIL

3709 MI Two Tier Server
3822 MI Chip 'n Dip
3702 MI Sugar and Cream
3647 MI Egg Cup
3607 MI Handled Divided Relish
3605 MI Covered Mustard w/Spoon
3822 MI Divided Relish
3601 MI Covered Jam Jar w/Spoon

New Hobnail Milk Glass pieces added in January 1970

Fenton Poppy Lamps

9100 LS 19" Student Lamp
9100 CU 19" Student Lamp
16" Lamps 9104 MI — Oil 9105 MI — Electric
18" Lamps 9104 CU — Oil 9105 CU — Electric
9100 MI 19" Student Lamp
9100 BA 19" Student Lamp

New Poppy pattern lamps in satin colors and milk — January 1975

2701 SH HONEYCOMB 21" STUDENT LAMP
1501 SB SATIN BLUE OVERLAY 21" STUDENT LAMP PEWTER FINISH
1401 HA COIN DOT 21" STUDENT LAMP
1406 HA COIN DOT 20" STUDENT LAMP
1306 SB BUBBLE OPTIC 20" STUDENT LAMP PEWTER FINISH

New student lamps in HA, SH, SB July 1976

143

DECORATION CODES
1956-1980

Listed below are the major decoration codes which can be found in three or more shapes. Other decorations which were extremely limited can be found listed under OTHER SPECIAL CODES.

AB — APPLE BLOSSOM
7/1969-12/1970 (see p. 84)
Pink Flowers on Silver Crest.

BB — BLUEBELLS ON HOBNAIL
1971-72 (see p. 83, 131)
Blue flowers on milk glass Hobnail.

BC — BLUEBIRDS ON CUSTARD
1977-1979 (see p. 115)
Bluebirds on custard satin glass. Same code used for black crest at a different time (1970).

BD — BURMESE WITH TRANSFER LEAVES
1970-1972 (see p. 81)
A transfer decoration of oak leaves on Burmese.

BD — BLUE DOGWOOD ON CAMEO SATIN
1980-1982 (see pp. 126, 127)
The story of the blue flowers with five petals which became "Blue Dogwood" is told on page 46.

BL — BLUE ROSES ON BLUE SATIN
1978-1983 (see p. 82)
Used first in 1973 on the 5140 egg in custard satin with blue rose.

BQ — BLUE ROSES ON CUSTARD
1981
A special assortment of small items; blue roses with green leaves.

BY — BUTTERFLIES
1977-1978 (see pp. 84, 115)
Delicate yellow and blue flowers and butterflies on milk glass.

CD — DAISIES ON CAMEO SATIN
7/1978-1983 (see p. 114)
Spray of rusty-orange daisies on a beige shade of satin glass.

CH — HOLLY ON CUSTARD
7/1972-1981
Holly spray on satin custard glass.

CV — CHRISTMAS MORN
1978 Christmas Classics (see pp. 82, 115)
A snowy church in the woods painted on custard satin.

CW — CARDINALS IN WINTER
7/1977-1979 (see pp. 84, 115)
Dramatic and popular red cardinals on milk glass.

DB — DECORATED BURMESE
1973-1980 (see p. 81)
A hand-painted scene with trees and hills.

DC — DAISIES ON CUSTARD
1975-1982 (see pp. 82, 114)
White coralene brown-eyed daisy sprays on custard satin.

DH — HOLLY ON MILK
7/1971-1975 (see p. 84)
Tiny sprays of holly on milk glass Hobnail.

DR — CHOCOLATE ROSES ON CAMEO SATIN
1979-1982 (see p. 82)
Brown roses on beige satin glass.

DV — DECORATED VIOLETS (VIOLETS IN THE SNOW) (1969-84 (see pp. 83, 113)
Tiny violets on milk glass or Silver Crest.

GH — 1980 "GOING HOME"
1980 only (see p. 128)
A horse-drawn sleigh scene for annual CHRISTMAS CLASSICS.

LC — LOG CABIN ON CUSTARD
1977-present (see p. 82)
Custard satin glass with log cabin in the woods.

LR — LOVE ROSE ON RUBY
1979-1980 (see p. 113)
A single white rose and the word "Love" on ruby.

LW — LOVE ROSE ON WHITE
1979-1980 (see p. 113)
A single pinkish rose and the word "Love" on milk glass.

NB — "NEW BORN"
1980 MOTHER'S DAY (see p. 124)
Baby bird on branch painted on custard satin.

NC — NATURE'S CHRISTMAS
1979 CHRISTMAS CLASSICS
Deer in the woods painted on custard satin.

OM — THE OLD MILL
1979-1980 (see p. 82)
River scene with old mill on custard satin—only 4 items.

PY — PINK ANEMONE or PINK BLOSSOM
(1973-PRESENT) (see pp. 102, 114)
Delicate pink coralene flowers on custard glass.

RB — ROSE BURMESE
1971-1980 (see p. 81)
Hand-painted pinkish roses on blown Burmese.

RC — ROSES ON CUSTARD
1977-1983
Pinkish roses on custard satin glass.

RD — ROSES ON RUBY
1979-Present (see p. 113)
White enamel roses on ruby.

RH — HOLLY ON RUBY
7/1972-1982
White enamel holly sprays on ruby.

RW — ROSES ON MILK
1974-1975 (see p. 84)
Pink enamel roses on milk glass (usually Hobnail).

SS —SUNSET ON CAMEO SATIN
   1980-1982 (see p. 126)
   Scene of rustic old barn with a pale orange sunset effect.

WD —WHITE DAISIES (ON BLACK)
   1972-76 (see p. 91)
   Enamelled white daisies on ebony.

YR —YELLOW ROSES
   7/1969 (see p. 84)
   Large yellow roses on Silver Crest.

COLOR CODES FOR 1955-1980

The forty pages of color found in this book are a satisfactory representation of the wide variety of colors and decorations made for the Fenton line from 1956 through 1980. But I must emphasize the word "representation," as a few colors and shapes were only in the line for a brief period. These examples are quite difficult to locate today, appearing occasionally at antique shows, flea markets, household auctions, garage sales, even second-hand shops, rummage sales and pawn shops. Astute collectors and dealers can pick them up for a fraction of their collectable value. The reasons that production was so limited at the time of their inclusion in the line are simple: poor sales or production problems. Today's rarities are yesterday's failures. However, from time to time the Fenton lines were changed to keep their offerings fresh and varied. Old colors were discontinued and new, more marketable colors were introduced.

AB —APPLE BLOSSOM
   1/1960-7/1961 (see pp. 65-84-85)
   This "crest" color code, first appearing in the 1960 catalogue, was discontinued by July of the following year, 1961. It combines milk glass with a spun edge of opaque pink glass. During the 1½ years offered, it was made in only eight items. This AB code was also used later for the "Apple Blossom" decoration on Silver Crest.

AG —APPLE GREEN (OVERLAY)
   1961 only (see p. 73)
   This combination of a light green over milk glass interior is especially lovely, and was used on the "Hobnail," "Jacqueline," "Wild Rose and Bowknot" and other special Victorian shapes. Even though the 1961-62 catalogue shows this color, production of AG was limited to 1961 only. The 1962 price list includes no items in AG.

AO —AUTUMN ORANGE (GOLD AVENTURINE)
   7/64 to 12/1967 (see p. 76)
   Another beautiful cased color, combining unusual Fall colors of brown and orange over milk white, which was part of Fenton's Vasa Murrhina line. 12 different items were offered in the 1965 catalogue, but this was cut back to only five shapes in 1967.

AR —AMBER (Antique Amber—see also CA)
   1/1959 to 12/1980
   This AR color code, used for their transparent amber, was first used in 1959 for a color called "Antique Amber" in the catalogue. In 1963, both codes AR and CA (Colonial Amber) were used, with the latter code settling in for the remainder of the color's life. Amber was used on a wide variety of novelties and lamps. The color was last offered in 1980 for a dozen assorted shapes in Hobnail.

BA —BLUE SATIN
   1973-1984 (see p. 79)
   This soft satin glass can be a base color of either "Blue Marble," with swirls of white in the glass, or a more homogeneous blue milk glass. The final appearance of the color code was in the 1984 catalogue, limited to two different POPPY pattern lamps and a line of decorated ware known as "Frosted Asters." The color was a staple used on the limited-edition annual "Christmas in America" (1970-81) and "Madonna" Mother's Day (1970-79) plates.

BC —BLUE CREST
   1963 only (see p. 85)
   The January, 1963 supplement offered a limited number of shapes (only 8) in three crest colors, including this milk glass with a spun blue edge, and the same shapes in Flame Crest (FC) and Gold Crest (GC). The blue edge is a more vibrant, darker color than that found on the old Aqua Crest made in the 1940's. Items made: 7428, 7329, 7228, 7429, 7294, 7474, 7321, 7213.

BK —BLACK
   (see p. 70, 91) 1968-1976; 1981-82
   Also called Ebony, this opaque "black amethyst" was brought back into the Fenton line in 1962 with a combination black and milk glass Hobnail salt and pepper set (see code BW). Six years later, four pieces of the "Thumbprint" pattern were made in black, and the use of the color expanded gradually afterward into other items. The peak year was 1969, with 13 items offered in black. Rarities in BK today include the "Grape & Cable" candy jar, the Mandarin and Empress vases and the No. 3872 Hobnail candle bowl. See also WD under decoration codes for "White Daisies" decorated black glass.

BM —BLUE MIST
   (see p. 76) 1964 only
   This "spatter glass" color combines blue and white in a crystal casing. Production of the Fenton line of this color was limited to only nine shapes in the year 1964.

BN — BLUE OPALINE
1960 only

This color is a light blue opaline, limited to only two shapes in the JACQUELINE pattern, the No. 9153 5″ vase and the No. 9152 7″ tulip vase. The pattern was expanded the following year into a number of other shapes and overlay colors, but the "opaline" colors (see also YN and PN) were discontinued.

BO — BLUE OPALESCENT
1959-64; 1979-1981

This color has been appearing and disappearing from the Fenton line ever since they started making glass in 1907. During the third quarter-century, BO was offered from 1959 through 1964, and then again from 1978 until 1981. Today, the firm offers a new shade of this treatment, called "Provincial Blue Opalescent" (Color Code: 00). Some "Hobnail" and "Coin Dot" items made brief re-entries in BO in 1959. In 1978-81, BO was made in several shapes in the Lily of the Valley pattern.

BR — BURMESE
1970-present (see p. 81)

This recreation of the long-lost Burmese color created and patented by the Mt. Washington Glass Works one-hundred years ago has remained in the Fenton line since 1970. The color was possible only in mold-blown ware until 1986, when BR was successfully introduced in pressed wares. The color was offered before 1980 in plain (BR), decorated (see DB) and with hand-painted roses (see RB).

BU — BLUE
1960-12/1963

This code for a pale blue transparent color was rarely used, applied mostly to the Nos. 9175 and 9176 modern "Swirled" ash trays (introduced 1960—discontinued 1970). In 1964 the color of blue made in these ash trays was changed to the darker Colonial Blue (see CB).

BV — POWDER BLUE OVERLAY
1961/62 (see p. 79)

Even though this light blue overlay encased with white was introduced in January, 1961 supplement, and was also shown in the 61-62 catalogue, it actually remained in the line for only one year. The color was not listed in the 1962 price list.

BW — BLACK AND WHITE
1962-12/1977

This code was used exclusively for the Hobnail salt and pepper shakers, one in black, another in white. These were introduced in 1962 and last appeared in the 1977-78 catalogue.

CA — COLONIAL AMBER
1962-80 (see p. 71, 87, 88, 89, 90)

A wide variety of patterns, novelties and lamps were made in amber, which has been called Antique Amber (AR) and Colonial Amber (CA). There is no difference in intensity between the two colors, despite the fact that both codes appear in the 1963 catalogue. See also AR.

CB — COLONIAL BLUE
1962-12/1979 (see p. 70, 87, 88, 89, 90)

This deep sapphire blue transparent color was used for many different items in the Fenton line. Colonial Blue can be found on most of the major table lines—Thumbprint, Fenton Roses, Valencia, and Hobnail. CB made its final appearance to date in a line of 11 hobnail shapes in 1979. The same formula was used also in a line of overlay, creating the Opaque Blue (OB).

CG — COLONIAL GREEN
1963-12/1976 (see p. 70, 87, 88, 89)

This shade of transparent green is "olive" colored, different from the emerald green color made earlier by Fenton. The major table lines and a wide variety of novelties and lamps were produced in CG. In overlay, with a white interior, the color was called Shelley Green (OG), used only on a line of lamps.

CI — CUSTARD HANGING HEART
1976 only (see p. 47, 95, 101)

True to form, the Fenton firm reached into its own history for the idea for this line, redeveloped by Robert Barber in 1975. See p. 47, 95. The shapes made are shown in this book on page 101, from the 1976 catalogue supplement. But the life of the pattern was short-lived, with the line being removed from the catalogue in 1977. Only ten items were made in CI and TH (Turquoise Hanging Heart), but being art glass, there are probably a number of experimental or sample rarities to be found. This was iridescent glass.

CK — CHOCOLATE
1/1976-12/1976 (see p. 45, 94)

This old "Greentown" color formula, created by Jacob Rosenthal (who worked for Fenton during most of the company's early years) was pulled out of mothballs and made a very brief reappearance for America's Bicentennial. In the Fenton line, the color was limited to the same seven shapes in which the Patriot Red (PR), Valley Forge White (VW) and Independence Blue (IB) limited editions were made. However, Fenton did make many other items for LeVay in this color, and a few test pieces are known to exist.

CL — CORAL
1961 only (see p. 73)

This peachy overlay color is often confused for the pink Wild Rose (WR) overlay color, but the two are entirely different (compare pages 72 and 73). Even though the color appeared in the 1961-62 catalogue, no Coral items were offered in the 1962 price list. Thus, production was limited to 1961 only. 14 different shapes were made.

CN — ORIGINAL FORMULA CARNIVAL
1970-1983 (see p. 93)

Even though the Fenton color codes sometimes describe this Carnival glass as "blue green," the true base color is a deep amethyst. The iridescent highlights are blue and green in nature. The color and iridescence are so much like the old Fenton carnival (from circa 1907 to 1920), that the glass must be held up to a bright light to check the base color. The Fenton trademark used on the "reintroductions" helps to protect the investment value of the company's original, highly collectable patterns. Each year, new items were added and others discontinued to keep the line of "carnival glass" fresh and interesting to new generations of collectors.

CO — ORANGE CARNIVAL
7/1971-12/1973 (see p. 118)

Often called "marigold" carnival by collectors, this color was made in 14 different shapes from July, 1971 to the end of 1973. Many of the items offered were reproductions from old molds, with the Fenton trademark carved into the base of the mold to aid collectors in identifying the correct production period. This color code was reassigned, see below.

CO — CAMEO OPALESCENT
1979-1982 (see pp. 100, 121)

Another color which was "reintroduced," after almost a fifty year absence, was the Cameo Opalescent, originally made by Fenton during the 1920's (see Fenton 1, p. 72). 28 different items were introduced in January, 1979, but only 15 were shown in the catalogue two years later (1981-82 catalogue). By 1983, the color was no longer being made.

CP — COLONIAL PINK
1962-1968 (see pp. 86, 87, 90)

This transparent "pink" pressed glass, different from the color of the popular machine-made "rose" colored glass of the depression era, was first shown in the January, 1962 catalogue supplement. Its final year was 1968. It was most commonly made in the Thumbprint and Fenton Roses table lines, but other novelties were occasionally offered in the color. It is slightly different from a new 1988 Fenton color, Dusty Rose.

CR — CRANBERRY OPALESCENT
1956-present (see pp. 67, 68)

Hobnail and Coin Dot are just two of several mold-blown designs made from their original introduction during the second quarter-century into the third 25 years. Cranberry Hobnail remained the longest, being discontinued (except for lamps) in December, 1977. Only 12 items remained in the line that year. However, the color was occasionally resurrected in a few items in Fenton's Connoisseur Collection.

CS — CRYSTAL SATIN
1972-1974

This code was first introduced in 1972 for a small (7 items) line of frosted crystal figurals. The Praying Boy & Girl and Happiness Bird remained in the line until 1974. A similar, softer satin crystal was introduced in 1977 and the name was changed to VE (Crystal Velvet).

CT — CUSTARD
1975-1976 (see p. 138)

Only two items in Hobnail, the No. 3872 candle bowl and a small 8″ crimped vase (No. 3958), were in the line in this color, which is the much-used custard satin (CU) without the acid finish. Undoubtedly a few test pieces were made in this color. Also made in the "Olde Virginia Glass" line in 1976.

CU — CUSTARD SATIN
1/1972 to present (see p. 102)

This popular color has remained in the line since it was introduced in 1972, and is used as a base color for a wide variety of decorations (Roses on Custard, Pink Daisies, Daisies on Custard, etc.) The long-lived Log Cabin on Custard is presently (1988) being offered in 5 different items, and a CU 9101 Poppy lamp also appears in the 1988 line.

CY — CRYSTAL
1956-present

This colorless, transparent glass has never been too successful for a company which is identified with colored glass production, but Crystal made a frequent appearance in the Fenton line. Certain occasional items, like the punch bowl ladle, the flower arranger and mayonnaise ladle, made the color code necessary in most of the catalogues. However, in January, 1968, 17 items in Fenton's best-selling Hobnail pattern were offered in crystal, (see p. 27), and the following year the Valencia line was offered in 10 different shapes in CY. With a satin finish, crystal was called Crystal Satin (CS) or Crystal Velvet (VE).

FC — FLAME CREST
1963 only (see p. 84, 85)

This is milk glass with a spun red-orange colored edge. Made in only eight different shapes, just as were BC and GC. A rare and desirable color on the collectors' market.

FO — FRENCH OPALESCENT
(1956-68)

Made intermittently and in limited quantities from 1956 to 1968 in both pressed and blown opalescent patterns, including Hobnail, Coin Dot and the Empress and Mandarin vases. In 1980, the color returned in plain and decorated ware and has remained in the line ever since. Recently called French Cream.

GB — AVENTURINE GREEN WITH BLUE
1964-68 (see p. 76)

One of the Vasa Murrhina colors, with green and blue encased in white, this color first appeared in 9 shapes in January, 1964. Four years later, only 5 shapes were being offered.

GC — GOLD CREST
1963-12/1964 (see p. 84)

Milk glass with a spun Colonial amber edge. The items in the line are those same eight shapes listed under Blue Crest (8 items only). Unlike BC and FC, Gold Crest was continued into the 1964 price list, being discontinued at the end of that year. It is thus easier to find on the collectors' market than its sister colors.

GD — GOLDENROD
7/1956 to 12/1956 (see p. 75)

This overlay color with a very limited life is very popular today, and a number of experimental or test shapes keep surfacing. Only seven shapes were shown in the July, 1956 Catalogue in GD, and one more (the No. 3859 Hobnail 8″ vase) offered in the accompanying price list. The color is basically the same formula used on the earlier Gold Overlay and Yellow Cased colors from circa 1949-50. The color on all three can range in intensity, from golden amber to bright yellow, depending upon the thickness of the casing. There were some production problems with the color, so it was taken out of the line by the end of 1956, and does not appear in the 1957 price list.

GN — GREEN
1/1960 (code changed to GR)

Fenton made a few different shades of green transparent glass, mostly the olive-shaded Colonial Green (CG) and the deeper emerald Springtime Green (GT). The codes GN and GR were both used to denote the dark transparent green in which the Nos. 9175 and 9176 "Modern Swirl" ash trays were made. The 1961 catalogue changed the code to GR for the same ash trays. In 1965, the green color used on these same ash trays was CG. The following year a cigarette lighter was designed to match, also made in CG.

GO — GREEN OPALESCENT
7/1959-7/1961 (see p. 68)

In July, 1959, 12 different items in Hobnail were added to the Fenton line in green opalescent (GO). For two years, this color was limited to Hobnail and the three shapes made in the "Beatty Waffle" (see Fenton 2, Fig. 504) design. The COIN DOT items shown in this book are in the earlier Lime Opalescent cased color, made before 1955.

GR — GREEN 7/1961 to 12/1962
(Code changed to GT in 1977)

See notes under GN above for this color code, which was limited only to two modern ash trays, and a single Hobnail 4″ vase in 1962. In 1965, transparent green returned with the introduction of Colonial Green. Then again, in 1977, emerald green returned in 10 different shapes (see p. 100-CR19), including the modern ash trays (re-numbered 7075 and 7076).

GT — SPRINGTIME GREEN
1977-78 (see p. 90)

A special line of ten shapes, also made in WT, CA and CB, offered only in the 1977-78 catalogue. All shapes made in GT are shown in the Wisteria assortment on page 100 of this book (CR19). Springtime Green is generally the same as the chemical formula used to create the colored glass for the codes GR and GN—in other words, transparent emerald green.

HA — HONEY AMBER
1/1961 to 12/1967 (see p. 73, 140, 141)
Lamps 1977-78

This golden amber color cased with milk is an overlay color, available in special designs like Bubble Optic, Wild Rose and Bowknot, the Wheat vase, and a variety of lamps. A number of items in Hobnail were also made in HA. As in all overlay colors, the items are made from a blown mold procedure, and cannot be pressed. The January, 1967 catalogue lists HA in the color codes, but no item is shown within its pages. Production was limited to three Rose pattern lamps, shown only in the 1967 Lamp Supplement. Then again, in 1977-78, there was a brief reappearance of the color in lamps only (see p. 99).

IB — INDEPENDENCE BLUE CARNIVAL
7/1974-12/1976 (see p. 94)

In anticipation of the nation's upcoming Bicentennial, a special blue carnival glass formula and a number of limited edition shapes, were offered in July, 1974 and in January, 1975. The color was so well received, that a line of regular Fenton items was made in 1976 in IB. The color was discontinued at the end of 1976.

JA — JADE GREEN
Early 1980 only (see p. 125)

In 1980, Fenton made an abortive attempt to reintroduce their Jade Green opaque color, popular in the 1920's and 1930's, but quality control standards fifty years later were quite different from the earlier period, and the line was quickly discontinued because of production problems. 20 different shapes were made in this color, all marked with the Fenton-8 logo of the 1980's. These same shapes were made in Peking Blue (PK).

JB — JAMESTOWN BLUE (CASED)
1957-1958 (see p. 75)

The next three colors were made from the same basic color formula, the first being cased in white. JB has an inner layer of white and an outer layer of blue. The No. 7350 5″ vase and the No. 7262 12″ vase have the same color characteristics as JB, but with the addition of the silver crest spun edge, they are listed in the catalogues and price lists as SJ (Silver Jamestown). Only six different items were made in this color during the 2 years of production.

JM — JAMESTOWN BLUE WITH MILK
1957-1958 (see p. 75)

This color code was limited to the No. 1021 Ivy Ball, with a milk glass base and a transparent Jamestown Blue ball. This same Ivy Ball can be found with an emerald green (GM) and a cranberry (RO) ball.

JT — JAMESTOWN BLUE TRANSPARENT
1957-1958 (see p. 75)

Without the inner white lining, the code JT was used. Introduced in 1957, the shapes in this color were expanded in 1958 to eight different items, some of which are quite rare today. A real find would be the No. 6080 candy box, which was first made in JT and RO in 1958. JT had a polka dot optic.

LC —CASED LILAC
7/1955-6/1956 (see pp. 65, 74)

This rare color was made only in a limited number of shapes during the transitional period from the second to the third quarter century of Fenton's history. Introduced in July, 1955 (see Fenton 2, p. 133), production continued through June, 1956. Only six different shapes were made in this cased color, which combines an outer layer of Turquoise and an inside layer of Gold Ruby. See also F2, Fig. 465.

LM —LIME GREEN
7/1974 to 12/1976

This color has the same formula as that used on Lime Satin and Lime Sherbet, but with no satin finish. This code was used on only two items in Hobnail, usually with a floral arrangement. First offered in 1974 in a special Christmas candle bowl arrangement (No. 3872), the color was discontinued in late 1976. The No. 3956 Hobnail 6¼″ vase was also made in Lime Green, with special artificial flower arrangements which complemented the color.

LN —LAVENDER SATIN
1977-1978 (see p. 80)

This opaque satin glass color was only offered for two years, made in sixteen different shapes during its lifetime. Ten shapes were shown in the 1977-78 catalogue, and six more added in the 1978 supplement. But by 1979, the color was discontinued. The limited production and unusual color make this color much desired by collectors. A rarity would be a test piece without a satin finish.

LS —LIME SHERBET
1973-80 (see p. 80)

Lime Sherbet was first listed in the 1973-74 catalogue. This opaque green satin glass, appropriately named, was dropped from the line at the end of 1980. A large number of shapes, including lamps, were made during the eight years of production.

MB —BLUE MARBLE
1970 to 12/1973 (see p. 78, 101)

In January, 1970, the new Fenton catalogue supplement showed three types of glass not offered to consumers for forty years or longer—Burmese, Carnival and Blue Marble. This last color, which was known as "slag" or "mosaic" to glass collectors for many years, was made in pressed ware which captured the liquid characteristics of molten glass before solidification. Each piece is different, with the swirls of white and blue "frozen" in varying positions. Without the milk glass, the color would be the base color used on Blue Satin (BA).

MG —MILK WITH DARK GREEN
1953-12/1956

Used exclusively after 1955 for the No. 1021 Footed Ivy Ball, which had a white foot and an emerald green ball. This was out of the line by 1957, but the MR (Milk with Ruby Overly) version remained in the line much longer. This same ivy ball can be found with a Jamestown Blue ball or an amber ball.

MI —MILK GLASS
(Continuous production)

This Fenton mainstay color needs no introduction. Without any doubt, with the remarkable success of the Hobnail pattern in this color, more Milk Glass color was made than any other during the third 25 years of the company's history. This color was also used as the interior color on many of the Overlay colors, and was the basic color of the popular Silver Crest line. Milk glass with a satin finish was called White Satin (WS).

OB —OPAQUE BLUE
1/1962-12/1965 (see pp. 72, 77)

This absolutely gorgeous overlay color, combining deep Colonial blue over milk, is one of my personal favorites. The number of shapes made in this color is substantial, including Hobnail, Bubble Optic, and a variety of "Rib Optic" items. The color first appeared in the January, 1962 Catalogue supplement in 16 different shapes, but this was drastically cut back to only seven in 1963. In 1964, only the 11½″ Bubble Optic vase remained available. In 1967 and 1971, lamps were offered in "OB", which is listed next.

OB —BLUE OVERLAY
(Lamps only) 1967 and 1971

The descriptive name for "OB" was changed between 1965 and 1967, when only lamps were being offered. Today, any lamp in OB would be considered highly desirable. This overlay color combines a dark colonial blue over a milk glass interior. In July, 1976, the color was still being made in lamps, but this time with a smooth satin finish (see HB under special codes).

OE —ORANGE SATIN
1/1968 to 6/1968

In January, 1968, the No. 8251 Mandarin vase and No. 8252 Empress vase, made from newly acquired Verlys molds, were produced in transparent Orange (OR) and also a rare Orange with satin finish (OE). Both were in the line for only six months. These were the only two items offered in this color in the January, 1968 price list, and the color treatment was not offered again in the July, 1968 list.

OG —SHELLEY GREEN OVERLAY
1967 only

This overlay color, used only on lamps, was named after Bill Fenton's daughter. OG combined a very beautiful outer casing of Colonial Green over white, giving the green color an entirely different appeal. Unfortunately we do not have a colored illustration of OG to show you in this book. It was listed only in the 1967 price list and is extremely rare today.

OP —OPAL
1969 only

In the 1969-70 Catalogue, the color code OP was

149

included. It was used to describe the color of the No. 3604 Hobnail Boudoir lamp (disc: 1970), and the No. 3608 Fairy Light, both shown on page 32 of that catalogue. In addition, the price list for 1969 lists the No. 7249 cup in OP. After that year, the code was never used again. OP had heat resistant qualities.

OR —ORANGE
1963 to 12/1977 (see p. 88, 89)

The transparent Orange color is a type of pressed "amberina," with variegating reddish-amber highlights. The 1963-64 catalogue presented it in only seven shapes, mostly blown items, but the 1964 supplement expanded the color into pressed shapes. All of Fenton's table patterns, including Hobnail, Thumbprint, Valencia and Roses, found many of their shapes being offered in OR at one time or another. The color did run its course, however, and made its final appearance in the 1977 price list in eleven Hobnail shapes. No OR was offered in 1978, being discontinued before the next catalogue was printed.

PA —PLATED AMBERINA
1/1962 to 12/1963 (see p. 77)

This reintroduction of another Victorian treasure was limited to only two years, being introduced in the January, 1962 Supplement, in five different items. This was cut back to only four in 1963, and the color discontinued at the end of that year.

PC —PEACH CREST
1940-12/1969

This perennial favorite (see Fenton 2, p. 48) has been offered every year in one form or another ever since it was introduced in 1940. Dozens of shapes were made during the color's lifetime. In 1958 and 1959, 21 different items were made, but by 1963 only 8 shapes were offered. Only five standard shapes were made in the final year (1969), some of which are identical to items introduced in the 1940's.

PK —PEKING BLUE
Early 1980 only (see page 125)

This light blue opaque color was a remake of the old PEKIN BLUE from the 1920's. When it was brought back in early 1980, the color name was changed to "Peking" blue, but because of the same quality control problems which surfaced on Jade Green, the color was soon taken from the line in mid-year, a rare occurrence.

PN —PINK OPALINE
1960 only (see p. 77)

This color is a light purplish-pink opaline, limited to two vases in the JACQUELINE pattern, the No. 9153 5″ vase and the No. 9152 7″ tulip vase. The pattern was expanded the following year into a number of other shapes and overlay colors, but the "opaline" colors (see also YN and BN) were discontinued. The color is sometimes confused by collectors for plum opalescent (PO), which was made from the same formula.

PO —PLUM OPALESCENT
1/1959-12/1962 (see p. 69)

In 1958, plum opalescent was discovered during an attempt to create a cranberry color in pressed shapes. The glass came out of the mold a deep purple, so a new and very different line was born and introduced to customers in 1959. In 1960, 15 different shapes were made. However, it was not an easy color to control, so the line was cut back and eventually discontinued at the end of 1962.

PR —PATRIOT RED
1976 only (see p. 94)

This rare opaque red color, popularly known as "red slag" is a reintroduction of the old "Venetian Red" made by Fenton in the 1920's and the "Mandarin Red" of the early 1930's. The shapes made are limited to the Bicentennial items shown on page 54 in color.

RE —ROSALENE
1976-78 (see p. 103)

In the 1890's and very early 1900's a few factories here in this country produced a heat-sensitive color which combines pink opaque with swirls of white (today called "pink slag"). These desirable pieces are either pressed or mold-blown. In 1976 Fenton brought this color back from the past with the creation of Rosalene. No two pieces are exactly alike, with the variegation of color different on each piece made. About 20 different shapes were offered in this color during the three year production lifetime, but during the final year (1978), only five items remained in the line. A satin-finished color known as Satin Rosalene (SR) in "Candy Stripe" lamps was also offered in 1977-78. (See p. 99).

RG —ROSE WITH AVENTURINE GREEN
1964-67 (see p. 76)

This cased "vasa murrhina" color combines pink and green with flakes of mica, encased with a white interior. Since the glass predates the use of the Fenton trademark, the few shapes in which this glass is found are occasionally confused for earlier Victorian pieces made at the turn of the century. The shapes made are the same as those found in the AO and GB colors.

RM —ROSE MIST
1964-1965 (see p. 76)

This spatter color, with pink and white encased in clear, was introduced along with Blue Mist in 1964, but unlike the latter was continued through 1965 as production ware. It was introduced in nine shapes and expanded into 12 shapes in the 1965 catalogue. The No. 6465 pitcher is especially sought after. Two similar treatments with more intense pink and white coloring were made for a special line for Sears, which they sold as a part of a "Vincent Price National Treasures" collection of antique reproductions in 1968. The colors were CC—Cranberry Mist Crest and CM—Cranberry Mist. (See p. 77).

RN — RUBY IRIDESCENT
1976-77 (see pp. 93, 118)

Fenton was one of the first American factories to produce a ruby pressed iridescent ware around 1914, now popularly known as "red carnival." In 1976, a limited number of shapes were produced in this treatment. The color was expanded to about 15 items shown in the 1977-78 catalogue, but the color was discontinued at the end of 1977.

RO — RUBY OVERLAY
1956-1974 (see p. 77)

The color known to collectors as "cranberry," but referred to in the trade as ruby overlay, has been produced at Fenton intermittently from their early years. With an opalescent treatment it was known as CR (Cranberry). If this is not confusing enough, when the non-opalescent color returned to the line in 1982 in new shapes, the name was officially changed to "Country Cranberry" (CC). These later pieces are trademarked, but since the color is always mold-blown, the Fenton mark is sometimes melted out and hard to see.

RP — ROSE PASTEL
1954-57 (see p. 74)

This transitional period color is shown in the second Fenton book, p. 51. Introduced in 1954, RP was kept in production through 1957. It is similar to a "shell pink" color made by Jeannette and Fostoria during the 1950's. With the addition of a crystal spun edge, the color was called Silver Rose (SR). A few additional shapes not shown in color in F2 are shown on page 34 in Turquoise (TU).

RS — ROSE SATIN
1974-1977 (see pp. 80, 103)

The formula used to make Rosalene was also used to make a number of mold-blown items in a pink opaque known as Rose Satin. The color does not have the swirls of white in the glass found on Rosalene, a pressed glass color with a shiny surface. Only about a dozen shapes were made in Rose Satin, which was discontinued at the end of 1977. Especially popular today are the lamps.

RU — RUBY
1966-present (see pp. 71, 87, 88)

Fenton has been producing ruby pressed glass off-and-on since 1914. It was especially popular during the 1920's in iridescent ware and in the 1930's in tableware (see F1, p. 74; F2, pp. 30-31). Then the color disappeared from the line until it was revived in 1966 for a virtual permanent return. Ruby was at first limited mostly to various shapes in the Thumbprint pattern, but was later used to produce special Hobnail items and a line of decorated (RD, RH) and iridescent glass (RI). In 1979, two sizes of heart-shaped nappies with spun milk glass crimped edges made a brief appearance as part of a special Valentine's Day assortment.

SC — SILVER CREST
1940-1986 (see pp. 85, 110)

The story of Silver Crest, a milk glass color with a spun crystal edge, stands beside Hobnail as a long-time staple of the Fenton line. The peak years were the "Kennedy Years" (1960-63), when almost 70 different shapes were being made. In 1968, the addition of the Spanish Lace design to some of the shapes increased the appeal of the color, with expansion of this pattern to more than a dozen different items. At this same time, hand-painting was introduced on several Silver Crest shapes, and with the added ornamentation of floral motifs (DV, AB, YR), production was increased on the color. But the number of items made was gradually cut back over the next two decades, with only 14 pieces shown in the 1986 catalogue.

SJ — SILVER JAMESTOWN
1/1957 to 12/1959 (see pp. 65, 75)

Only seven shapes were made in this color, which encased the Jamestown Blue color in white, with a spun "silver crest" edge. Most often the blue color is on the inside (5 shapes) but on two items the blue is on the outside, causing some collectors to confuse the color for JB (which lacks the spun edge). Sometimes confused for Silver Turquoise (ST), which also has the spun crystal edge.

SR — SATIN ROSALENE
7/1976-1977 (see p. 99)

This color is quite different from Rosalene and Rose Satin, although it was made from the same pink opaque formula. The code was limited to three "Candy Stripe" lamps, offered only from July, 1976 to the end of 1977. These lamps are quite desirable among collectors because of the limited production and their unique beauty.

SR — SILVER ROSE
1956-57 (see p. 74)

The formula used on the Rose Pastel (RP) color was combined with a spun crystal edge for a very limited number of shapes in 1956 and 1957. The order forms for those years list seven shapes as available in the rare color.

ST — SILVER TURQUOISE
1956-58 (see p. 74)

The Turquoise (TU) opaque color, with a spun crystal edge, was called Silver Turquoise. The color remained in the line a year longer than the SR treatment and was made in twice as many shapes (14) during the three-year production life.

TH — TURQUOISE HANGING HEART
1976 only (see p. 101)

The catalogue reprint on page 101 tells the story of this limited-production color, which was an off-shoot of the Robert Barber "Hanging Heart" design (see page 95). Production was limited to 1976. 13 different shapes were listed in the January, 1976 price list, three more than the number shown in CR21 reprint on page 101.

TO —TOPAZ OPALESCENT
1959-62; 1980 (see pp. 66, 67, 70, 124)

Collectors may be confused about whether this color is "vaseline" or "canary" opalescent, but the official Fenton name for this lovely yellow has always been Topaz Opalescent (TO). Very little was made prior to 1940, when production was expanded for the Hobnail pattern, until 1944, when the uranium needed to create the color was no longer available. In 1959, TO returned in a variety of patterns and shapes, including Cactus, Coin Dot and the ever-present Hobnail. A rarity from this period would be the Ogee ash tray in this color. Then for almost 20 years, no TO was offered in the line, when in 1980 it made a brief return to the market in the Lily of the Valley pattern and a variety of "CollectiBells" (see p. 124).

TU —TURQUOISE
1955-58 (see p. 74)

Many pieces of this opaque color are shown in F2, p. 58, with other shapes shown in this third book, p. 34. TU is sometimes confused for the similar Blue Pastel (BP) made in 1954. With a spun edge in crystal, it is known as Silver Turquoise (ST). The color made its final appearance in the Fenton line in the 1958 catalogue in a dozen shapes of the Hobnail pattern.

VE —CRYSTAL VELVET
1977-present (see pp. 122, 123)

This soft, satin-finished crystal is not shown in this book in color. Most of the items made in VE before 1981 can be seen on pages 122, 123 of this book. A wide variety of animal figures, patterns and lamps were produced in Crystal Velvet during this period. The popularity of the color is witness to VE still being in the line today (1988).

VR —VELVA ROSE
1980-82 (see p. 129)

In June, 1980, Fenton again searched their history for a color idea, bringing back the soft, pastel iridized Velva Rose (see F1, p. 65), originally made in the mid-to-late 1920's. It was a special limited edition color made to commemorate the company's 75th Anniversary, being specially marked with the new Fenton trademark for the 1980's (a small number 8 appears within the oval logo.) Below and outside of the trademark appears "75th". As promised in the 1980 supplement, the 13 shapes made in VR were discontinued at the end of that year, but 15 new items were produced in Velva Rose for the 1981-82 catalogue.

WR —WILD ROSE
1961-62 (see p. 72)

One of the most beautiful of Fenton's overlay colors, this creation combines an outer casing of cranberry with an inside casing of white. Nothing like it had been produced since Victorian times, and it is a testament to the remarkable talent of the Fenton glassworkers. The all-too-short life of this and the other overlay colors of this period (AG, HA, BV, CL) can be found in a variety of patterns and novelties, including Hobnail, Wild Rose and Bowknot, and Jacqueline.

WS —WHITE SATIN
1/72-present (see p. 92)

Milk glass with a soft satin finish presents a perfect form on which to add a variety of outstanding decorations. Thus, this color has remained a staple in the line ever since its introduction in 1972. However, the code WS was restricted to undecorated examples of this color. The color was used primarily for a variety of collector's plates, the Bicentennial items, and a few lamps, but when it was first introduced about eight different figural items were offered in WS.

WT —WISTERIA
1977-78 (see pp. 90, 100)

This soft lavendar pressed glass color was only offered during a single catalogue season, being discontinued at the end of 1978. The shapes are limited to those shown on page 100, CR-19, most of which were new shapes brought out that year, all of which were also produced in Springtime Green (GT), Colonial Amber and Blue (CA, CB).

YL —YELLOW OPALINE
1960 (see p. 77)

See notes under PN for information on the brief history of this scarce translucent yellow color, made in only two shapes and for only a single year.

Other Special Limited Codes

The codes listed below were used only on special items of such extremely limited production, or in so few shapes that they should be listed separately. Sometimes these codes were changed and expanded into a major line, with a new color code assigned, at a later date.

BF —BARBER ART GLASS
(PULLED FEATHERS) see p. 95

BH —BITTERSWEET HANGING HEARTS p. 95

BL —BLUE ROSE ON 5140 BL DECORATED
EGG 1/73

BN —BROWN ROSE
1973

Same decoration as found on DR, used only for the No. 5140 egg in custard satin glass.

CV —CASCADE (BARBER COLLECTION)
see p. 95

EG —EGG PAPERWEIGHT
see p. 95

FL —FLORENTINE TREATMENT
(Nativity Bell—1980) p. 128

DA —MI HOBNAIL FLOWER ARRANGER WITH
ARTIFICIAL DAISIES

GL —GOLD ON WHITE SATIN
1975 to 12/1978
Used for special gold-decorated Anniversary
Plates in white satin.

GR —GREEN ROSE
1973-75 Decoration on 5140 GR EGG

HB —SATIN BLUE OVERLAY
(lamps—7/76)
This is the same formula used on the OB, for
lamps only, with a satin finish.

HB —BUTTERFLY WITH BLOSSOM ON HONEY
AMBER (lamp 77-78) see p. 99

LB —LABYRINTH—BARBER COLLECTION
p. 95

MD —MILK DECORATED
1971-72
Code used for milk glass Hens on Nest with
decorated heads.

PB —PEACH BLOW
1939, 1952-57
This is cased glass with gold ruby encased in
white opal (milk). Made first in 1939. Replaced in
1940 by Peach Crest (PC). Made several hobnail
shapes from 1952 to 1957.

PF —MI HOBNAIL FLOWER ARRANGER WITH
PINK FLOWERS

PR —PURPLE ROSE
1973-74 (EGG DECORATION)

SB —SATIN BLUE OVERLAY
(lamps—1976-77)

SH —SATIN HONEY AMBER
(lamps 7/76)

SL —SILVER ON WHITE SATIN
1975-76—see p. 113
Used on 25th Anniversary plate only.

ST —SUMMER TAPESTRY—
BARBER COLLECTION see p. 95

TB —HAND-RUBBED BLUE-SATIN ON MILK
7/1969; 1980-82
Used on 9088 and 9188 originally; Called "AN-
TIQUE BLUE" in 1980.

TG —HAND-RUBBED GREEN-SATIN ON
CREAM BACKGROUND MILK GLASS
7/1969
Same two items as on TB color-satin.

TN —ANTIQUE BROWN
1980-82 (see p. 129) Currier & Ives
Unusual hand-rubbed shades of brown and tan on
milk glass.

TS —HAND-RUBBED BROWN SATIN ON
CREAM BACKGROUND MILK GLASS
Same two items as 1969 production of TB and TG.

VC —EGG "VIOLETS ON CUSTARD"
73-74

WB —BLUE ROSES
7/1972; 1977-78
An early code for BL (5140 egg); later for a decorated satin blue overlay lamp.

YF —MI HOBNAIL FLOWER ARRANGER WITH
YELLOW AND WHITE FLOWERS

INDEX